KU-007-474

COMPUTER FORENSICS AND CYBER CRIME

An Introduction

Marjie T. Britz, Ph.D.
The Citadel

LIVERPOOL
JOHN MOORES UNIVERSITY
AVRIL ROBARTS LRC
TEL 0151 231 4022

PEARSON

Prentice
Hall

Upper Saddle River, New Jersey 07458

Library of Congress Cataloging-in-Publication Data

Britz, Marjie.
  Computer forensics & cyber crime : an introduction / Marjie T. Britz.
      p. cm.
  ISBN 0-13-090758-8
  1. Computer security. [1. Computer crimes.] I. Title: Computer
forensics and cyber crime. II. Title.
  QA76.9.A25B77 2003
  363.25'968—dc21

                                           2003012102

Publisher: Stephen Helba
Executive Editor: Frank Mortimer, Jr.
Assistant Editor: Sarah Holle
Production Editor: Nicholas P. Angelides, Pine Tree Composition
Production Liaison: Barbara Marttine Cappuccio
Director of Production & Manufacturing: Bruce Johnson
Managing Editor: Mary Carnis
Manufacturing Buyer: Cathleen Petersen
Creative Director: Cheryl Asherman
Cover Design Coordinator: Miguel Ortiz
Cover Designer: Miguel Ortiz
Editorial Assistant: Barbara Rosenberg
Marketing Manager: Tim Peyton
Formatting and Interior Design: Pine Tree Composition
Printing and Binding: R.R. Donnelley & Sons

Copyright © 2004, by Pearson Education Inc., Upper Saddle River, New Jersey 07458. All rights reserved. Printed in the United States of America. This publication is protected by Copyright and permission should be obtained from the publisher prior to any prohibited reproduction, storage in a retrieval system, or transmission in any form or by any means, electronic, mechanical, photocopying, recording, or likewise. For information regarding permission(s), write to: Rights and Permissions Department.

Pearson Prentice Hall™ is a trademark of Pearson Education, Inc.
Pearson® is a registered trademark of Pearson
Prentice® Hall is a registered trademark of Pearson Education, Inc.

Pearson Education LTD., *London*
Pearson Education Australia PTY. Limited, *Sydney*
Pearson Education Singapore, Pte. Ltd.
Pearson Education North Asia Ltd., *Hong Kong*
Pearson Education Canada, Ltd., *Toronto*
Pearson Educacíon de Mexico, S.A. de C.V.
Pearson Education-Japan, *Tokyo*
Pearson Education Malaysia, Pte. Ltd.

10 9 8 7 6 5 4 3 2 1
ISBN 0-13-0907588

LIVERPOOL
JOHN MOORES UNIVERSITY
AVRIL ROBARTS LRC
TEL. 0151 231 4022

COMPUTER FORENSICS
AND CYBER CRIME

LIVERPOOL JMU LIBRARY

3 1111 01057 4174

As always, this book is dedicated in loving memory of my dad, Theodore Albert Britz, a truly great man who was taken too soon. It is also dedicated to Mom, Teddy, Marianne, and Ronnie who make my writing possible in so many ways, and to my angels, Taylor and Teigue, who bring sunshine to my world.

CONTENTS

4 COMPUTER CRIMES: COMPUTERS AS TARGETS—HACKING AND BEYOND 59

5 AVENUES FOR PROSECUTION AND GOVERNMENT EFFORTS 80

6 APPLYING THE FIRST AMENDMENT TO COMPUTER-RELATED CRIME 99

7   THE FOURTH AMENDMENT   113

8   FORENSIC TERMINOLOGY AND COMPUTER INVESTIGATIONS   142

9 DEVELOPING COMPUTER FORENSIC SCIENCE CAPABILITIES   157

10 COMPUTER INVESTIGATIONS: PRE-SEARCH ACTIVITIES   176

FOREWORD

I have never been accused of sugar coating my remarks and I'm not about to start now. That is why when I say this book by Dr. Marjie Britz is an excellent text, I am sincere. This text is an excellent first step for anyone who wishes to learn about the investigation of computer crime, and the forensic processing of seized computer data. It is also an excellent reference for major cases involving computer prosecutions.

It is for persons who are just starting their exposure to and taking their first classes in computer crime and computer forensics. The text provides excellent information for students, and those needing it for research and exposure to computer crime investigations. Fully explained for the newbie are technical terms that a person new to computer forensics needs to know. New terms are identified and defined with plenty of examples and explanations.

Dr. Britz provides an excellent background, history and terminology of computer crime. She has gone step by step, and assumed the reader is a novice at computer investigation. The text starts out by explaining what Cyberspace is, how the Internet, criminal behavior and computer crime has evolved, and how it all effects law enforcement.

She identifies the problems law enforcement has with maintaining state of the art investigations and support for the investigations. The lack of law enforcement resources in both financial and management support is brought to light. In addition she brings out problems identified with the lack of judicial consistency both in the laws and cases prosecuted.

When I first read this text I was impressed by the amount of excellent legal research and references for cases and case law. However, by the time you are reading this text the U.S. Patriot Act will have been passed. It will modify or enhance many of the statutes and procedures used in computer investigations. Nonetheless, Dr. Britz has done an excellent job of documenting the statutes and cases involving key issues in the investigation and prosecution of computer crimes. The primary Federal computer statutes used for prosecuting computer crime are well identified.

Everyone involved in the investigation of any type of crime is well aware of the responsibility of the investigator to uphold and support the Constitution while performing the investigations. The safeguarding of a persons First and Fourth amendment rights is covered throughout this text. There are entire chapters (six and seven) dealing with the First and Fourth Amendments as they relate to computer investigations, search warrants and seizure of computers.

Finishing the last two chapters with forensic and computer investigation terminology and procedures for conducting forensic analysis, Dr. Britz takes the reader through the basics of computer terminology relating to forensics and includes a significant number of technical terms which the investigator or analyst will have to know to conduct an analysis. Knowledge of these terms and how they relate to computer analysis will help the analyst properly prepare a successful prosecution.

And finally, in the last chapter the text explains how to develop forensic capabilities and some standard operating procedures for processing computer evidence. A typical computer lab setup is discussed, so the novice will have a starting point with which to supply his/her forensic lab.

The reader is given some basics on how to process computer evidence, and how to build procedures that will allow the analyst to properly defend his/her activity against defense challenges. Problems involved with finding, preserving and presenting digital evidence are discussed. One of the best parts of the last chapter is that it provides an excellent overview of procedures and suggestions on how to create a forensic process and make your process defensible in court.

All in all, I found this book to be very informative and an excellent text for anyone wanting to expand his/her knowledge in the area of computer crime investigation and computer forensics.

It fills the gap between those texts that assume the reader already has a full understanding of both the legal and technical knowledge necessary to get involved with computer forensics and investigations and those who know very little about what computer forensics is.

By providing a good basis of the legal considerations along with a basic overview of forensic processing, the reader is shown the first steps necessary to expand his/her knowledge base and become a proficient computer examiner. After reading the book, the analyst/investigator will go on to the more technical issues involved with specific subjects that are encountered in day-to-day analysis.

Dan Mares
IRS (ret.), owner,
Mares and Company LLC

ACKNOWLEDGMENTS

This book would not have been possible without the assistance of a variety of individuals in the trenches. Their assistance and patience proved tireless, and I am heavily indebted to each and every one. Thus, I would like to thank: Dan Mares, Maresware; Bruce Simmons, Mitre; Joe Mykytyn; Jimmy Doyle, NYPD; Jack Wiles, The Training Company; Chip Johnson, SLED; Amanda Simmons, SLED; Keith Lockhart, NW3C; Ben Lewis, NW3C; and, an assortment of other individuals too numerous to mention.

I would also like to thank the following reviewers: Dan Mares, Maresware, Lawrenceville, GA; Lt Chip Johnson, South Carolina State Law Enforcement Division, Lexington, SC; Scott Senjo, Weber State University, Ogden, UT. Dr. Ed Whittle, Florida Metropolitan University- Tampa, Tampa, Fl; and Karen Weston, Gannon University, Erie, PA.

Marjie T. Britz

COMPUTER FORENSICS
AND CYBER CRIME

INTRODUCTION

1

Historically, the world has experienced periods of great enlightenment and progress. The Industrial Revolution, for example, brought unprecedented knowledge and opportunities almost two centuries ago. This revolution, automating common tasks, provided previously unheard-of privileges and advances. Advances in transportation increased the array of vacation destinations, enabled families to remain in contact with distant family members, and decreased infant mortality rates as prenatal care became more accessible in remote areas. In addition, sharp advances in communication improved police efficiency and radically changed the courting behavior of lovers. Individuals, families and institutions were granted unprecedented access to luxury items like cooling systems, and improved household maintenance through power tools, yard equipment, and the like. The automation of printing and the introduction of mass media greatly enhanced information dissemination by increasing the availability of reliable and credible sources of knowledge. Unfortunately, it also increased levels of physical lethargy, obesity, complacency, desensitization, child poverty, and criminal behavior. Today, American society has experienced similar transformations as a direct result of the Information Revolution.

The introduction of the **Internet** has created unparalleled opportunities for commerce, research, education, entertainment, and public discourse. A global marketplace has emerged, in which fresh ideas and increased appreciation of multiculturalism have flourished. The introduction of computerized encyclopedias, international consortia, worldwide connectivity and communications has greatly enhanced quality of life for many individuals. Indeed, the Internet can be utilized as a window to the world, allowing individuals to satiate their curiosity and develop global consciousness. It allows individuals to experience those things that they have only dreamed about. Interested parties can visit the Louvre, devouring priceless artifacts at their leisure or take an African safari without the heat or mosquitoes. They can find answers to the most complex legal or medical questions or search for their soul mates. They can download coupons for their favorite restaurants or search for recipes to their favorite dishes. In addition, individuals, corporations, public organizations and institutions can more effectively advertise their products or services, using graphically highlighted information and providing links to supplemental information or support. In fact, computerized access to unprecedented information has cut across traditional boundaries.

Like other institutions, law enforcement has also benefited. The Internet has successfully created a non-threatening platform for information exchange by community residents. In addition, the speed and efficiency has enabled agencies to communicate with other agencies on a global scale, solidifying relationships and increasing cooperation. Indeed, law enforcement has been able to further its mission by simply extending its viewing audiences. Textual descriptions and graphic images of wanted suspects or missing persons can be viewed by anyone with an Internet connection, and concerned citizens can report suspicious activity in an efficient and effective manner. However, the Internet and the increasing reliance on digital technology and communications has also had negative repercussions—creating seemingly insurmountable obstacles for law enforcement. Indeed, the same technology that allows access to favorite recipes from Madagascar can be utilized to download blueprints for weapons of mass destruction. Those same individuals surfing the Web for vacation specials can stalk and harass targeted victims while enjoying the fruits of such searches. Indeed, the very advantages that make the Internet so attractive often pose the greatest risk.

Disadvantages to the Internet include an increasing dependence on cyber-information. Many undergraduate students rely exclusively on "knowledge" gleaned from electronic sources. Unfortunately, the quality of information found in cyberspace is often questionable, and displacement of humanity has resulted from this dependence on artificial intelligence. More importantly, new technologies have a history of breeding new forms of socially undesirable behavior while enhancing traditional ones. Just as the automation of the printing press and the introduction of mass media exponentially increased the distribution of and demand for criminal contraband, like pornography and illegal substances, the Internet has established a virtual cornucopia of child exploitation and obscenity and created an underworld marketplace for drugs and weapons. In fact, the level and prevalence of criminal behavior and exchange of visual or informational contraband have never been this high. Such advances in technology are also being utilized to commit low-level predatory crime in a new environment known as cyberspace.

CYBERSPACE AND CRIMINAL BEHAVIOR

Cyberspace may be defined as the indefinite place where individuals transact and communicate. It is the place between places (Sterling, 1994). Although originally coined in 1984 by science fiction writer William Gibson, it is hardly a new concept. In fact, traditional electronic communications have always fallen within this existential space. Telephonic conversations, occurring across time and space, were predated by wire exchanges. However, the new medium known as the Internet has monumentally increased the **physicality** of the virtual world, outpaced only by the exponential growth in the number of users. In fact, no other method of communication converges audio, video and data entities. Unlike traditional methods, the Internet combines mail, telephone, and mass media. As stated previously, it exposes individuals to a myriad of new ideas, and may serve as a social gathering place, a library, or a place to be alone. As such, the existential nature of the medium does not negate the reality of its consequences. Individual users have married, planned their lives, and stalked our children there. Unfortunately, this virtual world is often perceived as a painless alternative to worldly problems, where individuals shed their worries and become perfect in their profiles.

Privacy advocates have often overlooked the negative repercussions of this global medium, arguing zealously that the potentiality of emerging technology precludes governmental interests in monitoring citizens. Such supporters include luminaries like The Grateful Dead's David Barlow and Mitchell Kapor, co-inventor of the popular spreadsheet program Lotus 1-2-3 (Sterling, 1994). Both Barlow and Kapor have been most vocal in their defense of some of the most notorious computer hackers in the United States. They argue that the original thrust of the frontier police, directed at ne'er-do-wells intent on compromising the privacy of American citizens, has been refocused on the very individuals that they originally protected. In fact, the two created the Electronic Frontier Foundation offering to "fund, conduct, and support legal efforts to demonstrate that the Secret Service has exercised prior restraint on publications, limited free speech, conducted improper seizure of equipment and data, used undue force, and generally conducted itself in a fashion which is arbitrary, oppressive and unconstitutional" (Sterling, 1994: 11). While early actions by the U.S. Secret Service may validate some of these early concerns, the efforts of this organization have often overlooked the negative potentiality of this global marketplace that has reunited a society that had increasingly removed itself through suburbanization.

Just as the Industrial Revolution created an environment conducive to street or predatory crime through the concentration of the urban population, the Information or Digital Revolution has created a new forum for criminal activity. Ironically, this new environment all but negates security measures taken by individuals wishing to protect themselves from traditional crime. In fact, the introduction of the Internet is unlike other communication media, allowing predators to reach directly into a victim's home, circumventing the meanest of physical security systems. Such systems, a direct result of traditional street crime, are designed to protect individuals, families, and institutions from criminal victimization. They are characteristic of a growing suspicion of anyone unknown. This skepticism, not new or unique to the United States, has not established itself in cyberspace. In fact, the globalization of communications has led to a complacency diametrically opposed to traditional notions of privacy and security.

American society has long been characterized by its distrust of strangers. As media attention has focused on elevated levels of predatory crime perpetrated by non-acquaintances, this fear has been heightened. Cautionary admonitions to children have traditionally included warnings of strangers and locking of doors. However, the advent of technology has lowered traditional barriers, and actually served as an informal invitation for unknown visitors. Many have recognized only too late the dangers of their inattentiveness—victims of theft, stolen privacy, and the like. While others, yet to suffer negative consequences, remain blissfully unaware of their own vulnerability. In fact, most individuals, young and old alike, are seduced by the soft hum of a device that appears to be the gateway to worlds previously restricted. Unfortunately, this fascination may be exploited by those we try most to avoid—criminals and predators.

CLARIFICATION OF TERMS

Just as debates rage over the appropriate codification of crime committed via electronic means, controversy surrounds the actual semantics associated with the phenomenon. For clarification purposes, then, it is necessary to define the historical usage of terms associated with technological or electronic crimes. **Computer crime** has been traditionally defined as any criminal act committed via computer. Cybercrime has traditionally encompassed abuses and misuses of computer systems which result in direct and/or concomitant losses. Finally, computer-related crime has been defined as any criminal act in which a computer is involved, usually peripherally. While these terms will be used interchangeably throughout the text, students should be advised that a variety of definitions exist, and that such variations have resulted in confusion among legislators and investigators alike. Some authors, for example, argue that any crime that involves digital evidence may be characterized as a computer crime. This is misleading at best, and self-serving, at worst. Traditional kidnapping cases in which ransom demands are communicated via telephone will always represent a crime against a person and should not be characterized as a "telecrime." While it is desirable to establish an environment where computers are viewed as potential evidence containers in any case, to redefine traditional predatory crime as cybercrime or computer crime is absurd. Extortion is extortion and will remain such regardless of the method employed to communicate the threat. The result of such hyper-definition is to negate some emerging legislation. This is not to suggest that legislators should cease efforts to specifically criminalize computer-specific criminal activity. Indeed, further legislation should be pursued to enhance prosecutorial toolboxes, not to replace or supplant traditional mechanisms.

TRADITIONAL PROBLEMS ASSOCIATED WITH COMPUTER CRIME

Individuals seeking a crime have always displayed a remarkable ability to adapt to changing technologies, environments, and lifestyles. This adaptability has often placed law enforcement at a disadvantage, struggling to keep up with criminal innovations. Indeed, the law-enforcement community has often failed to recognize the criminal potentiality of emerging technologies until it is almost too late. This trend has proven to be true in contemporary society. Fortunately, much computer-related crime involves non-specialist users (e.g., child pornography, drug dealers, harassment, etc.). In fact, the earliest computer crimes were characterized as non-technological specific. Theft of computer components and software piracy were particular favorites. Hacking and technologically complicated computer crime came later.

Although the advent of technology has vastly changed the modus operandi of certain criminal elements throughout history, current advances have changed the very physical environment in which crime occurs. As such, the law enforcement community has experienced unprecedented periods of uncertainty and ineffectiveness. Many of these problems are associated with the comprehension of the nature of the emerging technology, while others involve questions of legality and sovereignty. Unfortunately, legislative bodies and judicial authorities have been slow to respond to such inquiries, and law enforcement has been forced to develop investigative techniques without adequate legal foundations. At the same time, the lack of technological knowledge traditionally associated with the law enforcement community hampers even the most mundane investigation. So, while the investigators of computer-related crime must display the levels of ingenuity comparable to sophisticated criminal entrepreneurs, traditional investigators are ill-equipped to do so.

Physicality and Jurisdictional Concerns

The physical environment that breeds computer crime is far different from traditional venues. In fact, the intangible nature of computer interaction and subsequent criminality poses significant questions for investigative agents. For example, what forensic tools are available for identifying entry points in data breaking and entering? Certainly, seasoned investigators recognize the utility of prymark analysis in home burglaries. But few recognize the how-to's and what-for's in abstract, intangible environments. In many cases, such differences in technique, and even approach, are further complicated by the lack of precautionary boundaries and restraints—both physical and virtual. Indeed, the intangibility of such environments creates unlimited opportunities.

The lack of physical boundaries and the removal of traditional jurisdictional demarcations allow perpetrators to commit multinational crime with little fear (or potential) of judicial sanctions. For the first time, criminals can cross international boundaries without the use of passports or official documentation. Whereas traditional criminal activity required the physical presence of the perpetrators, cybercrime is facilitated by international connections that enable individuals to commit criminal activity in England while sitting in their offices in Alabama. In addition, electronic crime does not require an extensive array of equipment or tools. It does not require vehicular transportation, physical storage capability, or labor-intensive practices, all of which increase the potential for discovery and enforcement. In addition, this shift from a corporeal environment, where items can be seen, touched, smelled, etc., to a virtual world where boundaries, concrete barriers and physical items are inconsequential, has further insulated the criminal from law enforcement. In fact, the sheer intangibility of crime scenes has all but crippled many criminal investigations.

A further concern regarding the physical intangibility of computer crime involves the traditional lack of cooperation inherent in law enforcement investigations. Issues of funding, political platforms, and the like have traditionally reduced communication and cooperation among jurisdictions. These issues are further compounded when international components are considered. The lack of consensus among international entities regarding the criminalization of certain behaviors and the appropriate sanctions associated with same often negate cooperative agreements. While some countries rate computer crime as a high priority, for example, others have embraced computer criminals, protecting them from international prosecution. Antigua, Caracas, and the Dominican Republic, for example, have all challenged American sovereignty over wagers placed by American residents through their online casinos and sports books. In addition, international councils that have been developed have been largely ineffective, and the momentum to develop such cooperation has waned in the wake of the Y2K nonevent.

Perceived Insignificance and Stereotypes

Investigators and administrators have displayed great reluctance to pursue computer criminals. A lack of knowledge coupled with general apathy towards cybercriminality has resulted in an atmosphere of indifference. Many stereotype computer criminals as non-threatening, socially challenged individuals (i.e., nerds or geeks), and fail to see the insidious nature of computer crime. The potentiality of weapons and narcotics trafficking, conspiracies of mass destruction, and the like are all but alien to those individuals not actively involved in computer investigations. In addition, those administrators and investigators who grudgingly admit the presence and danger of electronic crime tend to concentrate exclusively on child pornography, overlooking motivations and criminal behaviors apart from sexual gratification. Unfortunately, these perceptions are often directly opposed to the reality experienced by seasoned investigators.

In a study conducted by the Department of Justice (Stambaugh, et al., 2001), computer crime investigators recognized the threat posed by employees and insiders. Respondents indicated that businesses were perceived as the number one target for computer crime. Individuals and financial institutions placed second and third, respectively. Their typology of employees or insiders consisted of longer-term workers with extended hours (male and female) between the ages of 20-45 from a variety of social and economic backgrounds, with good computer skills, knowledge of company security procedures, and the ability to mask their intrusions. In fact, their commonality lies more in their motivations, which are usually characterized by revenge, greed, or resentment. Unfortunately, these individuals are most often trusted employees with authorized access. Thus, timely detection of their activities is often unlikely.

This study also revealed that even seasoned investigators believed child pornographers to be the most prevalent (criminal offenders and hackers ranked third and fourth). Typologies of these offenders included males between 16-57 (usually mid or upper 30s to 40s) with a minimum of high school diplomas (although college degrees were also common). These individuals were likely to display moderate to high tech ability, few prior arrests, and high-end computer equipment with large storage capacities. Unfortunately, the majority of Internet users fall squarely within this typology.

Prosecutorial Reluctance

Like their law enforcement counterparts, prosecutors across the country lack sufficient knowledge and experience to effectively prosecute computer crime. In addition, many do not perceive electronic crime as serious and often grant it the lowest priority. (As many prosecutors are strongly influenced by the concerns of their constituents, they are reluctant to deviate from the headline catching cases of street crime or other violent crime). This view is often created or exacerbated by the lack of judicial interest in these types of crime and the lack of training displayed by responding officers. Even those jurisdictions which have granted electronic crime high priority are often thwarted by a lack of cooperation in extradition requests, the victim's reluctance to prosecute, the labor intensive nature of case preparation, and/or the lack of resources for offender tracking.

Lack of Reporting

Although estimates vary, most experts agree that the vast majority of Fortune 500 companies have been electronically compromised to the tune of at least $10 billion/year. However, early studies indicated that only 17 percent of such victimizations were reported to law enforcement authorities (Center for Strategic and International Studies, 1998). At the same time, number of reported incidents handled by Carnegie-Mellon University (CERT–Computer Emergency Response Team) has increased from 1,334 in 1993 to 4,398 during the first two quarters of 1999 (U.S. General Accounting Office, 1998). It does appear that reporting is getting better; a survey of 521 security personnel from American companies, financial institutions, universities and government agencies revealed that 32 percent of respondents reported electronic crime to law enforcement. This represented an increase of 15 percent of the previous study. However, computer intrusion is still vastly underreported.

One of the primary reasons that businesses fail to report computer intrusions is their need to assure consumers of data security. This represents an absolute necessity to most businesses, as individual consumers need to have faith in the company's infrastructure. And, more importantly, need assurances that confidential information remains inviolate. Imagine the chaos that would result, for example, if Citibank or Chase Manhattan announced that a hacker had compromised the accounts of 10,000 customers. In addition, many corporations are uncomfortable with the release of information to any entity, including law enforcement, and want to maintain control of the investigation at all times. Unfortunately, law enforcement authorities can not extend promises of confidentiality of findings as the sheer nature of the American judicial system makes it legally impossible to hide or fail to divulge results of an investigation (i.e., it is all available in the public record). Thus, many corporations choose to handle things internally, including disciplining perpetrators. Some naively assume that criminal prosecution, if preferred, can be accomplished by simply sharing the results of their investigations with law enforcement agencies. This assumption is based in large part on the perceptions of security professionals who decry the need for proper law enforcement procedures, arguing that corporate investigations should not "waste" time attempting to maintain the chain of custody. The "professionals" argue that only 2 percent of incidents that are investigated necessitate that type of detail (e.g., Bill Spernow, 2001). Unfortunately, such internal investigations may all but negate the potential for criminal prosecution, as the incorporation and documentation of proper evidentiary procedures is essential in the judicial process.

A further reason that companies do not report is the perception that reporting will not result in capture or identification of a suspect. These companies fail to see a positive cost-benefit ratio. (Unfortunately, they may have a point, as 77 percent of surveyed departments reported that electronic crimes are assigned a low to medium priority at their agency, with the exception of child pornography (Stambaugh, et al., 2001). Many also find it difficult to determine the proper authorities or question the capabilities of law enforcement agencies, who are often stereotyped as technologically deficient or retarded. Interlapping and overlapping jurisdictions pose additional problems, as it is most rare that computer crimes occur within one state, let alone one jurisdiction. Even non-sophisticated computer criminals will access different services to disguise their location. Such circuitous activity often necessitates federal or international assistance. Finally, many intrusions are detected long after the violation occurred, making investigations more difficult.

Lack of Resources

Although computer intrusions have proven to be problematic within the corporate world, their unwillingness or inability to effectively communicate with judicial authorities has led to an increase in computer crime. Unfortunately, law enforcement and corporate entities desperately need to cooperate with one another. Unlike their civil service counterparts, the business communities have the resources (both financial and legal) necessary to effectively combat computer crimes. First, these companies, through their system administrators, have far more leeway in monitoring communications and system activities, and they have the ability to establish policies which enable wide-scale oversight. Subsequently, these entities have the ability to gather evidence with little or no resources expended (i.e., system monitoring software–keyboard logging, scripting logging, password maintenance, etc.). CADS (Computer Anomaly Detection Systems), for example, are designed to use the power of the computer to detect suspicious activity. In addition, these companies have the economic resources available to fund investigative efforts, while law enforcement agencies do not. Ideally, these two communities, sharing the same interests, would develop open lines of communication and cooperation. However, this has not yet occurred.

Due to the very nature of computer crime, an influx of economic support to local law enforcement agencies is sorely needed. Law enforcement has been seriously underfunded since its inception. This trend has been exacerbated with the advent of high-technology crime. Emerging technologies require perpetual training as the potentiality for computer criminality has exponentially increased. Wireless technologies and emerging encryption and steganography programs, for example, are increasingly complicating law enforcement investigations. As law enforcement budgets remain strained, it is virtually impossible for administrators to allocate training funds to update their officers on today's technology without assurances that the training would not become obsolete by tomorrow. This never-ending cycle is further complicated by the sheer cost of the training available. With the exception of federally sponsored programs, much of the training available is offered by private companies who charge exorbitant fees for their services. It is not unusual, for example, for a one-week training course on computer forensics to exceed $1500 per officer. Budgets are further strained by peripheral costs associated with training, like per diem expenses.

In addition to costs associated with training, administrators must consider three additional areas in support of computer crime investigations: personnel, hardware, and housing. By far, costs associated with staffing computer crime units far exceed the other two areas. While traditional expenses like salary and benefits are often overlooked, they become a very expensive component when establishing a new function. For every officer who is assigned new areas of responsibility, additional staff must be recruited, hired, and trained as a replacement in his/her original position. In addition, small agencies can scarcely afford to send officers to lengthy training courses or assign them exclusively to computer crime units, as their personnel resources are already stretched to the limit. As a result, many agencies have poorly trained computer investigators who are functioning in several capacities at once. Finally, the complexity of computer crime often necessitates the retention of individuals who exhibit a high level of technological competence and familiarity with computer infrastructures. Unfortunately, these skills are also highly prized within the private sector, placing poorly funded law enforcement agencies at a distinct disadvantage. While the private sector can offer elevated salaries and lucrative business packages, law enforcement, a civil service entity, is often precluded from offering differential packages to these individuals.

A further deterrent for many law enforcement agencies is the costs associated with the acquisition of appropriate equipment. As stated previously, technology is changing at a remarkable pace, and while computer components are decreasing in price, they quickly become obsolete, making large investments impractical for many departments. Twenty gigabyte hard drives, for example, were touted as a major revolution in 2000. Now, drives with four and five times that storage capacity are commonplace. Thus, it is essential for equipment to remain consistent with current technology, as imaging drives and storing criminal evidence require comparable space (and speed). Advances in microprocessors have also increased exponentially. Just as users were marveling over the speed of the Pentium III, Intel introduced the Pentium IV™. (Perhaps a Pentium V will be available by this text's publication date). However, CPU's are but one facet of the expense budget allocated for hardware. Printers, scanners, monitors, modems, storage devices, and the like, are all necessary for investigations. And, as in other areas in computer technology, expenses associated with equipment updating can be enormous.

Updating software can also be quite expensive. Upgrades to many of the most popular programs can reach as high as several hundred dollars per machine. Updates of operating systems can also be quite pricey. As with the update of hardware, it is absolutely imperative that investigative agencies remain abreast of developments in popular software, as criminal evidence may reside in these programs. In addition, investigative software is necessary to analyze and recover such evidence. At a minimum, agencies must invest in data duplication, data verification, data capture, data recovery, data preservation, and data analysis tools. Password cracking, text searching, and document viewing tools are also necessary. Unfortunately, many of the licenses to these programs, created exclusively for computer forensic purposes, require annual fees or significant costs for upgrades. New Technologies Incorporated (NTI), for example, grants licenses to individuals, not machines, and charges law enforcement annual fees for licensing and additional fees for upgrades. Thus, the majority of expenses associated with the creation of a computer crime unit are not only recurring, but increasing.

A further expense associated with establishing computer crime units concerns the creation of a computer laboratory (discussed in more detail in Chapter 10). Unlike previous expenses, such expenditures should represent a non-recurring expense for an agency's budget. Software and hardware expenses aside, the most significant portion of lab start-up costs is a one-time investment in a physical site. As office space is always at a premium in police departments, this investment may be the hardest to come by. However, it is the most important due to the unique and fragile characteristics of digital evidence and technological devices. These characteristics require the partitioning of traditional and technological evidence with special consideration given to the fragility of digital evidence, including temperature, moisture, dust, and static controls. Unfortunately, such high maintenance support is almost impossible at the local level as most resources are only available at the federal level. (Although half of all agencies recently surveyed reported the presence of an electronic crime "unit", many of these units were staffed by a single officer, often acting part-time in this capacity, without the support of a forensic laboratory.)

Federal resources have been increasing by leaps and bounds; the creation of regional investigative offices at the FBI and child exploitation and pornography task forces are but a few examples. The Secret Service has invested a considerable amount of time, resources, and training in this area. Many of these programs have proven invaluable to local jurisdictions struggling with dwindling resources and outdated technology. Unfortunately, the federal resources are stretched extremely thin. The exponential increase in computer activity in violation of federal statutes coupled with the inundation from local agencies has resulted in extended turnaround time and a denial of cases which are not deemed significant (i.e., those that do not threaten public safety, involve exploitation of children, or the like). In addition, this same lack of resources has led to an inability to respond proactively to the dawning era of the techno-criminal. Resources are so constrained that federal assistance traditionally are reserved for only the most serious of cases; avoiding local juristictions. (It must be noted, however, that the federal government has made a concerted effort to stem the flow of child pornography, aggressively investigating known offenders and surveying areas ripe for child pornographers.) In addition, many libertarians argue that this increasing reliance on federal resources violates constitutional safeguards that mandate jurisdictional capabilities, suggesting that concerns of federal power and police states can only be exacerbated by relieving local governments of such responsibilities and powers.

Jurisprudential Inconsistency

Unfortunately, the Supreme Court has remained resolutely averse to deciding matters of law in the newly emerging sphere of cyberspace. They have virtually denied cert on every computer privacy case to which individuals have appealed, and have refused to determine appropriate levels of Fourth Amendment protections of individuals and computer equipment. As such, the country is remarkably divided on fundamental elements of law—establishing a legality standard of behavior in one jurisdiction which negates or supersedes another.

EXTENT OF THE PROBLEM

Many computer crimes violate both federal and state statutes. Although the federal agencies are better equipped to deal with the complexities involved with high technology crime, state agencies are also inundated by increasing requests from local agencies for assistance in the investigation and detection of computer crime. The lack of resources coupled with the array of criminal perpetrators on the Web has all but overwhelmed investigative agencies at all levels of government. Crimes committed via computer fall on a spectrum ranging from nuisance activities (i.e., viruses, spamming, etc.) to computer-assisted criminal activity (i.e., home addresses, maps, family information, etc.) to computer-initiated criminal activity (i.e., wire transfers, fraud). Nefarious purposes include white collar crime, economic espionage, organized crime, foreign intelligence, terrorism, sexual deviance, and technologically innovated traditional crime. Perpetrators range from suburban teenagers to disgruntled employees to incarcerated felons. To make sense of this myriad of activities, motivations, and individuals, computer crimes may be divided into three categories: 1) computer as a target; 2) computer as an instrument; and 3) computer as an incidental. While these categories often overlap, they are most useful in discussions of high technology crime.

The earliest examples of computer crime involved activities in which computers or computer components were targeted by criminals. "Phreaking," an activity in which telecommunications systems are manipulated and ultimately compromised, was the precursor to today's hackers, while viruses and worms have become a daily concern for corporations, civic organizations, and individual users. Trojan Horses and other popular hacking tools are now readily available on the Web , and the theft of data has become increasingly popular. Government entities and financial institutions, in particular, have proven especially vulnerable to data theft. While much of the activity involves recreational entertainment for savvy computer users, implications for international security and wide-scale financial fraud are looming concerns. Additional criminal activities which target computers or their components include software piracy and trafficking in stolen goods.

Organized crime groups have recognized the potential profit from the black market in computer chips, and various cases have involved organized Asian gangs trafficking in high dollar computer chips.

Computers have also proven to be *the means* for many criminally minded individuals. Removing traditional physical boundaries, and perhaps more importantly, removing international borders, the Internet has vastly increased the potential both for traditional crimes and technology-specific activities. The appearance of anonymity creates the façade of a shield which seems to negate possible repercussions. Thus, the opportunities for embezzlement, stalking, and gambling, to name a few, have been exponentially elevated with the introduction of electronic commerce and communications. In addition, the prevalence of child pornography has skyrocketed as it has become more accessible. In fact, many individuals argue that the Internet has actually created this increase in child pornography as some individuals actually become child pornographers through experimentation—an activity which they would not have engaged in if the information had not been so accessible.

Additional crimes that have become more accessible to the masses include counterfeiting and forgery. The introduction of high-end scanners and printers have created at atmosphere ripe for the illegal reproduction of American currency and corporate or government checks. Sophisticated graphics software, popular among virtually all computer users, enable criminals to cut and paste, rearranging and transposing figures at will. Thus, computers can be the instrument in a variety of criminal activities.

Finally, computers can be containers or storage warehouses for crime unrelated to technology. Drug dealers and bookies, for example, may utilize popular spreadsheet programs like Lotus or Excel to more effectively organize their records. Even burglary or homicide investigations may include evidence recovered from a computer. Indeed, as computers reach every crevice of American life, it is likely that digital evidence will be found at an increasing number of crime scenes, unrelated to computer crime. Thus, it is essential that all investigators, not just those involved in high-technology units, recognize the elevated possibility of computers as evidence receptacles.

As stated, individual actors engaged in computer crime range from suburban teenagers to disgruntled employees to incarcerated individuals, while motivations range from recreational to financial to ideological. Targets may include, but are not limited to, individuals, military or intelligence institutions, banking or financial organizations, utility or service companies, colleges or universities, and telecommunications networks. And, crimes may range from simple trespass or voyeurism to bank fraud to child pornography to international terrorism. However, one of the most common types of computer crime is unauthorized use or computer intrusion.

Estimates of the costs associated with computer intrusions range from $15 billion (Datamonitor, 2001) to $250 billion (Radcliffe, 1998). Estimates of the proportion of businesses attacked are just as diverse, ranging from 25 percent to almost 99 percent. Although this does not present a realistic picture, even the lowest estimates reveal the seriousness of this phenomenon. Ironically, these studies also reveal the reluctance of corporations to expend funds on data security. In fact, it is estimated that more than half of businesses spend 5 percent or less of their IT budget on security. This is reflected in the diversity of corporations which have fallen victim to computer intrusion. Nike's Web site (*www.nike.com*, for example, was hijacked and redirected to a political site in 2000). Government sites have proven equally vulnerable. In March 2000, a 19-year-old Houston cracker pled guilty to one count of conspiracy to commit teleconferencing fraud and computer cracking after hacking into various government sites, including the White House and (this individual was a member of GlobalHell, a notorious hacking group).

Another popular form of computer crime which often affects both government and corporate entities is the spread of computer viruses. The "Love Bug" virus, for example, affected at least 45 million computers and caused billions of dollars in damages. Victims included government agencies, educational institutions, financial corporations, and individual users alike. The systems most vulnerable to such attacks have proven to be MS Windows NT, Linux or variations, and Sun Solaris, in descending order. Recent years have also been characterized by an increase in denial of service attacks. Scott Dennis, a former computer system administrator for U.S. District Court in Alaska, launched three denial of service attacks against the U.S. District Court for the Eastern District of New York to illustrate the vulnerability of the system and prove his worth.

Perhaps the most disconcerting of all computer crime involves the visualization of the sexual exploitation of children. In 1998 alone, child pornography cases under investigation by the Cybersmuggling Unit of the Department of Customs in Sterling, VA increased by 185 percent (Radcliffe, 1998). Unfortunately, this trend is continuing. An investigation in Medford, MA in 2000, uncovered a local area network supporting 12 incoming telephone lines on a BBS named "The Eagle's Nest." This underground board offered hundreds of images of child porn to subscribers, and was accessed by over 250 users a day (SEARCH, 2000). The instances of this type of activity are only expected to increase as Web users are added daily.

EXTENT OF PROBLEM:

- 25 percent of respondents detected external system penetration
- 27 percent detected denial of service
- 79 percent detected employee abuse of Internet privileges
- 85 percent detected viruses
- 19 percent suffered unauthorized use
- 19 percent reported ten or more incidents
- 35 percent reported two to five incidents
- 64 percent of those acknowledging an attack reported Web site vandalism
- 60 percent reported denial of service
- over 260 million dollars in damages were reported by those with documentation.

www.securitystats.com, Datamonitor, 18 January 2001.

CONCLUSIONS

Just as the introduction of the telephone gave American society the first wave of heavy breathers, telemarketers, and rapid response, the creation of the Internet has resulted in a myriad of developments, some positive, others negative. Individual users can travel all over the world at the touch of a button. They can access the latest sports scores, stock prices, and international news, while downloading their favorite music or photographs. On the surface, computers increase the independence and autonomy so prized in American society. Indeed, the ability to pack an entire briefcase on a floppy and conduct business from off-site locations like the beach or the mountains is a wondrous thing. This autonomy, however, masks an ever-increasing reliance on technology in which the masters become the slaves and the slaves become the masters. Unfortunately, this overreliance on technology creates an extremely tenuous situation, in which computer failures can prove all but disastrous. This environment proves especially conducive to manipulation by those with nefarious intentions. Thus, an increase in antisocial and pathological behavior is all but inevitable. However, law enforcement authorities are struggling with outdated technology, a lack of significant resources, and administrative and public apathy.

TERMS DISCUSSED

computer crime   internet   physicality

DISCUSSION QUESTIONS

1. How can the intangibility of computer crime complicate investigations and subsequent prosecutions?
2. How has computer crime been characterized in the past? Do these perceptions hinder investigations? How?
3. Why are individual victims reluctant to report computer crime? What about private corporations?
4. What are some of the general costs associated with the investigation of computer crime? How do these compare with traditional investigations? What suggestions can you offer to increase the resources available for such?
5. Discuss the problems associated with the limited resources available in most police departments across the country. What can be done to alleviate some of these problems?
6. What is meant by jurisprudential inconsistency?

COMPUTER TERMINOLOGY AND HISTORY

2

COMPUTER LANGUAGE

Generally speaking, there are three basic components of every computer system: **hardware, software,** and firmware. (It must be noted that the following definitions are intended to simplify understanding of complex terms for undergraduates and non-computer specialists. They are not intended to represent the sophistication and complexity of the computer world. Rather, they are intended to provide an elementary framework for informational digestion.)

Computer Hardware

Hardware is composed of those components that are physical or tangible in nature. It includes common devices such as scanners, zips, modems, monitors, etc. It may be categorized as input, output, or storage devices, although these categories are not always mutually exclusive. Input devices are those mediums through which information is introduced to the computer. They include, but are not limited to the following. **Modems** are electronic devices which connect a computer and telephone line to enable communication between computers by converting binary data to analog tones and voltages communicable over an analog communications cable and vice versa (can also be an output device). **Keyboards** are devices through which commands and information are introduced to the computer. They are, perhaps, the most recognizable of all. In fact, keyboards tend to be somewhat universal, and are usually clearly marked. Unfortunately, this type of familiarity often breeds complacence. Investigators should remember that keyboard configuration is easily manipulated. As such, they should be aware that the suspect may have reconfigured the standard keyboard layout creating "not keep" which may have consequences ranging from the nusance to the catastrophic. Any move might prove to be the case's undoing. Additionally, investigators should consider the possibility that remote users may use keyboards to manipulate a suspect system. Thus, it is extremely important that investigators recognize potential hazards posed by keyboards.

The *mouse (plural mice)* is a device which moves a cursor on the screen when moved by hand. The **scanner** is a device for making a digital image of any graphic, for reproduction or processing by the computer.

Other input devices, such as microphones and the like are also commonly used (Shnier, 1998). Output devices are those devices that produce and/or display information that has been processed by the computer for dissemination to the user. (In operation, a computer is both hardware and software. One is useless without the other. The hardware design specifies the commands it can follow, and the instructions tell it what to do.) Some of the most common of these are: *Monitors,* originally called Cathode Ray Tubes (CRT). The modern monitor's precursor dates all the way back to 1895 (Kovacich, et al., 2000). Contemporary monitors on desktop computers are usually separate from the **Central Processing Unit** (CPU). However, some manufacturers combine CPU's and monitors. Generally speaking, computer monitors are devices that communicate to users, in a digestible format, the results of their commands. *Printers* are devices that create printed documents, per the computer's instructions, to reflect the results of computer commands. For investigators, printers can hold invaluable, yet often overlooked, criminal evidence. Thus, investigators should be sure to check all printers at the scene, and those computers which may be networked in remote areas (i.e., imagine yourself running to and from the computer, depressing the print key multiple times, desperate to have success. If the computer and its peripherals are turned off at night, and yet jobs are sent to the printer during the interim–voila–evidence). *Central processing units* are the single integrated circuit actually interpreting program instructions and the processing of data in a computer. (Original eight-bit processors had eight pins for accessing their external data buses. As in other cases of technology, processor capabilities have developed at exponential rates. Intel's Pentium processors, for example, are capable of transferring 64 bits (or 8 bytes) simultaneously!). **Buses** are multiple connections consisting of several parallel wires between chips and memory chips. These parallel electrical connections permit the transfer of several bits of data simultaneously. **Motherboard** is the primary circuit board of a PC to which all other elements are connected. These components include the processor memory chips, BIOS, and Read Only Memory (ROM). *PC Cards* (originally *PCMCIA* for the organization that developed it, i.e., Personal Computer Memory Card International Association) refer to plug-in boards originally designed for laptops. Initially the size of a thick credit card, their capabilities include: hard drives, network interfaces, flash memory cards, modems, SCSI,[1] CD-ROM and audio drives. These may also be used in desktop computers.

Computer Software

Generally speaking, the term *computer software* refers to a series of instructions that performs a particular task. More specifically, software is the interpretation of binary byte sequences represented by a listing of instructions to the processors. The two

---

[1]SCSI (Small Computer Interface System), increasingly popular, provides interfacing for up to seven peripherals (actually, as an eight-bit bus interface, but the host adapter which connects to the computer's bus also counts as a device), and allows communication between any two devices simultaneously. Relied upon for speedy transfers, wide SCSI provides up to 40 MB/sec!

major categories are system software and application software. Semantically speaking, there are a variety of terms used to represent certain elements within the realm of software. *Programs,* for example, represent the sequence of rules through which software operates; **source code** refers to the set of instructions written in programming language; **object code** is what is actually executed by the computer; and so on, and so on. **Malware** or *malicious programming code* refer to a code that causes damage to computer systems. Within this definition lies an entire subfield of terminology. **Trap doors,** for example, are codes that allow a user to enter a system without authorization (also referred to as a "back door"); a **Trojan horse,** nicknamed after the Greek myth of old, is a program that on its face has a legitimate purpose, but also has a hidden feature, such as a trap door or hidden program. Unlike viruses and worms, Trojan horses do not replicate themselves. Such programs may include those which can be triggered to cause damage or alter information; a **virus,** usually attached or inserted into a file or the boot sector of a disk, is a rogue computer program which is designed to disperse copies of itself to other computers for destructive purposes by attaching itself to programs and replicating. (A boot sector virus can also infect a hard drive, where it is much more dangerous.) They are introduced to computer systems as part of an infected COM, EXE, or boot sector program file, or through network downloads as macros, set-up files, or e-mail attachments (Randall, 1999). While most computer users are familiar with the term, many do not recognize that viruses reside on a continuum of destruction, ranging from the relatively harmless, designed to prove the superiority of its creator, to the catastrophic. In fact, some are so dangerous that they require a complete shutdown of businesses. Viruses are never accidental. They are always intentionally and deliberately designed to perform certain functions, and all are harmful in some way. For example, all consume disk space, memory and other resources which directly affect the speed and efficiency of an individual machine, and at a minimum, their proliferation has all but required the necessity of space-draining antivirus programs (Randall, 1999). They are inherently dangerous, in that they are uncontrollable. Once initiated, even the writer or creator cannot control the infestation that will result. The motivations for such creations range from boredom to retribution; **worms** are self-contained programs (or sets of programs) which may spread functional copies of themselves or their segments to other computer systems (usually via a network connection). Although many individuals synonymize worms with viruses, they are quite distinct. Unlike viruses, worms do not need to attach themselves to a host program nor are they designed to alter or erase files. However, system crashes may result due to their ability to infest machine space. There are two types of worms: network worms and host computer worms. **Network worms** consist of several segments operating on different machines that use the network for several communication purposes. Once activated, these worms will scan for connections to the host node. Such vulnerabilities will enable the worm to spread throughout the network. **Host computer worms,** on the other hand, are entirely contained on the computer they run on. These worms only use network connections to copy themselves to other computers. Some variations include self-destructive programs. These "rabbit" programs terminate themselves after launching a copy on another host. Thus, at any given time, only one copy of the worm is operating on the network.

Droppers are programs that are created to avoid anti-virus detection, usually by encryption that hinders detection. Their typical function is to transport and install viruses when an infected computer performs a certain function; **bombs** are usually built into malware as an activation mechanism. Like droppers, bombs are designed to activate when a specific action occurs. *Time bombs* are those bombs which are activated at a specific time on the infected system's internal clock. For example, many individuals feared that virus writers would create bombs programmed for New Year's Eve, 1999. *Logic bombs,* on the other hand, are programs which are designed to activate upon a series of events. For example, this type of program may be activated the nineteenth time a user launches Microsoft Office. In other words, bombs are malicious scripts or scheduling programs (Randall, 1999).

Perhaps the most important piece of software for any user is the **operating system**. Written in Assembler or C, the operating system is a piece of software that runs user applications and provides an interface to the hardware. Traditionally, almost all personal computers with the exception of Macintosh products contained some version of DOS (Disk Operating System), allowing for a maximum of four different operating systems on the same physical drive. Currently, the majority of PC's in the United States contain some form of *GUI* (pronounced gooey, stands for Graphical User Interface) or *WIMP* (Windows, icons, multi-tasking, and pointing device). Originally created by Xerox™, such "point and click" technology is now the norm due to its user-friendly platform. (Unfortunately, this reliance has resulted in a lack of knowledge of disk structure and underlying foundations by those individuals responsible for investigations.)

● NETWORK LANGUAGE

Increasingly, network language is dominating the computer landscape. While many low-end users are familiar with the acronyms, few recognize (or care) what particular terminology refers to. However, it is essential that computer investigators understand the language behind the technology. Here are but a few examples of the most commonly used terms: **TCP/IP** *(Transmission Control Protocol/Internet Protocol* refers to the suite of protocols that define the Internet. More specifically, TCP is a method of communication between programs which enables a bit-stream transfer of information. Originally proposed and designed as the standard protocol for ARPAnet (the precursor of today's Internet), TCP/IP software is now available for every major kind of computer operating system, although most DOS-based systems require the purchase of additional software. To be truly on the Internet, your computer must have TCP/IP software. Luckily, it is now built-in to many of the most common operating systems (i.e., Microsoft Windows 95, NT, etc.).

IMAP *(Internet Message Access Protocol)* is a method of accessing electronic mail or bulletin board messages that are kept on a (possibly shared) mail server. In other words, it permits a "client" e-mail program to access remote message stores as if they were local. For example, e-mail stored on an IMAP server can be manipulated from a desktop computer at home, a workstation at the office, and a notebook computer while traveling, without the need to transfer messages or files back and forth between these computers. This technology is increasingly important as reliance on electronic messaging and use of multiple computers increase, but this functionality cannot be taken for granted: the widely used *Post Office Protocol* **(POP)** works best when one has only a single computer, since it was designed to support "off-line" message access, wherein messages are downloaded and then deleted from the mail server. This mode of access is not compatible with access from multiple computers since it tends to sprinkle messages across all of the computers used for mail access. Thus, unless all of those machines share a common file system, the off-line mode of access that POP was designed to support effectively ties the user to one computer for message storage and manipulation.

Routers are defined as special-purpose computers (or software packages that handle the connection between two or more networks. Routers spend all their time looking at the destination addresses of the packets passing through them and deciding which route to send them on. Routers are analogous to switches found within telephone systems—the same switches that have proven irresistible to phone phreakers and their contemporary counterparts. **Hubs** are central switching devices for communications lines in a star topology. They may add nothing to the transmission (passive hub) or may contain electronics that regenerate signals to boost strength as well monitor activity (active hub, intelligent hub). Hubs may be added to bus topologies; for example, a hub can turn an Ethernet network into a star topology to improve troubleshooting.

Packets are defined as units of data exchanged between host computers. Typically, they are further distinguished as headers and data. (*Packet Switching* refers to the method used to move data around on the Internet. In packet switching, all the data coming out of a machine is broken up into chunks, each chunk has the address of where it came from and where it is going. This enables chunks of data from many different sources to commingle on the same lines, and be sorted and directed to different routes by special machines along the way. This way many people can use the same lines at the same time). The different headers are appended to the data portion as the packet travels through the communication layers; **cookies** are small pieces of information that an HTTP server sends to the individual browser upon the initial connection. (Not all browsers support cookies. However, most popular browsers do: MS Internet Explorer 3.0 or higher and Netscape Navigator 2.0 and higher.) These cookies are stored on an individual hard drive for retrieval by a particular site. Theoretically, this storage is to simplify things for individual users so that their preferences and personal information do not necessarily have to be re-entered upon return access.

More succinctly, a "cookie" refers to a piece of information sent by a web server to a web browser that the browser software is expected to save and to send back to the server whenever the browser makes additional requests from the server. Depending on the type of cookie used, and the browser's settings, the browser may accept or not accept the cookie, and may save the cookie for either

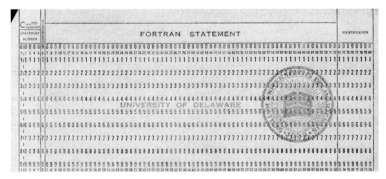

Eighty-column punch card originally used by IBM is still called the Hollerith card.

a short time or a long time. Cookies might contain information such as login or registration information, online "shopping cart" information, user preferences, etc. When a server receives a request from a browser that includes a cookie, the server is able to use the information stored in the cookie. For example, the server might customize what is sent back to the user, or keep a log of particular user's requests. Cookies are usually set to expire after a predetermined amount of time and are usually saved in memory until the browser software is closed down, at which time they may be saved to disk if their "expire time" has not been reached. Although many users naively believe that cookies are capable of reading individual hard drives and sending the user's life history to the CIA, they are simply intended to gather more information about a user than would be possible without them. Thus, cookies do not *steal* information; they simply act as storage platforms for information which a user has supplied.

Cookies operate primarily through the application of *attributes* which instruct the browser which servers to send them to. *Domains,* for example, tell browsers which host names that cookies should be returned to. A computer's **DNS (Domain Name System) entry** is based on a group of computers on a common network defined by a commonality of Internet Protocol (IP) Addresses. These networks are governed by common rules and procedures and treated as a unit. Prior to the implementation of the Domain Name System, the *translation of host names to IP addresses was done by the IP software doing a look-up in the file* /etc/hosts *or* /etc/inet/hosts *(on UNIX computers)* or hosts.txt *(on PCs)*. This system proved to be unworkable and impossible to administer with the virtual explosion of the Internet (Schnier, 1998). Thus, the introduction of DNS was essential for the fluidity of electronic communications. Generally speaking, DNS eases the translation of IP addresses through the utilization of hierarchical principles. Traditional top-level domain names include *com* (commercial organization), *edu* (educational institutions), *gov* (government organizations), *org* (nonprofit organizations), and *net* (internet access providers). Foreign countries and state organizations are increasingly using two- and three-letter codes.

A BRIEF HISTORY OF COMPUTERS

If computer is defined in its simplest sense (i.e., a device used to ascertain an amount or number by calculation or reckoning), the earliest computers were invented by the Chinese over 800 years ago. These devices, known as abacuses, were unsophisticated instruments designed exclusively for mathematical computations. Comprised of rows of colored beads, abacuses were useful for only the simplest of tasks. However, the precursors of contemporary computers were not developed until the nineteenth century.

Much of today's technology may be directly attributed to ideas proposed by Londoner Charles Babbage (1822 and 1871). Babbage designed an analytical engine that was designed to receive instructions from punch cards, make calculations with the aid of a memory bank and print out mathematical solutions. An unprecedented ideal, Babbage's device was a dismal failure due to the lack of a technological infrastructure—a necessity for any novel invention (Microsoft, 2000). (If such support had existed, this mechanism would have undoubtedly revealed our earliest computers). However, the credit for today's machines is most often attributed to the work of Herman Hollerith. Indeed, Dr. Hollerith was the first to successfully introduce a device exclusively designed for data processing. This machine, developed an ocean away from Babbage, was created to tabulate the 1890 Census in the United States. Like many government employees before and since, Dr. Hollerith soon left his civil assignment (1896) and developed his own company, the Tabulating Machine Company, IBM's immediate predecessor. Although a monumental discovery, Hollerith's device bears little resemblance to the machines of today. However, his vision and foresight laid the foundation for a virtual explosion in communication, processing, and digital technology.

Subsequent developments in technology soon replaced the rather elementary machine created by Hollerith, and a virtual army of inventors has refined and perfected the rudimentary technology. Interestingly, many of these innovations have been partially, if not completely, funded by government initiatives. The first modern digital computer, for example, was built at Iowa State University by John Atanasoff, professor of physics and mathematics, and his graduate student, Clifford Berry, and was funded with federal monies. The Atanasoff-Berry Computer (ABC, for short) had capabilities which included binary arithmetic, parallel processing, separate memory, regenerative memory, and basic computer functionality.

This technology, passed on to John W. Mauchly and John Presper Eckert, eventually resulted in the development of the Electronic Numerical Integrator and Computer (ENIAC). Built at the University of Pennsylvania's Moore School of Electrical Engineering, this device was responsible for calculating firing and bombing tables for the United States military. Fully assembled in 1945, ENIAC was composed of 30 separate units, coupled with separate power supplies and air conditioning units, and weighed 30 tons! In addition, it utilized 19,000 vacuum tubes, 1500 relays, and required 200 kilowatts of electrical power to operate (Microsoft, 2000). Despite its monumental size, ENIAC was the prototype for most modern computers, mainframes and PC's alike.

A TASTE OF HACKING TERMINOLOGY

Back door—a hole in security deliberately left within a program or software which enables nonauthorized access.

Bit bucket—final destination of discarded, lost or destroyed data.

Black hat hacker—term which refers to evil crackers.

Cracker—term originally coined by hackers which usually refers to those individuals violating secure systems for illicit purposes rather than fun. (**Hackers** claim to be motivated purely by intellectual pursuits, while "crackers" exploit systems for economic reasons or other forms of personal gain. Crackers are often referred to as "cyberpunks.")

Phreaking—art and science of cracking the phone network (i.e., making illegal phone calls).

Red hat hacker—tongue-in-cheek reference to a flavor of the Linux operating systems.

Sneaker—individual hired by a company to test its security systems by attempting to violate them.

Spaghetti or kangaroo code—complex or tangled code.

Time bomb—subspecies of logic bomb that is triggered by reaching some predetermined time or is set to go off in the event that a programmer is fired and not available to suppress action.

Trojan horse—malicious, security-breaking program designed to appear benign. Like the historical Trojan horse, these programs effectively hide something quite dangerous.

Vulcan nerve pinch—keyboard combination that forces a soft-boot or jump to ROM monitor. In many microcomputers, the combination is Ctrl-Alt-Del. Sometimes called the "three-finger salute."

Wedged—often mistakenly synonomized with crashes – refers to the inability of a computer to make progress. Unlike a crash, a computer which is wedged is not totally nonfunctioning.

Wetware—term used to refer to humans operating computers (as opposed to hardware and software).

White hat hackers—term used in the industry to designate "good" hackers.

Developments in mainframe technology were accompanied by innovations in other areas of computer technology. Created around the same time as ENIAC, Colossus I was built at a secret government lab in Buckinghamshire, England by Professor Max Newman. Unlike American innovations, Colossus I was designed exclusively for cryptanalysis. Using punched paper tape to scan and analyze 5,000 characters per second, this device proved to be invaluable in World War II as it broke the heretofore impenetrable "Enigma" codes used by the Nazi forces. This development, coupled with the design of the ABC and the ENIAC, led to an explosion of mainframe technologies in the 1960s and 1970s, when mainframe devices became in vogue across university and corporate landscapes. Finally, the ad-

Known as the founder of IBM or "Big Blue," Thomas J. Watson transformed the Computer-Tabulating-Recording Company (CTR) into one of the largest conglomerates in the world. (*Getting Images, Inc.—Hulton Archive Photos.*)

vent of PC's (originally containing operating systems like DOS and UNIX[2]) combined with the emergence of GUI platforms (like Windows™ and many Macintosh products) created a world accessible to technologically challenged individuals.

REALMS OF THE CYBERWORLD

Basically speaking, there are three different levels of networked systems: *intranets*, *internets*, and the *Internet*. *Intranets* are small, local networks connecting computers which are within one organization and which are controlled by a common system administrator. *Internets*, on the other hand, connect several networks, and are distinguished in the literature by a lower case *i* (i.e., internet as opposed to Internet). These networks are usually located in a small geographic area, and share a common protocol (usually TCP/IP). The *Internet*, on the other hand, is the largest network in the world, an international connection of all types and sizes of computer systems and networks. It is a system of small networks of computers linked with other networks via routers and software protocols. This TCP/IP-based network links tens of millions of users, across more than 45,000 net-

---

[2]UNIX, created in 1969 in Bell laboratories, was initially exclusive to large corporations and universities. Unix is especially well-suited for telecommunication systems, and creates an environment particularly seductive to hackers and phreakers. Originally designed for multi-user and multi-tasking computers, this operating system is gaining in popularity due to its stability and inexpensiveness.

works, in countries spanning the globe. Originally, this system was funded in large part by the U.S. government, and was not available for commercial usage.

A BRIEF HISTORY OF THE INTERNET

Although the infamous Cold War is fast becoming a distant memory, the 1960s were characterized by government suspicion and social hysteria. The threat of nuclear war and mass destruction were such that government entities focused on developing electronic communication systems that would remain viable even if large portions were somehow destroyed. The beginning was a project of the *Advanced Research Project Agency Network* (**ARPANET**) sponsored in 1969 by the Department of Defense. Primarily designed to overcome threats from a blackout of communication in the event of a nuclear war, this computer network linked four universities (UCLA, Stanford, UC Santa Barbara, and the University of Utah) and was intended to facilitate communications between computers over phone lines regardless of system characteristics (Baladi, 1999). Initially used by researchers, engineers, computer experts, and the like, the system proved to be rather cumbersome (and complicated). Interactive sessions were not possible. Rather, the method of communication required users to post suggestions in papers titled 'Requests for Comments' (RFC for short), and await responses or amendments to their documents. The first RFC (RFC0001) was written on April 7th, 1969—the closest thing to a 'start date' for the Internet. There are now well over 2000 RFCs, describing every aspect of how the Internet functions.

ARPANET was opened to non-military users later in the 1970s, and early takers were the big universities—although at this stage it resembled nothing like the Internet we know today. International connections (i.e., outside America) started in 1972, but the "Internet" was still just a way for computers to talk to each other and for research into networking; there was no World Wide Web and no e-mail as we now know it. By the mid-80s, this network was further expanded with the introduction of the NSF Net, established under the National Science Foundation by a small group of supercomputer research centers and researchers at remote academic and governmental institutions. This network was highly supported by the government, which encouraged researchers and institutions to avail themselves of this communication tool. This collaboration proved to be invaluable to the development of both online and offline computer communities, as well as the creation of a myriad of software which included **UNIX OS** (developed by Bell laboratories); **Mosaic Interface** (a multi-media interface for information retrieval) and **Eudora** (an e-mail system) contributed by the University of Illinois; **Gopher** (information retrieval tool) contributed by the University of Minnesota; **Pine** (e-mail), University of Washington; **CU-SeeMe** (low-cost video conferencing), Cornell (Adams, 1996). Such software innovations, coupled with (and often facilitated by) government grants, created a more user-friendly cyber-world.

By the mid-1980s, the Commercial Internet Xchange (CIX) had emerged, and midlevel networks were leasing data circuits from phone companies and subleasing them to institutions (Adams, 1996). Eventually, this small network had expanded into networks of networks, until the contemporary phenomenon known as the Internet emerged. During this period, the services we use most now started appearing on the Internet. In fact, the concept of "domain names" (e.g., *www.microsoft.com*), was first introduced in 1984. Prior to this introduction, computers were simply accessed by their IP addresses (numbers). Most protocols for e-mail and other services appeared after this.

The part of the Internet most people are probably most familiar with is the World Wide Web. This is a collection of hyperlinked pages of information distributed over the Internet via a network protocol called HTTP (hypertext transfer protocol). This was invented in 1989 by Tim Berners-Lee, a physicist working at CERN, the European Particle Physics Laboratory, who created the Web so that physicists could share information about their research. Thus, the Web was introduced as a restricted means of communication between scientists. Although it was originally a text-only medium, graphics were soon introduced with a browser called NCSA Mosaic. Both Microsoft's Internet Explorer and Netscape were originally based on NCSA Mosaic.

This graphical interface opened up the Internet to novice users and in 1993 its use exploded as people were allowed to 'dial-in' to the Internet using their computers at home and a modem to ring up an 'Internet Service Provider' (ISP) to get their connection to this (now huge) network. Prior to these developments, the only computers connected were at Universities and other large organizations that could afford to wire cables between each other to transfer the data over. Currently, there are several quick and inexpensive ways to connect to the Internet. At the minimum, users simply need a computer, a modem, a telephone line, and inter-computer communication software. These basics allow users to connect via Internet Service Providers (ISP). New trends, however, reveal that consumers are increasingly attracted to service-oriented ISP's—sometimes referred to as "Online Service Providers." These organizations provide consumers with navigational tools especially attractive to nontraditional users. Such accessibility has created unprecedented growth.

Internet growth has grown exponentially in the past decade—from 300 host computers in 1981 to over 36 million in 1998 (Doherty, 1999). Internet users have risen from 10–25 million in 1991 to 157 million in 1998; over 34 percent of households in the United States actively use the Internet. (The magnitude of use in the U.S. was recently apparent in the wake of Independent Counsel Kenneth Starr's report to Congress. Internet sites carrying the document were quickly overwhelmed and were, in effect, immobilized shortly after its release). The popularity of this medium has been fueled by the diversity of information available on the Web. Users' interests range from real-time information (i.e., scores of sporting events, current stock prices, etc.) to transactional services (i.e., banking, airline reservations, etc.) to entertainment (i.e., horoscopes, movie reviews, etc). Such popularity has also emerged due to the multitude of communications media including: e-mail, bulletin boards, newsgroups, or the most popular, the World Wide Web. The Web's popularity stems from the effortless nature of its communications. Even novice users can easily transmit audio, video, and graphic files.

● CATEGORIZING INTERNET COMMUNICATION

World Wide Web

The **World Wide Web** may be likened to an electronic marketplace where electronic storefronts of businesses, individuals, civic groups, and governments market both tangible and intangible products. Each electronic storefront established on the Internet is known as a Web site. These sites have a variety of goals. While many are profit-driven, others are developed for informational purposes only. Government agencies, public interest groups, educational institutions, and the like, often use this medium as an alternative to traditional means of information dissemination that may be costly and/or labor intensive. Regardless of motivation, each Web site may be identified by its *Uniform Resource Locator* **(URL).** These URLs are used for traffic control and Web management. Appearances range from the very basic texts only sites to sophisticated visual and audio configurations. In fact, these storefronts are only limited by the proprietors' imagination. It is anticipated that this marketplace will continue to experience exponential growth at the rate of 200 percent per year. Such growth may be primarily attributed to relatively low overheads associated with cyber capitalism. Not surprisingly, the presence of criminal elements within this realm is expected to increase proportionately.

Newsgroups/Bulletin Boards (Usenet Groups)

Two of the oldest methods, and certainly the most cumbersome, of digital communications are bulletin boards and newsgroups. (Although an accurate accounting is all but impossible, estimates for the number of bulletin boards in 1990 were approximated at 30,000 within the U.S. boundaries alone. By this publication, this number could have increased tenfold.) These communications involve posting services often likened to a community bulletin board where individuals or groups post meetings, information, or the like. More succinctly, bulletin boards may be characterized as a medium of computer exchange whereby individuals may have the capability of accessing software, posting personal information and exchanging electronic mail. This medium has proven especially popular among subversive and/or racist organizations, because it is much cheaper than printed publications and because complete globalization is possible. The lack of regulations and the perception of First Amendment protection also increase the viability for criminally minded individuals. Finally, utilization of validation controls by systems operators (i.e., collection of personal and other identifying information, such as home address or telephone number) further insulates deviants from law enforcement, and makes it extremely difficult for successful infiltration or investigation.

Message boards are popular media for exchanging information. Users range from sports fans to organized crime groups.

Bulletin boards vary based on the amount of time, energy, and supervision expended by the *sysop* (i.e., an abbreviation for a system operator who is an individual with authority to review and delete any information on the board). They also vary based on their degree of anonymity. Anonymous boards, for example, issue "handles" to users to protect their identities. Moderate boards, on the other hand, are those in which the sysop knows (or thinks s/he knows) the true identity of the users, but simple members or posters do not. And, finally, known user boards are those in which role playing and pseudonymous postings are forbidden.

Bulletin boards may also be grouped by their degree of immediacy. Some boards, commonly known as chatlines, allow users to connect and "chat" simultaneously, while single-phone-line boards store messages serially in order of their posting time. Because of their reliance on the level of sysop attention and operation, others only operate during designated periods. These same characteristics determine the size and accessibility of bulletin boards. Some boards, for example, are strictly private, restricted to friends or known associates of the sysop. These boards are especially popular among criminals and deviants. Other boards are more open, and allow users access based on the operator's discretion. However, many of these boards also reserve private areas. Thus, while a variety of individuals are permitted to join, they are restricted to certain portions of the board. These types of situations may also signal the presence of illicit materials or activities. Unfortunately, these types of boards may be especially problematic for law enforcement as favored individuals having unlimited access may actually serve as remote sysops, gaining control of the board via remote methods. As in previously discussed situations, this may create jurisdictional hazards for local law enforcement, particularly in those cases where the board is physically located in one jurisdiction, but is accessed, changed, or deleted remotely. These concerns are further exacerbated in situations involving national or international boards (e.g., CompuServe), which run on mainframe computers.

A final method of categorization involves the level of community found within postings, users, and system operators. Some boards are rather sterile and antiseptic, little more than software storage dumps where individuals download and/or upload software, but have no contact with other users or sysops. Other boards, however, are designed to facilitate interpersonal communications while protecting the anonymity of each poster and obscuring the contents from public dissemination, while others are designed as community affairs which emphasize public exchanges and forbid "lurkers" (i.e., those individuals who do not actively engage in communication, but simply watch those that do). Even these boards, however, may conceal nefarious activities. In fact, fringe groups abound on bulletin boards. Hackers, Satanists, anarchists, Nazis, pedophiles, child pornographers, and the like have found homes throughout the bulletin board landscape. Many on these boards, regardless of motivation or manner, attract users through the posting of pirated software (i.e., *wareZ*). Purely underground boards have proven to be transient and elusive, appearing and disappearing relatively quickly.

Internet Relay Chat

Internet Relay Chat (IRC), most commonly characterized by online discussions in "chat rooms", is increasing exponentially. Far less expensive than telephonic conversations, IRC provides users with the opportunity to talk longer to more peo-

TECHNOLOGICAL DEVELOPMENTS IN COMMUNICATIONS

- 60s—Lasers, copy machines, satellites (Echo 1, Telstar, Early Bird), fax machines.
- Early 1970s—fiber optics, videotape recorders, Intel 4004, Intel 8008.
- 1975–1980—TCP/IP spec, satellite (GPS), Apple and Microsoft developed.
- 1980s—300 baud, cell phones, IBM/PC, MacIntosh.
- 1985–1990—2400 baud, pagers, 286 Processor, 9600 baud, 386.
- 1990s–486, Modems 28.8K baud then 56K baud, Satellites (Iridium), Pentiums I, II, III, cable modems.

ple. Unlike traditional telephonic communications, chat rooms allow users to interact with several others at the same time, regardless of time and space differentials. In essence, a chat room is a technologically evolved party line.

Chat rooms are structured so that users may observe and participate in real-time conversations while "identifying" the nicknames of the individuals on the channel and their corresponding Internet Protocol (IP) addresses. Although some IRC may be located on generic servers, for the most part these chat rooms (or channels) are facilitated by Online Service Providers (OSPs). Categorized by topic, users can visit rooms designed for a variety of individuals ranging from singles to gardeners. Similar to a social gathering, individuals then have a variety of options. They may simply choose to observe (yes, wallflowers exist even in cyberspace); they may choose to participate in group discussions; or, they may choose to engage in a private conversation with one user—either by finding a corner of the room or stepping outside. On the surface, these rooms are provided by OSPs as a service to their customers, intended to group individuals with similar interests. In this "safe" environment, individuals may exchange ideas or information without fear of social reprisals or embarrassment. Indeed, the assurance of anonymity allows users to experiment with social (and legal) boundaries, while masking their identities and, perhaps, their intentions.

Topics in Internet chat rooms range from the innocuous to the profane. Online predators often use this medium, as it enables them to mask their identities with handles and develop relationships with unsuspecting victims. In fact, solicitations for sex are quite common in "teen" rooms.

While major online service providers facilitate this electronic dialogue, they fail to warn users of the potential for deception. In fact, most of these OSPs deny any responsibility (ethical or legal) for communications between users while promoting vacation packages and OSP social functions (For example, America Online encourages members to meet other users—developing singles' cruises and conventions in Vegas and the like.) Perversely, this ambiguity leads to further trust on the part of users, and provides an atmosphere conducive to criminal manipulation and sexual victimization—especially on the part of minors.

FUTURE ISSUES AND CONCLUSIONS

Advances in computer technology have increased exponentially in recent years. Ideas or visions once thought to be unattainable or fantastical are now considered to be overly simplistic or rudimentary. Simultaneously, new innovations or proposals which had originally been met with skepticism are now established mechanisms of digital communication. Indeed, technological inventions have only been slightly outpaced by their conception. The concept of cable modems, for example, was originally met with outright disbelief. However, the implementation of cable modem technology is currently sweeping the country. As in other areas of computer technology, such advances have been accompanied with significant side effects. While users delight in the speed and 24-hour connectivity of the medium, individual ne'er-do-wells have exploited stagnant IP addresses. (Unlike traditional dial-ups, cable modems are characterized by individual IP addresses, independent of internet service providers (ISPs). Unfortunately for users, 24-hour accessibility equates to 24-hour vulnerability. This is contrary to traditional systems in which users were only vulnerable for the actual period of their online activity. In addition, Windows systems have proven to be especially vulnerable, as they provide network sharing systems. Thus, the majority of individuals who embrace contemporary technology remain blissfully unaware that these same technologies are accompanied by system vulnerabilities.

TERMS DISCUSSED

ARPANet	IMAP	scanner
bombs	keyboards	software
bulletin boards	Malware	source code
buses	modems	TCP\IP
Central Processing Unit	motherboard	trap doors
cookies	network worm	Trojan horse
DNS	object code	URL
droppers	operating system	virus
hardware	packets	World Wide Web
Host Computer Worms	POP	worms
hubs	routers	

DISCUSSION QUESTIONS

1. Briefly discuss the history of the Internet, including major developments and advancements.
2. How can bulletin boards be categorized? Why are they favored by some deviant subcultures?
3. Discuss the advantages and disadvantages of global connectivity.
4. What are some of the methods of data destruction employed by malicious users? How are they spread, and what are the implications for the future?

3

HISTORY OF CRIME AND COMPUTER CRIME

INTRODUCTION

Like traditional areas of criminal behavior, a continuum of criminal activity, sophistication, and innovation exists among computer deviants. Ne'er-do-wells in both worlds range from novice to expert. Street criminals who leave a physical trail of evidence in their wake, for example, are no different from their technological counterparts who naively rely on the promise of anonymity posed by the vastness of cyberspace to secure them from the detection of law enforcement. At the same time, individuals from both areas may hinder discovery by engaging in criminal subterfuge or traditional camouflaging techniques like the donning of ski masks or gloves. In fact, the virtuosity and tangibility of such items are the only distinctions. Unfortunately, many investigators are not properly prepared to appreciate or even conceptualize such similarities, and have consequently overlooked the potentiality of criminal automation and innovation.

TRADITIONAL PROBLEMS

As stated in previous chapters, the advent of digital communications has greatly enhanced various aspects of American life. Advances in medicine, increases in academic knowledge, and the amplification of communication technology have significantly improved the quality of life for many individuals across the country. However, these advancements have not been accomplished without substantial side effects. Like their legitimate counterparts, criminal entrepreneurs have embraced this new sphere, augmenting their traditional arsenals and altering their *modus operandi* and staking a claim in this newly created world. Unfortunately, the real world and its consequences have not kept pace with its virtual counterpart. Thus, the criminal justice system in general and police administrators in particular have been forced to confront contemporary problems (i.e., the lack of criminal physicality and the intangibility and vulnerability of criminal evidence) with antiquated tools.

Traditionally, criminal statutes were predicated on the vicinage of the criminal act. Travel and location, for example, were assumed to be spatially based. Issues or concerns of jurisdiction only extended to the identification and maintenance of appropriate legal avenues and government sovereignty (e.g., state vs. federal interests). However, cyberworlds, with the potential for global connectivity, tran-

Just as Bonnie and Clyde used the newly invented automobile to flee from law enforcement authorities, today's
criminals are increasingly using computer technology to
thwart the police. *(CORBIS)*

scend traditional spatial boundaries and all but obscure legislated jurisdictions.
Thus, identification of the actual **vicinage** (i.e., location of the physical act) is often quite difficult. Take, for example, an American citizen residing in the state of
Tennessee who places an illegal wager on a sporting event by "purchasing" gaming software from a site located in the Canary Islands. To complicate matters, let's
assume that his funds to wager and any winnings earned are withdrawn and de-
posited electronically at a bank in Las Vegas. While he has violated both state and
federal statutes through his *possession* of an illegal gaming device (i.e., the gaming software), it is unclear whether any illegal wagering actually occurred. Thus,
the lack of physicality regarding the actual wagering has created a variety of jurisdictional disputes and legal conundrums (i.e., was criminal activity actually
committed? If so, which government agency holds jurisdictional sovereignty? Etc.).
This issue is further compounded by the absence of international guidelines for
cyber-activity. Indeed, many international entities have become havens for individuals or companies who intentionally circumvent the extant cyber-laws of the
United States. These countries, beneficiaries of exorbitant taxes and fees from
such corporations, have consistently failed to recognize the interests of the United
States and others. Such government apathy has even extended to cooperation on
criminal investigations in which they have no fiduciary interest. Unfortunately, a
modicum of cooperation is essential even in those cases in which vicinage is
firmly established. Take, for example, an individual in Washington, D.C., who
uses a server in Canada to send a threatening e-mail to the President of the United
States. To complicate matters, let's assume that this individual utilizes an

anonymizer[1] located in Germany, although the perpetrator and the victim are located in the same area. The cooperation of authorities in Canada and Germany may be essential to determine this "anonymous" individual. Thus, international cooperation must be created to eradicate the seduction of anonymity which confounds even the simplest of criminal investigations.

The promise of anonymity coupled with the dearth of inter-jurisdictional communication creates an environment in which many individual users naively assume that their identities are safely protected, thereby encouraging deviant activity. Such seduction enhances the potentiality of criminal and nefarious activities, as both criminals and their victims are lured into a blanket of security. Online harassment, stock manipulation, and child pornography have increased exponentially as such feelings have been intensified by the increase in anonymous e-mail accounts and re-mailers. While many individuals create cyber-identities to engage in harmless flirtations or role-playing, others hide behind handles to stalk innocents or defraud victims. Interestingly, those same individuals who create false identities for harmless entertainment fail to recognize that privacy may be a double-edged sword. Those same portals which failed to request or verify *their* subscriber information also failed to verify those with whom they are communicating.

Anonymous re-mailers also increase the susceptibility and vulnerability of naïve users, and frustrate the efforts of law enforcement. These "anonymizers" are designed to strip the source-address information from e-mail messages.[2] While privacy advocates and civil libertarians argue that these resources provide a nurturing environment for the First Amendment, many re-mailers appeal to those with prurient or less than academic interests. Some even target or direct their services to those self-same individuals, claiming that their site protects users from law enforcement and intelligence agencies. Thus, the promise of anonymity and the lack of international cooperation encourage criminal activity independently of user sophistication. Unfortunately, more sophisticated approaches have been employed by those individuals who are technologically savvy.

Individuals displaying elevated levels of savoir-faire have further frustrated the efforts of law enforcement via the utilization of encryption and steganography. Like other masking devices, digital encryption, the act of transforming structured data into indecipherable code, was originally intended to protect the online confidentiality of law-abiding citizens. Employed by financial institutions, government entities, retail establishments, and the like it was employed to prevent the theft of personal and financial information. As encryption programs have become increasingly available for public consumption, however, they have been utilized by criminals to hide their activities, both on- and off-line. In fact, the proliferation of encryption software, coupled with the increasing awareness of Internet security,

---

[1] Anonymizers are sites which enable users to mask their IP addresses through rerouting, remailing, or deletion of header information. This successfully conceals the sender's identity.

[2] Many of these services differ in their level of security. For example, some will hold messages for a period then send them out randomly through a multitude of other re-mailers, while others may simply strip the information and send the messages.

will most likely result in even greater usage. Although the federal government has proposed legislation which would make encryption keys discoverable under court order, current investigations are often stymied by the absence of such keys. In addition, some law enforcement agencies lack adequate resources to even identify the presence of online criminal activity. Such agencies are unable to detect criminal violations until it is too late.

Unlike traditional crimes where victimization is usually obvious, detection of computer crime is often delayed due to the self-same masking devices previously discussed. Although skilled investigators can usually divine the time and location of computer crime over time, technology is changing at a rate most favorable to the criminal mind. In fact, it has always proven difficult to identify the source and destination of communications on computers (Stambaugh, et al., 2001). However, the exponential increase in the multitude, diversity, and variance of telecommunication systems coupled with the advent of wireless communications has made it extremely difficult for investigators to respond within time constraints necessarily imposed by the volatility of digital evidence. (Unlike traditional communication carriers, internet service providers are not required to maintain transmission records. Although some do, the advent of bulk billing, eliminating the need for recording transmission information, has resulted in a lack of maintenance of transactional information). In addition, digital evidence has proven to be easily modified or deleted, and its voluminous nature has proven quite daunting for criminal investigators.

The investigation of computer crimes is often accompanied by unique obstacles. While investigators have struggled to keep abreast of recent technology, they have been hindered by a lack of judicial interest, administrative apathy, and cultural skepticism. For these reasons, a complete picture of the criminal landscape has yet to emerge. Indeed, the sheer potential of technologically supported criminal activity has yet to be realized. Although many of the obstacles appear at first glance to be insurmountable, an historical perspective of criminal behavior in general reveals similar periods of law enforcement uncertainty and criminal innovation. The introduction of the telephone, for example, allowed individuals to fine-tune their harassment of victims, plan criminal activities, and conspire across jurisdictional boundaries, while creating a plethora of law enforcement problems for authorities. In fact, early police were forced to rely on antiquated codes of behavior before the legislature passed specific legislation targeting criminal activities committed via telephone, like the Wire Act. Thus, law enforcement agencies should look to traditional statutes and federal legislation to prosecute computer crimes in the absence of technology-specific legislation.

⬤ RECOGNIZING AND DEFINING COMPUTER CRIME

It is unclear exactly when and where the first "computer crime" actually occurred. Contextually, theft of an abacus or a simple adding machine would constitute a computer crime. It is safe to assume that these types of activities occurred long before written or formal documentation was in vogue. However, the first documented instance of computer sabotage occurred in the early Nineteenth Century, when a textile manufacturer named Joseph Jacquard developed what would soon become the precursor to the computer card. His invention, which allowed repetitive automation of a series of steps in the weaving of special fabrics, was not popular among his workers, who feared for their continued employment. Thus, they dismantled his invention (United Nations, 2000). Unfortunately, such discussion does not adequately establish definitional parameters for criminal activity involving computers nor does the literature extend clarification. In fact, not all crimes involving computers can be characterized as "computer crime." It would not be appropriate, for example, to categorize a residential burglary as a computer crime, even if a computer was among the items stolen. At the same time, the hijacking of an entire shipment of computer hard drives is more appropriately situated elsewhere. And, finally, the theft of millions of dollars via computer hacking is most properly denoted as a "cybercrime." However, in all of these situations, a forensic computer scientist may be helpful. Accordingly, this book has attempted to identify those crimes in which a computer specialist might be helpful, and has used the terms *computer crime* and *computer-related crime* interchangeably.

THREE INCIDENTS

Although the threat of wide-scale criminal activity via computer has existed for decades, government officials tended to overlook the seriousness of **phreaking** and hacking prior to the mid 1980s. In fact, computer crime was all but ignored until a variety of cases exposed the vulnerability of data systems and outlined potential cataclysmic repercussions for national security. Unfortunately, such legislative and enforcement apathy created an environment conducive to criminal activity.

The first event to signal the potential of computer crime occurred in 1986, when an accounting error of less than one dollar was investigated by a dedicated employee at the University of California at Berkeley. This internal investigation revealed that a German hacker in the employ of the KGB had tapped into a military database and obtained sensitive (but not classified) information. Using only a personal computer and a basic modem, this individual was able to connect to Berkeley computers via an independent data carrier (i.e., Tymnet). Once connected, the hacker was able to move about the MILNET system with remarkable ease and relative impunity. The fact that such vulnerability existed within data systems was especially disconcerting to administrators because of its almost accidental discovery. In fact, without the efforts of this employee, it is highly improbable that this activity would have been uncovered. While his efforts were largely directed at accounting discrepancies, his findings resulted in the recognition of information risks associated with open systems. Governmental entities, traditionally lax in computer security, soon initiated measures to protect electronically stored information, especially military secrets. However, they continued to overlook the economic dangers associated with computer networking.

In 1988, only two years after the MILNET fiasco, legislators were forced to recognize additional threats to computer security after a program developed by a Cornell University student crippled over 6,000 computers and caused between $5 and $100 million in damages. This program, called the "Morris worm" (after its inventor, Robert Morris), was intended to attack computers via the Internet. This incident, the first of its kind, exploited security holes in the Unix operating system, infecting 10 percent of all computers connected to the Internet (Stambaugh, et al, 2001). Such wide-scale infestation created a major stumbling block for this newly emerging medium, unforeseen by all, even its creator. (It seems clear that Morris did not intend the havoc that was subsequently unleashed. In fact, when he recognized the possible implications of his actions, he released an anonymous message to programmers which instructed them how to disable the worm. Unfortunately, this message did not reach many of the intended recipients as the worm had already overloaded many systems.) Morris was subsequently convicted of violating the Computer Fraud and Abuse Act (CFAA), and sentenced to three years probation, 400 hours of community service, and fines of more than $10,000.

The destruction caused by Morris' worm was soon overshadowed by the crash of AT&T, then America's number one telephone provider. Although not entirely unprecedented, the magnitude of this crash, coupled with the lack of a particularized physical reason, signaled the beginning of hacking hysteria. Unfortunately, this hysteria was reminiscent of the "satanic panic" of the early 1980s in which American cities became besieged by rumors of robed worshipers slaughtering innocents. Suddenly, all technological failures were incorrectly attributed to a dark force of computer geniuses. In fact, most experts agree that the problem precipitating the crash had nothing to do with hackers al all, but was actually the responsibility of AT&T software. However, the possibility that hackers could disrupt vital services led to the persecution of several hacking groups, most notable of which was the **Legion of Doom** (LoD).

The Legion of Doom (LoD) derived its name from Superman comic books which glorified the antics of a circle of super-villains headed by criminal mastermind, Lex Luthor. Like their fictional counterparts, members of LoD relentlessly promoted themselves, boasting of their exploits on a variety of bulletin boards, including: The Legion of Doom Board, Plovernet, The Farmers of Doom Board, Metal Shop, Blottoland, Atlantis, Digital Logic, and Hell Phrozen Over. In addition, individual members created boards of their own, including *Silver Spy's* Catch-22, and *Mentor's* Phoenix Project. Originally, members of this group were expert phreakers, not hackers. However, as technology expanded, so did the activities of LoD.

Although it is impossible to determine the number of members formally associated with LoD and to pinpoint their activities, it is clear that law enforcement incorrectly assumed that all hacking activities could be attributed to the group. While the group certainly enjoyed the infamy and notoriety associated with these assumptions, most members were not malicious or criminally minded. In fact, many of these individuals nobly proclaimed themselves as public servants, pointing out security flaws in institutional systems so that repairs would be made, while others eventually sought employment at the self-same institutions that they had victimized (For example, longtime LoD member *Control-C* was actually hired by Michigan Bell after victimizing them for several years. The situation proved most beneficial to Michigan Bell, because hackers were dissuaded from attacking the techno structure that their friend had been hired to protect.) Unfortunately, some members of the group did not abide by the common ethos, and did, in fact, actively exploit systems for personal gain. These individuals, namely *Fry Guy* and *The Atlanta Three* (*Prophet*, *Urvile*, and *Leftist*), were directly responsible for the downfall of the group. Ironically, *Fry Guy*, described as an LoD wannabe, had never even met the Atlanta Three.

The beginning of the end for LoD was initiated by the arrest of petty hacker and braggart extraordinaire, *Fry Guy*, following his threat that LoD would crash the national telephone network on Independence Day. Armed with criminal evidence of his manipulation of switching stations and wire fraud and credit card fraud, the Secret Service gained his cooperation in which he revealed the "plot" by LoD to crash the phones on "a national holiday." His proclamations appeared to be on target when a blackout occurred on Martin Luther King Day, 1990. (However, this failure appears to have been nothing more than an irony of coincidence.) Based on his proclamations, the Secret Service obtained pen registers on the phones of The Atlanta Three—Prophet, Urvile, and Leftist. Both Urvile and Leftist agreed to cooperate, naively, and arrogantly, believing that their activities did not constitute criminal behavior.

However, Prophet, a Unix programming expert with a criminal history, had circumvented the security measures of AT&T, and downloaded and forwarded numerous copies of a document identified as *Bell South Standard Practice 660-25-104SV Control Office Administration of Enhanced 911 Services for Special Services and Major Account Center*. Copies were subsequently forwarded to the editor of *Phrack* (i.e., *Knight Lightning*), the "Phoenix Project", and a variety of other admirers of LoD. In fact, numerous outlets carried the infamous documents, and wide-scale searches were soon initiated by the Secret Service. One such search of a sysop's computer uncovered the existence of a board called *Illuminati*—a full-service board, owned and operated by Steve Jackson Games, Inc., which offered services ranging from electronic messaging to role-playing simulation.

The subsequent search of Steve Jackson Games, Inc. (SJG) resulted in one of the first legal rulings regarding the application of the Fourth Amendment to computer systems. This seminal case, *Steve Jackson Games, Inc.* v. *U.S. Secret Service, et al.*, 36 F. 3d 457, 463 (Fifth Cir., 1994), proved to be an embarrassment to the United States Secret Service. Agents were accused of Gestapo-like tactics after they seized virtually everything, including business records, private electronic mail, the entire bulletin board, and the drafts of forthcoming games and their accompanying literature. Their arguments that the bulletin board was a medium for the exchange of hacking information was subsequently ruled as unfounded, and their execution of an *unsigned* search warrant were harshly criticized by the Court.

The legal criticisms originally levied by the Fifth Circuit were soon echoed in the private sector as well. The Electronic Frontier Foundation, hosted on "The Well", was created by Grateful Dead member David Barlow, and the co-creator of Lotus 1-2-3, Mitchell Kapor. Their articulated mission was to protect the privacy

A SAMPLING OF INFAMOUS HACKERS

Terminus—a Unix programmer and AT&T minicomputer expert, adopted this particular handle to proclaim his hacker superiority. Although he eventually became a telecommunications programmer, his early career included the development of the first telco scanning programs. In addition, Terminus had victimized telecommunications providers for years, pirated AT&T proprietary software and stole electronic messages stored on their systems.

Shadowhawk—notable for his expertise and braggadocio at hacking the AT&T system, received a sentence of nine months and a fine of $10,000 for breaking and entering into a computer at U.S. Missile Command. While the government contended that his activities resulted in the theft of millions of dollars of data, Shadowhawk never sold or profited from the sale of any of the software illegally appropriated.

Kyrie—one of the few females achieving hacker notoriety, specialized in abusing corporate voice mail. Unlike Terminus and Shadowhawk, Kyrie aggressively used her skills for profit, compiling a group of 150 phone freaks who paid her for her information regarding long-distance dialing codes with stolen credit card numbers. Kyrie's activities were further compounded by the fact that she included her children in her wrongdoing, denying them a legal identity and depriving them of formal education. Like those before her, Kyrie's excessive bragging led to her downfall. After phoning to taunt Assistant Attorney General Gail Thackeray, Kyrie was sentenced to 27 months for her activities.

of American citizens and to encourage the growth of the World Wide Web. These individuals were soon joined by several cyber-luminaries and computer entrepreneurs including Steve Wozniak (Apple Computers) and John Gilmore (Sun Microsystems). These trailblazing efforts resulted in the creation of a variety of communication platforms designed to protect the privacy of the electronic frontier. One of the most recognizable is the Electronic Privacy Information Center (EPIC), which serves as an information clearinghouse on pending and current legislation, judicial leanings, and activities of government agencies. While it recognizes the vulnerability of sensitive information, hardware, and computer systems, this organization seeks to limit the amount of government intrusion and oversight.

CONTEMPORARY CRIMES

Just as law enforcement tended to overlook the seriousness of hacking and phreaking in the 1980s, legislative bodies have been slow to respond to the potentiality of contemporary computer crime in the Twenty-first Century. In fact, the strides made in electronic communications and the increasing emphasis on point-and-click platforms have enabled a variety of criminally minded individuals to expand their horizons. Traditionally, computer crime was comprised mainly of trafficking in stolen equipment or falsification of records. Although certain types of computer crime were possible prior to the introduction of cyberspace, the marriage of computer and telecommunications has resulted in an explosion of crime. The impression of anonymity has proven all but irresistible to criminally minded individuals. In fact, it may be argued that some individuals who had previously been deterred by the fear of exposure are more susceptible to the temptations posed by this type of platform. Indeed, preliminary estimates of Internet gambling, illegal in virtually every area of the country, suggest that the Web, with its promise of anonymity, has encouraged criminal activity among the masses. To wit, individuals who would never walk into an adult book store in search of photographs or videos of bestiality or child pornography, readily download those same materials in the privacy of their home[3]. Those unwilling to walk into a bank with a gun may feel comfortable altering bank records or manipulating stock records. Those same individuals who were dissuaded from seeking revenge through traditional avenues, may feel completely confident in posting embarrassing or compromising information on the web.

Even hackers, whom many authorities believed to be a relic of the 1980's, are increasingly dangerous. Recent cases indicate that computer dependency and communication globalization have been exploited by individual, group, and government hacking entities. A group known as *Global Hell*, for example, is suspected of hacking into a variety of government sites including the U.S. Department of the Interior, the United States Army, the Federal Bureau of Investigation, and the White House. Although their motivations appear to be a simple quest for notoriety as opposed to the destruction of government property, implications for national security are tremendous. Other implications of computer crime include:

1. financial losses,
2. personal security (i.e., identity theft),
3. industrial espionage,
4. international security, and,
5. public safety.

In fact, threats to public welfare and personal safety may surpass national security concerns. (Britain and Italy, for example, lost vital information from hematology studies and one year's worth of AIDS research, respectively. While in the United States, one large Northeast hospital lost over 40 percent of all patient records due to a virus.)

---

[3]Ostensibly, the primary purpose of newsgroups and bulletin boards is to disseminate information to a wide audience. This dissemination is usually directed at individuals sharing a common interest. The courts have likened these posting boards to newspapers or television broadcasts. As such, they have accorded these institutions a greater level of protection than other forms of electronic activity. Accordingly, the Privacy Protection Act all but precludes the seizure of the physical hardware involved in operating a BBS.

SEEKING REVENGE

Computers have proven an effective means of retaliation for terminated employees. Unlike workplace violence, the manipulation of computer systems provides a mechanism for dismantling entire corporations, leaving individual employees unharmed. Systems manager Donald Burelson, for example, employed a logic bomb which targeted the commission records for over 60,000 independent insurance agents. This logic bomb was predicated on personnel records, and was activated when his employment status was changed in the system.

CATEGORIZING COMPUTER CRIME: TARGETS, MEANS, AND INCIDENTALS

The categorization of computer crime for ease in explanation is, at best, cumbersome. However, there are three general categories of computer crime: targets, means, and incidentals. Please note, that while these categories are intended to be inclusive of the myriad of computer-related crime they are not mutually exclusive, as many computer crimes involve a multiplicity of intentions. For example, insiders may target a computer system for destruction due to perceptions of mistreatment, and, at the same time, may use the computer as a means of committing embezzlement. In hacking activities, one computer provides the means for the criminal activity, while another serves as the target. Finally, an individual may improperly gain access to a computer (i.e., unauthorized use) to steal information which resides therein. Thus, s/he would be targeting a computer, while at the same time, using it as an instrument to commit criminal activity. (Chapter Four will explore computers as targets.)

Phreaking and Telecom Crime—the earliest pattern of computer crime?

As stated previously, phreakers were the precursors of today's computer hackers. Initially, the motivation was simply to break the system—a system which claimed to be impenetrable. Like their evolved counterparts, phreakers routinely held conferences in which they discussed their exploits and shared their successes. Often times, these individuals would build "bridges", illegal conference calls of numerous individuals around the world billed to someone else. However, many of these incidents were overlooked by a law enforcement population which was hopelessly overwhelmed by an increase in predatory crime and a lack of personnel, economic resources, and political assistance. Unfortunately, this allowed this unique population to flourish. (In 1994, for example, it was estimated that 150,000 physical attacks on pay telephones occurred.) Thus, the 1980s and 1990s became a virtual playground for hackers and phreakers alike.

By definition, phreaking involves the manipulation of telecommunications carriers to gain knowledge of telecommunications, and/or theft of applicable services. Also identified broadly as *telecommunications fraud*, phreaking includes any

INFAMOUS HACKING AND PHREAKING BOARDS

8BBS—One of the first hacking boards, 8BBS, went online in March, 1980 and became especially popular on the West Coast. This group sponsored "Susan Thunder" and perhaps, most notably, "the Condor". In fact, the Condor's activities were so self-serving that his fellow hackers turned him in to the police. (Many of his activities have reached epic proportions. Unfortunately, such propagation has all but obscured the truth of his criminal behavior.) By all accounts, this board was not developed to facilitate criminal activities. However, some individuals attracted to the board could not resist the temptation to utilize their hacking skills for illicit purposes. The board was effectively shut down after it was discovered that some of their technology had been purchased via credit card fraud.

Plovernet—East Coast hacking board, Plovernet, was owned and operated by a teenage hacker who was known by the handle "Quasi Moto." It was a breeding ground for hacking groups like Legion of Doom. (Lex Luthor, the LoD founder, was at one time a co-sysop.)

414 Private—A hacking group of teenagers whose antics attracted national attention (some of the first), after they hacked into the Los Alamos military computers and Sloan-Kettering Cancer Center in 1982.

ALTOS—Considered in underground circles to represent the epitome of sophisticated, international hacking, ALTOS was originally formed in Bonn, Germany.

activity that incorporates the illegal use or manipulation of access codes, access tones, PBXs, or switches. According to accomplished phreakers, the theft of telephone access codes is the bottom rung of phone phreaking, due to the absolute lack of technical expertise required. By far the easiest way to steal access codes is to simply "shoulder surf," stealing the code from unsuspecting individuals while they are dialing. A more sophisticated approach, war-dialing, involves random number generators which test numerous codes until one is successful. One of these programs running throughout the night may generate several hits which are then compiled into a large database. The programs which enable these computerized code thefts have quickly found their way to the Internet, and are readily available for downloading. Both of these techniques have proven especially popular in college dormitories, military establishments, and traveling road crews (Sterling, 1994). Unfortunately for many criminals, surveillance technology is now available to identify computerized dialing, making war-dialing for access codes rather obsolete. However, it is currently popular among Third World immigrants in the United States. In addition, a slightly modified technology is now being employed by computer hackers.

Another method of defeating the telephone company, employed by such notables as Steven Jobs and Steve Wozniak, the founders of Apple Computer, Inc., involved the invention of hardware devices (Sterling, 1994). These *Blue Boxes*, as they were known, were devices which "tricked" switching systems into granting free access to long distance lines. These devices were also extremely popular among college dorms, and were considered by users as harmless. However, the telephone company saw it otherwise, and was directly responsible for the bankruptcy of *Ramparts*, an underground magazine which printed a do-it-yourself guide to blue-box creation. Fortunately, blue boxes have become outdated, largely ineffective since the advent of digital switching. However, other mechanisms, devices, technologies and *targets* of telecommunications frauds have emerged.

By the mid-80s, AT&T, tired of excessive losses to phone phreaking and telecom fraud, created ANI (Automatic Number Identification) trace capability. This technology successfully dampened the spirits of many phreakers who soon found easier targets in the Baby Bells, long distance competitors, among others. Phreakers have also infiltrated locally owned PBXs and voice mail systems, concealing themselves in hidden and unallocated places. One popular practice is to "divert" messages, saving the long distance charges. This practice involves infiltrating a private branch-exchange system, mimicking the same system, and dialing across the world. Thus, the victim actually suffers twofold: intrusion and fraud. Others simply regenerate a dial tone through a PBX or voice mail system. This strategy has been employed against such technological giants as Unisys and IBM to the tune of $300,000 and $400,000, respectively (SEARCH, 2000). While the economic benefits attract some phreakers, others are attracted to the challenge. These phreakers often wreak havoc among vulnerable systems, deleting voice mail messages and denying legitimate users access. Many companies feel so threatened by these criminals that they actually acquiesce to any demands made by them, while contemporary law enforcement authorities tend to minimize the seriousness of phreaking and even deny its very existence. Unfortunately, there is virtually no evidence to support the supposition that phreaking is outdated or decreasing in popularity. In fact, the lines between telephone phreaking and computer hacking have become increasingly blurred.

Many of the methods employed by early phreakers are now prevalent within the hacker community (many of whom started their hacking "careers" as phreakers). Patrick W. Gregory, for example, pled guilty to one count of conspiracy for teleconferencing fraud and computer cracking for his role as a founding member of a hacking ring called Global Hell. Allegedly causing over $1.5 million in damages to various U.S. corporations and government entities including the U.S. Army and the White House, his plea included charges of stealing telephone conferencing services from AT&T, MCI, and Latitude Communications and holding conference calls for over two years. Thus, while traditional mechanisms involving black boxes or recording devices to mimic long distance tones have become passé, new methods involving the manipulation of PBX systems have emerged.

Innovative ways of utilizing stolen PBX codes are also being employed by individuals involved in organized crime syndicates. Known as "call-sell" operations, pre-paid calls are sold on the street using stolen access or PBX codes. These scams

TRADITIONAL PHREAKING TOOLS

RED BOX	generates tones for free phone call
BLACK BOX	callers do not pay a charge for incoming calls
BEIGE BOX	lineman's handset
GREEN BOX	generates coin return tones
CHEESE BOX	turns a personal phone into a pay phone
AGUA BOX	disables government tracing
BLAST BOX	phone microphone amplifier
BLOTTO BOX	shorts out all phones in your area
BLUE BOX	generates a 2600-hz tone
BROWN BOX	creates a party line
BUD BOX	taps into a neighbor's phone
CHATREUSE BOX	uses electricity from phone
CHROME BOX	manipulates traffic signal
COLOR BOX	records phone conversations
COPPER BOX	causes cross talk interference
CRIMSON BOX	acts as a hold button
DARK BOX	reroutes calls
DAYGLO BOX	connects to neighbor's phone line
DIVERTER BOX	reroutes calls
DLOC BOX	creates a party line
GOLD BOX	dial out router
INFINITY BOX	remote activated phone
JACK BOX	touch-tone key pad
LIGHT BOX	in-use light
LUNCH BOX	AM transmitter
MAGENTA BOX	connect remote phone line to another
MAUVE BOX	phone tap without cutting a line
NEON BOX	external microphone
PARTY BOX	creates a party line
PEARL BOX	tone generator
PINK BOX	creates party line
RAINBOW BOX	kills trace

are highly organized, and cost telecommunications providers an inestimable sum in damages. A similar scam has also been applied to recent innovations in cellular technology. This type of activity is possible due to the reprogrammable nature of cellular chips. Thus, it is relatively easy for criminals to present false caller identification to avoid billing. In addition, this activity allows criminals to avoid traditional law-enforcement wiretapping, making it especially popular among drug dealers and organized crime figures. This activity is increasing in popularity, and it is not unusual to find pirate cell phones being sold from the back of trucks across the country (Sterling, 1994).

PHREAKING—MAKING A RED BOX

Various Internet sites provide tutorials of how to engage in hacking and phreaking, providing the essentials and instructing amateurs to avoid detection and prosecution—even including instructions on how to make boxes for nefarious purposes.

A "Red Box", one of the premier tools of phreaking, allows users to generate tones so that users can avoid toll charges.

Necessary Equipment

Available at local electronics retailers:

- Tone dialers
- 6.5536 Mhz Crystal

Steps

- Simply open up dialer and replace the 3.579545 crystal with the 6.5536 mhz one.
- Simply play the number of tones requested by the operator using the following schematic
  - $.25—five times
  - $.10—three times
  - $.05—once

Other Methods

Simply buy a phreaking program like *Fear's Phreaker Tools* or *Omnibox* and record the tones from computer speakers.

Note

Regardless of method, Red Boxes (and many other phreaking tools) only work on public telephones which use Automated Coin Toll System (ACTS) or operator assisted calls.

Traditional methods also included the use of "Customer Owned Customer Operated Telephones (COCOT's) where users (or abusers) could receive free calls by dialing an (800) number, waiting for the operator to hang up, and then dialing the number directly.

Internet Scams

Like telemarketing fraud, the amount of money consumers are losing to Internet fraud is increasing dramatically. More specifically, losses total in the millions, with one consumer watchdog agency reporting losses as high as $3,387,530. In addition, it is estimated that the average loss per person rose from $310 in 1999 to

$427 in 2000 (source: *http://www.fraud.org/internet/lt00totstats.htm*, last accessed on 10/2/01). Newly emerging patterns of telecommunications fraud include *web-cramming* and *ISP-Jacking*, both of which are similar to the 1-800 and 1-900 scams of the late 80s and early 90s in which callers were not informed of per-minute charges which were incurred for "free" phone services.

Web-cramming is most often accomplished when criminals develop new web pages for small businesses and non-profit groups for little or no expense. While advertising their service as free, these criminals actually engage in unauthorized phone charges on their victim's accounts. The most common scam involves the use of "rebate checks." These checks, when cashed, transferred the consumer's ISP, placing monthly service charges on their telephone bill. Web-cramming is possible because telephone companies contract to provide billing and collection services for other companies that sell telecommunications-related services. **ISP-Jacking,** on the other hand, involves disconnecting individual users from their selected Internet Service providers and redirecting them to illegitimate servers. In these cases, users are lured into downloading software which surreptitiously disconnects their chosen Internet service provider, silences their modem, and reconnects them to a remote server. Increasingly common, this type of scam has traditionally been overlooked by law enforcement authorities. However, the creation and implementation of computer crime units has helped somewhat. In 1999, the Royal Canadian Mounted Police, for example, uncovered a complicated scam in which Canadian users were rerouted through Moldova (a republic in the former Soviet Union) and other international locations to Dallas, Texas—resulting in thousands of dollars in long distance charges. As a result of their investigation, at least two Web sites (*www.sexygirls.com*) and (*www.erotica2000.com*) were shut down. Unlike other scams which tend to focus on customers of pay-for-porn scams, this particular type of scam does not require the posting of credit card information, and therefore, is more insidious as even the most cautious users are snared. Unfortunately, telecommunications fraud is often given a low priority among local and state authorities, as a result techno-cowboys remain relatively free to wreak havoc on unsuspecting victims. Such is the case in the burgeoning marketplace of Internet scams, where auction fraud, credit card fraud, get-rich-quick schemes, and "work at home" scams are common occurrences.

While Internet scams have taken on a variety of appearances and may appear quite innovative to the untrained investigator, many of them are simply new tricks from an old dog. Get-rich-quick and work-at-home schemes have simply found a new home on the information superhighway. Job, scholarship, and loved-one searches requiring advance fees have replaced the sometimes nefarious gumshoes of the past. In fact, individuals and entities which have traditionally preyed on the vulnerable within society have simply developed new, more sophisticated modes of operation. Such is the case with the *Nigerian found money* and *advance fee* scams. These scams are highly organized, and are perpetrated by individuals involved in the Nigerian organized crime syndicate. Long a mainstay of this group, these types of scams have emerged in the techno-landscape with a vengeance, rendering traditional investigative methods and prosecutorial avenues moot. More succinctly, gang members have simply changed the mode of communication from traditional postal operations to electronic platforms. Unfortunately, the scams appear to be just as successful in this arena, as their scams have enabled them to defraud individuals and businesses without the complication of oral or personal communication.

Nigerian Advance Fee Scheme. Known internationally as "4-1-9", the section of the Nigerian penal code which addresses fraud schemes, this scam is usually directed at small and medium-sized businesses or charities. Quite elementary in nature and execution, the *4-1-9 scam* has six primary steps:

1. Victims are identified and targeted through sources ranging from trade journals, professional directories, newspapers, etc.
2. Individual or company receives e-mail from a "government or agency official" (such as a senior civil servant in one of the Nigerian ministries, like the Nigerian National Petroleum Corporation).
3. The e-mail informs recipient that this government or agency is willing to transfer millions of dollars in "over-invoiced contracts", if:
4. recipient provides blank copies of letterhead, banking account information, and telephone/fax information. (These letters, in turn, are used to seduce other victims—these are often used to obtain a travel visa from the American embassy.
5. As the scam involves cultivating the trust of the recipient, more official documentation is received from the "government or agency" (i.e., authentication letters with official looking stamps, government seals or logos which support the claims).
6. Once trust is obtained, up-front fees are requested for taxes, government bribes, attorney fees, or the like (Grennan, Britz, Rush & Barker, 2000).

Of course, there is no money, but these scams remain wildly successful due primarily to American and European greed. Designed to delude the victim into thinking that he or she had been singled out or is extremely lucky to be the beneficiary of such grandiosity, these scams are also successful because victims are loathe to report their sheer gullibility. Unfortunately, individuals and corporations have been divested of millions of dollars before they realize the error of their ways. Such individuals, wishing to make a quick buck (in this case, several million), fall victim to these hoaxes even though warning signs are all around. Some even fall victim to a secondary scam known as the *Nigerian recompensation scam.* Just like the original scam, this fraud is initiated through an unsolicited electronic communication, in which the perpetrators claim to be members of the Nigerian government's recompensation unit—a unit designed to make restitution to victims of Nigerian scams. Once again relying on official-looking documents and titles, victims are asked to forward sums of money to cover administrative costs. Amazingly, many of those previously victimized are easy prey for this secondary assault!

Below is an actual copy of an e-mail received from one of the author's students. Although these scams are anything but new, the method for distribution is changing. Note the misspellings and grammatical errors.

From: "DON CYRIL" <*don_cyrilcc@email.com*>
To: *xxxxxxxxxxxxx@hotmail.com*
Subject: URGENT AND CONFIDENTAIL
Date: Thu, 31 Oct 2002 01:22:07-0500

3/5 RIDER HAGGARD CLOSE,
JOHANNESBURG,
SOUTH AFRICA.
Phone: 874762864167
Fax: 874762864168

SUBJECT: {URGENT TRANSACTION PROPOSAL} RE: TRANSFER OF $126,000,000.00USD. {ONE HUNDRED AND TWENTY SIX MILLION UNITED STATES DOLLAR}.

With due respect and humility, I write to you this business transaction proposal. I am Mr DON CYRIL, the auditor General of a bank in South Africa. During the course of our auditing, I discovered a floating fund in an account opened in the bank in 1990 and since 1993, nobody has operated on this account again. After going through some old files in the records, I discovered that the owner of the account died without a heir/next of kin or any close relation. I am writing following the impressive information about you through one of my friends who run a consultancy firm in your country.

The owner of this account is Mr. Gordon G. Scott, a foreigner, and a sailor. He died in 1993 in a road accident and no other person knows about this account or anything concerning it. The account has no other beneficiary and my investigation proved to me as well that Mr. Gordon G. Scott until his death was the manager Diamond Safari Company(pty) South Africa.

According to our Banking policies and guideline here which stipulates that if such money remained unclaimed after five years, the money will automatically be transfered into the Bank treasury as unclaimed fund. The request of foreigner as next of kin in this business transaction is occasioned by the fact that the customer was a foreigner and a citizen of south Africa cannot stand as next of kin to a foreigner.

We will start the first transfer with twenty six million {$26,000,000.00usd}. Upon successful conclusion without any disappointment from your side, he shall re-apply for the payment of the remaining amount to your account. The amount involved is {USD126M} One hundred and twenty six million United States Dollars. Only I want to first transfer $26,000,000.00 {twenty six million United States Dollar} from this money into a safe foreigner's account abroad before the rest, but I don't know any foreigner, I am only contacting you as a foreigner because this fund cannot be approved to a local account for the deseased owner is a foregner. It can only be approved into a foreign a/c.

The management of the bank is ready to release this fund to any person who has the correct information about the account. With my influence and the position of the bank officials, we can transfer this money to any foreigner's reliable account which you can provide with assurance that this money will be intact pending our physical arrival in your country for sharing. The bank officials will destroy all documents of transaction immediately we receive this money leaving no trace of the fund to any place. Two of us will fly>to your country immediately after the fund is remmited into your account.

I will apply for annual leave to get visa immediately I hear from you that you are ready to act and receive this fund in your account. I will use my position and influence to obtain all legal approvals for onward transfer of this money to your account with appropriate clearance from the relevant ministries and foreign exchange departments.

At the conclusion of this transaction, you will be given 35% of the total amount, as a foreign partner, in respect to the provision of a foreign account, 60% will be for me, while 5% will be for reimbursement of any expenses incured during the curse of the transaction.

Therefore to enable the immediate transfer of this fund to you as arranged, you must apply first to the bank as relation or next of kin of the deceased, indicating your bank name, your bank account number and location where the fund will be remitted.

Upon the receipt of your reply, I will send to you by fax or email the text of the application. I will not fail to bring to your notice that this transaction is hitch free and that you should not entertain any atom of fear as all required arrangements have been made for the transfer. You should contact me immediately as soon as you receive this letter. Trusting to hear from you immediately through this very email address.
DON_CYRIL10@LYCOS.COM
Thanks and best regards,
DON CYRIL

In addition to the 4-1-9 scams, there are six additional patterns of Nigerian fraud:

1. disbursement of money from wills;
2. transfer of funds from over invoiced contracts;
3. conversion of hard currency;
4. purchase of real estate;

5. contract fraud (C.O.D. of goods or services); and,

6. sale of crude oil at below market prices.

Unfortunately, each pattern of criminal activity shares similar characteristics which ensure their success and profitability. First, each of the scams has an aura of urgency and the ephemeral, in which the victims are encouraged to work with utmost haste before this lucrative (albeit slightly illegal) opportunity evaporates. Second, targets precipitate their future victimization (i.e., the victim becomes the aggressor), in which they become willing to expend greater funds if the deal is threatened. Third, victims are seduced into silence—reluctant to share their "good fortune" with others. Finally, victims are dazzled by documents in which inferences of corrupt government officials or corporate officers support their very authenticity—remember: many of these forms are actually byproducts of previous scams (Grennan, Britz, Rush, and Barker, 2000).

Collectively, these scams cost American corporations and private citizens millions of dollars. The problem has become so pervasive that the United States Secret Service has established "Operation 4-1-9." This international effort, documented at *www.treas.gov/usss/alert419.htm* (last accessed 4/18/01), receives approximately 100 calls and 300-500 pieces of related correspondence per day! In fact, the United States Secret Service has even established a presence at the American Embassy in Lagos in an attempt to improve the efficiency and effectiveness of their investigations and countermeasures. Unfortunately, the lack of international cooperation and the lack of adequate prosecutorial avenues (i.e., federal laws specifically prohibiting mail fraud do not apply to electronic communications) have made it extremely difficult for law enforcement authorities.

Non-Phreaking, Neo-Traditional Crime

While the Internet has increased the potential for interpersonal crime via computer, comparable advances in printing technologies, software capabilities, digital cameras, and the like have increased the sophistication of non-Internet criminal activity. Traditional methods of counterfeiting currency, defrauding financial institutions, viewing child pornography, and the like, have all been supplanted by more advanced approaches. Techniques for manipulating stocks, exchanging radical platforms, and criminal solicitation are increasingly modified to incorporate advances in technology. These advances mirror those found in legitimate markets. The same printers, copiers, and scanners which have greatly improved the ability of illegitimate users to counterfeit stock certificates, official documents, and even currency have also been utilized to create more sophisticated security measures for American currency, making watermarks passé.

Fraud and fraudulent instruments

As stated previously, advancements in technology have greatly improved American life, while creating innovative opportunities for deviant members of society. **Counterfeiting** and **Forgery,** the act of creating a fraudulent document and the act of falsifying a document (including the falsification of signatures) with criminal intent, respectively, have been made far easier with the advent of high-level graphical software and hardware advances. As with other areas of computer crime, organized crime groups have aggressively utilized such advances to create new modes of illegitimate enterprise. Many of these groups have successfully used computer programs not only to create fraudulent checks, but also to generate the forged signatures necessary for authentication. In Long Beach, California, for example, members of the North Vietnamese Triads used computers to forge payroll checks against major banks in excess of $20 million. Criminals have also used these techniques to perfect counterfeit currency with high-end printers and scanners. Unfortunately, this method of counterfeiting is much easier than traditional methods which required the making of printing plates. In fact, even novice computer criminals can manufacture counterfeit currency with a minimal investment of time and expense.

Non-traditional methods of fraud are also emerging due to the advances in technology. **Data Diddling,** for example, is becoming increasingly popular, and can be committed by anyone having access to an input device. Generally speaking, *data diddling* refers to any method of fraud via computer manipulation. More succinctly, data diddling usually refers to the deliberate manipulation of an existing program to redirect or reroute data representing monies or economic exchanges. This level of criminal activity is more sophisticated that the average counterfeiting scheme, and is extremely hard to recognize. With few exceptions it is committed by company or government insiders who exceed their authorization or by outsiders utilizing Trojan horses. One of the most notorious cases of data diddling involved the **salami technique** or the redirection of thin slices of accounts into a designated location. In this case, an individual preying on a systemic flaw which kept track of money to the 1/100 of a penny, redirected this infinitesimal amount into his personal bank account to the tune of several million dollars! Even government entities have not proven immune to economically motivated electronic fraud. The Veterans' Affairs Administration, for example, was swindled for close to $50K by an employee who directed funds to fictitious corporations which he had established just for this purpose (Andreano, 1999), while in Marin County, California, Fire Chief Richard Mollenkopf electronically embezzled three-quarters of a million dollars.

Similar type activities which do not require insider status or a comparable level of sophistication have also increased due to the growth of electronic banking (i.e., money transfers, direct deposit, electronic billing, etc.). Unlike traditional methods of remote banking, electronic banking relies on the electronic verification of personal identification without exception. Electronic thieves may use traditional techniques of fraudulent identification (i.e., routing phone calls to suspect's house) or the new method of *IP spoofing* to gain control of a targeted account. **IP spoofing** involves the manipulation of packets (i.e., messages that are exchanged between computers). These communications are indirectly routed across varying systems. Addresses attached to these messages verify the sender and the recipient organization, respectively. Necessary for the synchronization of transmissions, this also enables technology savvy individuals to more successfully mimic an innocent victim, as many electronic authentication platforms rely exclusively on IP verification. Thus, criminals may gain access to large amounts of money simply by disguising their computers. IP spoofing may also be used to redirect Internet traffic. *Domain Name Hijacking* is especially popular among political hacktivists and petty vandals, and is committed when individuals change domain name ownership by *spoofing* messages to domain name registrars like *Network Solutions™*. This approach has been used to attack several corporate giants. *Nike™*, for example, was successfully targeted in June, 2000, when visitors to the company's site were redirected to the environmentally conscious *www.s11.org* (who denied any connection to the rerouting). It has also been employed by individuals involved in stock manipulation.

Securities fraud and stock manipulation

While the emergence of the "information superhighway" has exponentially increased knowledge among many users, it has also created a false sense of empowerment in others. This is especially true among *day traders*. Although **day trading** (the process of buying and selling highly speculative stocks within one trading day) has existed since the creation of the New York Stock Exchange (NYSE), it was mainly reserved for brokers. In fact, for many years, brokers or licensed traders were the only individuals with the capability of accessing real-time trading information. However, the Internet has made it possible for untutored individuals to *instantly* access stock values and statistics. So there has been a marked increase in the number of individuals engaging in day trading. Unfortunately, many of these individuals do not fully understand the securities in which they are investing nor the market conditions which bear upon stock prices. As such they are extremely vulnerable, as many found out when the bottom fell out of tech stocks. This susceptibility has proven disastrous in many cases, and has even resulted in violence.

Though not all day traders lose their life savings and become homicidal, many are seduced by bullet in boards or web pages which claim to promise expert investment advice. While the majority of these pages are created by and subscribed to by stock novices seeking their fortune, some are actually created by criminals. One criminal fraud involves the creation of web pages to solicit money for unfounded investment advice. In early 2000, for example, the Securities and Exchange Commission (SEC) filed charges against "Tokyo Joe" (Yun Soo Oh Park) and his company "Tokyo Joe's Societe Anonyme." Together, this scam netted $1.1 million in fees from members in exchange for investment advice, daily stock

---

TRAGEDY IN ATLANTA

In the last several years, fortunes have been gambled and lost on the increasingly volatile stock market. For the most part, these losses are strictly financial. However, one tragic case in Atlanta involved an individual who lost his life savings on highly speculative stocks, killed his wife and children, and then targeted employees at a financial firm.

picks, and membership to a private chat room. Unfortunately for investors, he only promoted stocks in which he held an interest.

False information is another method in which unwitting investors are parted from their money. The first identified case of this type of Internet stock manipulation involved an individual who circulated false information regarding PairGain. By posting fraudulent information regarding the takeover of the company by an Israeli company and by providing a link to a fraudulent Web site which appeared to be a legitimate news server, this individual caused the stock to increase in price by 30 percent with trades totaling seven times the average volume! Unfortunately, those investors who bought the stock at the inflated price suffered significant losses. The perpetrator was subsequently found guilty of securities fraud and sentenced to five years of probation, five months of home detention, and over $90,000 in restitution to his victims. An additional example of false information involved the manipulation of Emulex. Mark Simeon Jakob, 23, was charged with nine counts of securities fraud and two counts of wire fraud after he falsely posted information on Internet Wire, Inc., his former employer. Jakob made over $200,000 by selling Emulex stock short after disseminating information which claimed:

1. Emulex was under investigation by the SEC.
2. Emulex's CEO was resigning.
3. that the company's revised earnings showed a loss.

This information caused the stock to tumble from $110 to $43 in less than one hour, and temporarily cost the company $2 billion in market value. Although the company's stock is now secure and their financial situation soundly framed, many individual investors, some of whom sold their shares at a 50 percent loss, did not recover.

Insider trading is also increasing due to the proliferation of day trading activity. In March, 2000, 19 people were arrested in a massive insider trading scheme. This scheme was predicated on the advice of one "insider" who solicited interested individuals in chat rooms, offering them inside advice for a percentage of their profits. Over a 2 ½-year period, this individual communicated insider information via chat rooms and instant messages, netting a profit of $170,000 for himself and $500,000 for his partners. Although authorities subsequently identified and prosecuted some of the individuals involved in this scheme, there are an indeterminate number remaining. (The North American Securities Administrators Association estimates that Internet related stock fraud costs investors approximately $10 billion per year or $1 million per hour!) While most of this fraud is conducted electronically, some schemes actually involve threats of violence.

Organized crime groups have manipulated stocks and exchanges by employing traditional strong-arm tactics outside the realm of cyberspace. Japanese crime groups, in particular, have been quite successful at extorting money, securities, and/or insider information through the art of *Sokaiya*, a process where individuals are threatened with violence or loss of reputation. In fact, many authors attribute much of Tokyo's bubble economy to the Yakuza's grip on the Japanese

Peter Gotti, seen here in the custody of federal agents, headed a family who actively used technology to further their criminal enterprise. Recent convictions of Gambino soldiers and associates suggest that the group was involved in a gamut of on-line criminal behavior, ranging from stock manipulation to child pornography. (Frankie Ziths/*AP/World Wide Photos*)

stock exchange (Grennan, et al., 2001). Russian and Italian groups have also made inroads into the market. Although the vast majority of their involvement has been via traditional (i.e., non-electronic) means, it is anticipated that their emergence in the techno-world is a foregone conclusion.

Other Web-Related Crime

Cyber-squatting is another form of criminal activity which is specific to the technological age, although many question the justification for its illegality. Basically, **cyber-squatting** may be defined as the practice of infringing on trademarked property via electronic means. The first method of cyber-squatting involves the purchase of domain names consistent with established companies or businesses (e.g., *www.toysrus.com* or *www.thegap.com*). The second includes the purchase of domain names which represent common misspellings or typographical errors of same (e.g., *www.toysareus.com* or *www.tgegap.com*). Specifically outlawed by The Anti-Cybersquatting Consumer Protection Act of 1997, this type of activity has been characterized as the epitome of techno-capitalism by some, but branded criminal by government authorities. Characterization notwithstanding, this Act has been utilized against individuals like John Zuccarini, who purchased thousands of domain names which represented common misspellings of popular businesses and *mousetrapped* accidental visitors (e.g., opening advertising boxes which require users to click on, and therefore look at, the advertisements to make them go away).

Internet Gambling. In keeping with the give-me-more-right-now environment so common in the United States, it is anticipated that fingertip accessibility will result in a virtual cyberboom of gambling activity. Protected by its very sophistication, Internet gambling has thus far proven to be too cost-intensive and too technologically advanced for local and federal authorities. In fact, both jurisdictions have refused sovereignty. As a result, the legality of such enterprises remains unclear. The language of the federal legislation which may be applicable is far too antiquated, and alternative legislation has been slow to emerge. One exception, Senator John Kyl's (Rep.- Arizona) Internet Gambling Prohibition Act of 1997—which specifically addressed internet wagering—has failed to bear fruit. State-level politicians have fared a little better. Minnesota and Missouri courts have both provided judgments adverse to the World Wide Web of gambling. However, the future remains unclear, and many constitutional scholars argue that the method of prosecuting internet gamblers and bookmakers (i.e., The Wire Act) is not consistent with emerging technology. Thus, the legality of online bookmaking and casino games is in doubt.

Legal questions notwithstanding, both local and federal enforcement authorities have identified and prosecuted individuals for Internet gambling via traditional fraud statutes. Missouri Attorney General Jay Nixon, for example, obtained a civil injunction and damages totaling over $65,000 against Interactive Gaming and Communications, Inc., while Minnesota Attorney General Hubert Humphrey III has pursued Las Vegas-based Granit Gate Resorts for false advertisement, as it led citizens to believe that Internet gambling was entirely legal. In addition, both the Wire Act and the Crime Control Act have been used to pursue individual bookmaking organizations. (Jay Cohen was the first defendant convicted of illegally operating a sports betting business which accepted wagers on sporting events via Internet. However, many more cases are pending.) However, the absence of regulatory oversight encourages dishonest or criminal practices. It is entirely possible, for example, for a virtual casino to simply roll up the proverbial carpet if enforcement efforts become intense or if their net-to-debt ratio becomes unfavorable to the owners. In fact, individual gamblers gamble simply by providing their credit card information to unknown entities. Thus, law enforcement officials and legislative bodies must establish guidelines for Internet gambling, while recognizing that enforcement of such regulations may prove impossible.

Cyberstalking and harassment. Computers have also provided the means for many individuals to more effectively stalk and harass their targeted victims. Just as its real-world counterpart, the insidious nature of this type of activity has remained unrecognized. In fact, individuals were free to verbally, physically, and sexually harass and terrorize objects of their attentions. However, Congress enacted legislation in 1994 which prohibited this type of behavior, due primarily to the attention garnered in the wake of the stalking and murdering of actress Rebecca Shaeffer in 1990. In the most general sense, *stalking* may be defined as the willful, malicious, and repeated following and/or harassing another person in an effort to inflict or cause fear of actual harm through words or deeds. By extension, **cyberstalking** is the same form of activity committed via electronic communications. *Cyberharassment,* on the other hand, focuses on actual harm suffered, including defacement of character, and the like. In fact, the distinctions between the two are subtle at best. In a general sense, the primary differences between the two involves actual harm suffered. Cyberstalking statutes, for example, are directed at activities which *may* be threatening or *may* result in injury. Cyberharassment statutes, on the other hand, involve activities which are threatening, harassing, or injurious on their face. Due to the lobbying of many Hollywood heavyweights, stalking is often treated more harshly, and is usually treated as a felony. Fortunately, federal authorities and many state legislators have passed anti-stalking legislation. However, both have failed to fully incorporate all of the activities which may be committed in this increasingly sophisticated age. For example, the Interstate Stalking Punishment and Prevention Act of 1996 (18 U.S.C. { 2261A) made it a federal offense to

> *travel across a State line or within the special maritime and territorial jurisdiction of the United States with intent to injure or harass another person, and in the course of, or as a result of, such travel places that person in reasonable fear of, or serious bodily injury to . . . that person or a member of that person's immediate family shall be punished as provided in section 2261 of this title.*

Although this has been used successfully, other federal legislation directly targeting online stalking have not passed Congressional muster (two bills, introduced in the 103rd and 104th Congress died in committee). These bills would have amended the Federal Telephone Harassing Statute to include communications by modem or other two-way wire, and would have forbidden anonymous interstate or foreign communications made *with the intent to annoy, abuse, threaten, or harass any person at the called number.*

Some states have been more proactive in the prevention of electronic stalking (e.g., Alaska, California, Massachusetts, Michigan, Oklahoma, Washington, and Wyoming) and cyberharassment (e.g., Alabama, Arizona, Connecticut, Delaware, Hawaii, Illinois, Indiana, Maryland, New Hampshire, New York and North Dakota) by passing legislation specifically designed to address electronic activities. In addition, other states have passed legislation or rendered traditional statutes technology-neutral. However, there appears to be a lack of consensus regarding the insidious nature of harassment and stalking activities overall, and third-party harassment and/or stalking has not been addressed. Thus, new legislation at all levels is desperately needed as online stalking will almost certainly outpace offline stalking due to the perceptions of confidentiality and the empowerment of anonymity.

Many individuals, including both law enforcement and civilians, continue to perceive that cyberstalking is less dangerous than physical stalking. However, cyberstalking has the potential to be far more insidious and pervasive as the popularity of remailers, anonymizers, ease of access, mass distribution capability, and the like, increase. As with other crimes, individuals who may not be tempted to engage in physical retribution or stalking of a particular victim may be lured into cyberstalking. In addition, such activities may lead to physical or real-world stalking activities. In 1998, a study indicated that 19 percent of all women and almost one-half percent of all men were stalked each year. In the general public, these numbers would represent over 1 million women and 370, 990 in the United States every year or 8 percent of women and 2 percent of men (Packard, 2000). However, the LAPD District Attorney's Office and NYPD's estimates of cases that include physical stalking predicated on previous electronic communications are 20 percent to 40 percent, respectively. (In Great Britain, the figures included 58 percent of men and 41 percent of women as victims). Generally speaking, empirical evidence indicates that cyberstalkers mirror their offline counterparts. They are usually male, the majority of their attentions are focused on women, and they are usually known to their victims. In addition, their motivations appear to be remarkably similar. Some pursue these criminal activities out of obsession, jealously, anger, or a desire to control (Packard, 2000).

The actual process of cyberstalking may take many forms, including tracking the victim's online activity or sending them a barrage of threatening e-mails, while cyberharassment activity may include abusive e-mails or the posting of fictitious or slanderous information in a public forum. In the late 1990s, for example, an image of Jeanne Mentavolos, one of the first female cadets at a traditionally male institution, was distributed across the world via the Internet. The image involved an altered photograph of the victim in which she appeared to have male genitalia. Often times, the motivation behind harassment is one of retaliation, as in the case of Gary Dellapenta. Dellapenta, a former security guard, actually solicited the rape of a woman who had rejected his advances by posting rape fantasies on a variety of pages while impersonating the victim. He even provided her address, and methods of bypassing the victim's security system. However, the courts have been reluctant to establish electronic boundaries of the First Amendment, and have narrowly interpreted cyberstalking and cyberharassment legislation.

As stated, the courts have been reluctant to identify certain communications as threatening, arguing that a strict scrutiny of individual cases is necessary to protect constitutional provisions. For example, in 1995, Jake Baker (a.k.a. Abraham Jacob Alkhabaz), University of Michigan student, electronically communicated with an individual in Ontario, Canada, plans to abduct, torture, rape, murder, and other assorted actions. He also posted a story about his classmate in which he and a friend torture, rape, and sodomize her with a curling iron before setting her on fire. *Jerry continues to maul at her breasts. He pulls them as far away as they'll go away from her body, twisting them to cause even more pain . . . Jane howls out loud. It's not even a human sound. Her eyes glaze over from the pain and torture (Alkhabaz,* 104 F.3d at 1498). Upon a consensual search, investigators also found e-mails between Baker and Arthur Gonda of Ontario, Canada, which fantasized about the abduction, bondage, torture, humiliation, mutilation, rape, sodomy, murder, necrophilia of a variety of individuals—including generalized teens and one individual from Baker's hometown—which stated:

> *I would love to do a 13 or 14 year old. I think you are rights . . . not only their innocence but their young bodies would really be fun to hurt. As far as being [sic] easier to control . . . you may be right, however you can control any bitch with rape and a gag (Alkhabaz, 104 F.3d at 1499).*

Initially the pair were charged with 18 U.S.C. 875(c), which prohibits the interstate communication of threats to injure or kidnap another person and a superseding indictment charging them with an additional five counts. However, a lower court quashed the superseding indictment arguing that the e-mail's were not "true threats" under the First Amendment as they were communicated to a third party. The sixth Circuit upheld the ruling (*U.S.* v. *Alkhabaz* 104 F.3d at 1499). In essence, the court ruled that their communications did not constitute a "threat" under the provisions of the act as the fantasies were not specifically communicated to the alleged victims. More specifically, the court argued that fantasies or musings, regardless of nature, were not criminal activities absent a specific expression of intent. To wit, their e-mail communications could refer to any 13- or 14-year-old, and was thus too indeterminate to satisfy *Kelner's* specificity requirement. Unfortunately, the requirement of specific intent nullified this action, as well as many future actions.

Child Pornography and the Seduction of Innocents. Perhaps one of the most common criminal activities which is facilitated through bulletin boards is the most unsettling. The introduction of electronic bulletin boards has allowed pedophiles and child pornographers to flourish with relative immunity and has resulted in a virtual explosion of child pornography. While traditional mechanisms for enforcement against such persons included Federal and state regulations, the boundaryless nature of cyberspace has protected peddlers from traditional measures and has raised questions regarding the legality of prohibitions. In addition, it has hampered law-enforcement efforts by insulating those inclined from enforcement by negating traditional methods of distribution which exposed perpetrators to third parties.

While electronic news groups and bulletin boards have probably facilitated increased knowledge, they have certainly created an atmosphere most conducive to criminal networking. Where else could pedophiles or child pornography peddlers meet and exchange information with little or no threat of prosecution? Many individuals with deviant tendencies have found others similarly stimulated via posting services or electronic bulletin boards, and are protected under the umbrella of the First Amendment because of their capability of performing "common carrier" functions—like the telephone company or the post office[5] (Winick, 1994). Such judicial perception, coupled with the increase in Internet communications, has resulted in an explosion of child pornography and the exploitation of children. In fact, this apathy has all but encouraged the development of associations dedicated to the exploitation of children. NAMBLA (the National Association of Men and Boy Lovers of America), for example, is an organization which proudly proclaims that its mission is to forge relationships between men who love boys! Sponsoring a Web site, this organization is no longer forced underground, but has an established presence on the web.

Unfortunately, they are not alone. Numerous bulletin boards, newsgroups, and chat rooms are dedicated to this type of behavior, and remain hidden behind the First Amendment. According to SEARCH (2000), the typical offender is an individual who requires children for sexual gratification. Like traditional pedophiles, they often find it necessary to maintain trophies of their victims or visual stimuli and may graphically articulate elaborate fantasies through writings or such. Their typical prey includes those individuals who express frustration with parental controls or who appear particularly naïve or vulnerable. These include children who are confused about their own sexuality or who express feelings of ostracism. Typically, the victims are youngsters who enjoy access to unsupervised computer communications. While many of them are actively seeking associations with adult suitors, others are unsuspectingly lured into fictional relationships which encourage dangerous liaisons. Such was the case with a Connecticut teen who was raped by Francis Kufrovich, a California man posing as a teenager. Unfortunately, it is anticipated that this type of behavior will increase in pace with the availability of Internet communications. However, proactive law-enforcement initiatives may result in the identification and prosecution of offenders.

Although many pedophiles searching the Internet for victims usually practice with the expectation of limited enforcement, proactive, cursory investigations may allow investigators to surprise the unsuspecting predators. Fortunately for law enforcement, many of these perpetrators assume that: 1) the individuals to whom they are communicating are accurately representing themselves, and 2) their behavior is hidden behind a Web of anonymity. In fact, these perceptions have proven to be shortsighted as even non-criminals mask their identity, and the First Amendment does not protect anonymous communications. These characteristics may be exploited by proactive law-enforcement agencies like the San Jose Police Department, who may create fictitious organizations or identities to seduce the seducer.[4] (In addition, law-enforcement agencies may find evidentiary support in the forensic analysis of seized media from the suspect's home as most child pornographers keep their collections within arm's reach.)

Online pharmacies—drug dealing under the guise of legitimacy. The emergence of a worldwide marketplace and the lack of applicable regulations have resulted in an explosion of questionable capitalist enterprises. Online pharmacies, for example, benefit consumers by encouraging competitive pricing with non-cyber outlets, but offer little protection against fraud. Virtually all of the available online pharmacies claim legitimacy, arguing that transactions require valid prescriptions. However, many of these sites operate illegally, maintaining no license at all or dispensing medicines in states in which they are not licensed. Some do not even require a valid prescription, prescribing medicine to individuals who complete short questionnaires, while others simply dispense medicine upon demand.

Although many legitimate, non-cyber pharmacies have used the Internet to enhance customer convenience, others exist solely in cyberspace (some offering drugs that have been banned by the FDA). To see one such Web site, go to *www.onlinepharmacy.com*. Unfortunately, enforcement of online illegal drug transactions is all but impossible at the present time, as pharmacies are licensed by states and are exempt from FDA regulations. Although efforts have been made by many agencies including the Drug Enforcement Administration to combat this

---

[4]Dean Lambey and Daniel DePew were captured in a sting operation by San Jose police before they could abduct a 12-year-old boy. Their plan involved the filming of a snuff film with their intended victim in the starring role (Search, 2000). Fortunately, they shared their intentions with an undercover investigator, and were captured after they purchased acid to dispose of the body (SEARCH, 2000).

sort of activity, specific legislation is necessary to solidify enforcement efforts and establish clear jurisdictional boundaries.

CONCLUSIONS

Increases in technology have dramatically changed contemporary society. For the most part, such changes have been positive. Increasing knowledge, enhancing communication, and encouraging competitive markets have all been byproducts of the information revolution. However, such advances have been accompanied by similar innovations among criminally-minded individuals. Such modernization has frustrated the efforts of law-enforcement agencies across the world, as they struggle with jurisdictional complications, legislative apathy, and judicial inconsistencies. Consequently, the majority of technologically savvy deviants have operated with virtual impunity, creating a landscape rich in criminal diversity.

As stated, computers may serve as the target or the means for criminals. They may be attacked for the information contained therein or as a form of retribution against an individual or organization. In addition, they may actually represent the instrumentality of the crime, serving as the proverbial smoking gun. Or, they may simply serve as a repository of criminal evidence, containing a hacker's list of stolen access codes or a bookmaker's list of customer accounts. Utilization aside, the use of computers exponentially increases the potentiality of economic loss and the magnitude of victimization. Thus, it is essential that law-enforcement agencies and legislative bodies recognize the insidious nature of computer crime, and allocate resources accordingly.

TERMS DISCUSSED

anonymizer	data diddling	phreaking
counterfeiting	day trading	salami technique
cyberstalking	IP spoofing	vicinage
cyber squatting	ISP-jacking	Web-cramming
forgery	Legion of Doom	

DISCUSSION QUESTIONS

1. Discuss the evolution of criminal behavior in the United States, including in your answer the utilization of technological advances.
2. What are anonymizers, and what is their relevance to computer crime and investigations?
3. What events precipitated the development of enhanced data security measures taken by the Federal government?
4. What are the three categories of computer crime? What are some of the individual crimes included in each?
5. How have organized crime syndicates utilized computer technologies to further their criminal interests? What are the implications for the future?
6. What are some of the laws which have specifically targeted online criminal behavior? Have they been employed effectively? Why or why not?

COMPUTER CRIMES: COMPUTERS AS TARGETS—HACKING AND BEYOND

4

COMPUTERS AS TARGETS

While hacking, phreaking, and the theft of sensitive information have garnered a great deal of both national and international attention, the theft of computer hardware and the infringement of software copyrights have been all but overlooked. However, these activities have become quite popular as computer components become smaller and more valuable.

Hardware

Increasingly, computer components are worth more than their weight in gold (or even platinum). However, these same components tend to be less protected than even the most inexpensive of metal commodities. Computers, accessible to employees, students, and sometimes, the public at large, are extremely vulnerable to theft. In fact, many valuable computer components may be concealed in areas as small as a shirt pocket. Many computer chips worth several hundred dollars, for example, may be hidden within a briefcase, a shirt pocket, or even a small wallet. A simple screwdriver, dress shirt, and a little know how, are the only tools needed to successfully steal thousands of dollars of material. No other criminal heist requires so little. In addition, unlike high-dollar jewelry, which may be identified by gem maps for appraisals, integrated circuits are difficult to trace. Thus, computer thieves have traditionally been able to market their stolen goods as legitimate. The increase of Internet auctions has only increased this possibility. Without the requirements imposed on traditional pawnshops, auctions such as eBay carry no responsibility for facilitating the transfer of stolen computer components.

In its most basic sense, the term *computer components* represents a variety of equipment, but is usually reserved for the smallest portions of computer technology, like integrated circuits. Larger components, of course, are the most obvious: CPU's, storage media, computer chips, etc. Although CPUs are often not thought of as easy targets, their size, utility, and value are dependent upon demographic

Although the size of CPUs and monitors often diminish their desirability for computer thieves, a sizeable black market for them still exists in many areas. (Courtesy of James Doyle/*NYPD,* ret.)

characteristics and local market value. (A CPU worth $1,000 in the U.S. might go as high as $3,000 in the UK.) Although many computers are made by large manufacturers who serialize CPUs and the subsequent components, identifying information is often superficial—able to be manipulated quite easily (e.g., stick-on serial numbers, etc.). The sheer magnitude of computer transactions makes it virtually impossible to trace many units reported stolen. Even more profitable, however, tend to be the circuitry found within computer systems in general. It is more economically advantageous, by far, to steal a CPU and sell the individual circuitry. Motherboards, ethercards, and the like, tend to bring a greater return due to the inability to trace these components. In addition, integrated chips, serial ports and drives (external and internal) prove almost impossible to trace.

The theft and resale of integrated chips has proven to be the most lucrative of component theft. Resale of such computer chips may return as much as ten times on their investment (which sure beats the stock market). One of the primary reasons that resale of this particular equipment is so lucrative is the basic law of supply and demand. While Americans have become socialized to expect a ready supply of the latest technology, other portions of the globe are not as fortunate. International residents may actually salivate at the purchase of technology that is already outdated in the United States. Thus, illegitimate global marketplaces have emerged. These marketplaces may be categorized as to their level of criminal culpability or organization.

Black market dealers are the most organized groups trafficking in stolen computer components. These individuals or groups may be likened to full-service restaurants—carefully soliciting orders and preparing merchandise as requested. Thus, their targets are selected only after they receive an order for particular merchandise. These groups actively participate in the theft itself. **Grey Market dealers**, on the other hand, are often legitimate businesses with questionable, and illegal, practices. Most often, these businesses are those which specialize in made-to order computers (i.e., non-standard or knock-offs). They represent a major customer for thieves, providing a ready outlet for their illegal wares. Buying the components at a significant discount, these companies claim ignorance. In fact, some of them resell these questionable components to other dealers. Another activity that is popular with both black market dealers and gray market dealers involves the fraudulent sale of counterfeit goods. These items, marketed and packaged as legitimate products, are often labeled as higher performance or more expensive components. Unfortunately, these types of activities are on the increase, as the profitability sharply outweighs potential risks. The sheer volume of personal computers and informal transactions coupled with legal requirements for search warrants all but negate the possibility of random identification. Thus, law-enforcement officers are forced to focus their investigations on the identification of individuals or corporations who sell an unusually high number of drives, circuits, or the like, without selling the accompanying equipment.

Software

In August 2001, the Federal Bureau of Investigation arrested four men and seized over $10 million worth of counterfeit Microsoft software. These arrests, the result of a 14-month investigation, revealed the increasing sophistication and organization displayed by computer criminals as many of the counterfeit items included disks with replicas of Microsoft's new hologram technology. Thus, this technology, designed exclusively to prevent software counterfeiting, is proving ineffective due to the high costs associated with obtaining licensed copies (e.g., Microsoft Office 2000, $599). Although highly lucrative, this activity is not as pervasive (or costly to manufacturers) as individual *piracy* (i.e., the unauthorized copying of software).

THEFT OF COMPUTER COMPONENTS

In February 2001, Samuel Williams and Dion Wilson, employees of SoftBank (now ClientLogic), illegally diverted more than $700,000 of computer products to drop zones across upper New York. Although they eventually pled guilty to conspiracy to commit wire fraud and to transport stolen property, their light sentences reflect the enticing nature of this activity. (Eight to twenty-four months versus a payout of $700,000!) Interestingly, if state statutes for larceny or theft of property had been applied, their activities would have carried heightened penalties (*www.cybercrime.gov/williams_wilson.htm*).

In 2001, IBM, a perpetual target of thieves and assorted other ne'er-do-wells, was victimized when over $4 million in disk drives was stolen from their San Jose location. These drives were later recovered in Southern California.

Although many thieves are now marketing high-technology merchandise, many of their traditional storefronts are still in place. As you can see, some criminals prefer the time-tested practice of selling stolen merchandise out of the back of a van. (Courtesy of James Doyle/NYPD, ret.)

Making multiple copies for personal use or distributing copies to friends or colleagues has become so commonplace that many individuals fail to appreciate, or even recognize, the illegality of their actions. The ease of replication, greatly enhanced through the advent of CD-RWs, has further exacerbated this problem as more and more users find the transportation of expensive programs readily available. However, the greatest contributor to this activity may simply be a lack of knowledge regarding software licensing.

Most retail programs are licensed for use at just one computer site or for use by only one user at any time. By buying the software, an individual becomes a licensed user rather than an owner. While this individual user may be allowed to make copies of the program for backup purposes, it is against the law to distribute copies to friends and colleagues. **Software piracy** is all but impossible to stop, although software companies are launching more and more lawsuits against major infractors. Originally, software companies tried to stop software piracy by copy-protecting their software. This strategy failed, however, because it was inconvenient for users and was not 100 percent foolproof. Most software now requires some sort of registration, which may discourage would-be pirates, but doesn't really stop software piracy. An entirely different approach to software piracy prevention was the introduction of a new category of licensed software. Unlike expensively packaged and mass merchandised software products, **shareware** acknowledges the futility of trying to stop people from copying software and instead relies on people's honesty. Shareware publishers encourage users to give copies of programs to friends and colleagues but ask everyone who uses a program regularly to pay a registration fee to the program's author directly.

Commercial programs that are made available to the public illegally are often called wareZ.

WareZ sites are extremely popular on the Internet. These sites enable visitors to download software illegally in violation of copyright protections. Unfortunately, many of these sites are created and maintained by highly sophisticated, well-educated administrators. Perhaps the earliest example of such activity was David LaMacchia, a student at M.I.T. who developed two bulletin boards on M.I.T.'s network named "Cynosure"and "Cynosure II". His system enabled individuals to upload popular software applications, like WordPerfect and Excel, to "Cynosure" and download those applications and more from "Cynosure II" with a valid password. Indicted for violating the Federal Wire Fraud Statute, LaMacchia was released after a Court ruled that the Statute did not apply to his activities. He remained at M.I.T. where he pursued a five-year master's program in electrical engineering and computer science.

Hacking

As mentioned previously, computers may be the intended target of a criminal or may actually represent the instrumentality of the crime. Hacking activities may fall into either category. Unfortunately, the characterization and subsequent discussion of such activity may not be neatly packaged. Like more traditional criminal behavior, the methodology employed, the motivation expressed, and the sophistication displayed are but a few characteristics which may vary drastically. Thus, hacking activities are most appropriately situated on a continuum. On the low end, there may be some individuals who take particular delight in entering systems for the sheer fun of it. Their activities may range from snooping around their neighbors' computers or searching the recesses of top-secret government databases. On the high end of the spectrum reside individuals who enter these same systems with destruction or treason in mind.

Although difficult to measure, some studies have suggested that the number of computer intrusions in the United States alone number in the millions, while others suggest that the cost to the public is in excess of several billion dollars. However, hacking is a global phenomenon not restricted to the United States. **Hackers** have been found in virtually every country in which computer technology is available. Remarkably, these individuals, irrespective of national origin, display startling similarities.

Traditionally, these individuals were young, socially retarded males who initially became enamored of computers and computer technology through role-playing games. Such entertainment, necessitating excessive downloads, led these individuals to manipulate telephone exchanges. (Prior to the mass introduction of Internet Service Providers and unlimited access, calls via modem tended to be quite costly.) Common justifications for their actions included an anti-establishment ideology that inferred that corporate structures and government entities were designed to abridge individualism and discourage collective unity. (Thus, hacking organizations may be likened to Christian identity groups which believe that a government conspiracy to exploit American citizens is furthered by corpo-

LIST OF 1980s HACKER ORGANIZATIONS
(compiled by Phrack in 1988)

The Administration; Advanced Telecommunications, Inc.; ALIAS; American Tone Travelers, Anarchy Inc.: Apple Mafia; The Association; Atlantic Pirates Guild.

Bad Ass Mother Fuckers; Bellcore; Bell Shock Force; Black Bag.

Camorra; C&M Productions; Catholics Anonymous; Chaos Computer Club; Chief Executive Officers; Circle Of Death; Circle Of Deneb; Club X; Coalition of Hi-Tech Pirates; Coast-To-Coast; Corrupt Computing; Cult Of The Dead Cow; Custom Retaliations.

Damage Inc.; D&B Communications; The Damage Gang; Dec Hunters; Digital Gang; DPAK.

Eastern Alliance; The Elite Hackers Guild; Elite Phreakers and Hackers Club; The Elite Society of America; EPG; Executives Of Crime; Extasy Elite.

4A; Farmers Of Doom; The Federation; Feds R Us; First Class; Five O; Five Star; Force Hackers; The 414s.

Hack-A-Trip; Hackers of America; High Mountain Hackers; High Society; The Hitchhikers

IBM Syndicate; The Ice Pirates; Imperial Warlords: Inner Circle I; Inner Circle II; Insanity Inc. International; Computer Underground Bandits.

Justice League of America; Kaos Inc.; Knights of Shadow; Knights of The Round Table.

League of Adepts; Legion of Doom; Legion of Hackers; Lords of Chaos; Lunatic Labs; Unlimited.

Master Hackers; MAD!; The Marauders; Md/PhD; Metal Communications, Inc.; MetalliBashers, Inc.; MBI; Metro Communications; Midwest Pirates Build.

NASA Elite; The NATO Association; Neon Knights; Nihilist Order; Order of The Rose; OSS.

Pacific Pirates Guild; Phantom Access Associates; PHido PHreakers of America; Phortune 500; Phreak Hack Delinquents; Phreak Hack Destroyers; Phreakers, Hackers, And Laundromat Employees Gang (PHALSE Gang); Phreaks Against Geeks; Phreaks Against Phreaks Against Geeks; Phreaks and Hackers of America; Phreaks Anonymous World Wide; Project Genesis; The Punk Mafia; The Racketeers; Red Dawn Text Files; Roscoe Gang.

SABRE; Secret Circle of Pirates; Secret Service; 707 Club; Shadow Brotherhood; Sharp Inc.; 65C02 Elite; Spectral Force; Star League; Stowaways; Strata-Crackers.

Team Hackers '86; Team Hackers '87; TeleComputist Newsletter Staff; Tribunal of Knowledge; Triple Entente; Turn Over and Die Syndrome (TOADS); 300 Club; 1200 Club; 2300 Club; 2600 Club; 2601 Club; 2AF; The United Soft WareZ Force; United Technical Underground. Ware Brigade; The Warelords; WASP.

The rising cost of software coupled with the decreasing cost of CD-RWs has resulted in an explosion of counterfeit software. Unlike other areas involving stolen or compromised property, individual users are often fully aware of the nature of the merchandise as unsophisticated counterfeit copies are easily identifiable. (Courtesy of James Doyle/*NYPD*, ret.)

rate assistance.) In addition, early hackers emphasized the virtuality of cyberspace, arguing that the Internet is a sphere of unreality, where nothing is concrete and everything if simulated. Finally, hackers around the globe share a sense of overwhelming empowerment in which they are the keepers of all knowledge.

> *Yes, I am a criminal. My crime is that of curiosity. My crime is that of judging people by what they say and think, not what they look like. My crime is that of outsmarting you, something that you will never forgive me for. (The Mentor, Phrack, v1 i7, phile 3, as quoted in Sterling, 1994.*

Contemporary hacker communities have lost much of the ideological superstructure. The lure of easy money, revenge, and personal notoriety have significantly tempered the righteous indignation expressed by early desktop cowboys. At the same time, traditional levels of misogyny have been reduced as more and more female code writers have emerged. This rhetorical shift and the lack of ideological consistency has resulted in an increase in hacking for profit. In addition, the proliferation of private hacking toolkits and software have spawned a generation of unskilled, financially motivated intruders (e.g., NetBus, Back Orifice, Deep Throat, etc.). Thus, the virtual explosion of remote-access software released on the market has dramatically changed the characterization of hackers. While traditional definitions included assumptions of motivation and skill, contemporary definitions have been altered to include any individual who intentionally accesses a computer without or in excess of authorization irrespective of knowledge or stimulus.

Classification by Motivation

National origin, ideology or demographics aside, there appear to be six primary motivations for computer intrusion or theft of information: boredom (*informational voyeurism*), intellectual challenge (*mining for knowledge—pure hackers*), revenge (*insiders, disgruntled employees, etc.*), sexual gratification (*stalking, harassment, etc.*), economic (*criminals*), and political (*terrorists, spies*). The least destructive, but no less insidious, category of hackers are the informa-

BACK DOORS AND TROJAN HORSES

Unfortunately, back doors and Trojan horses like Back Orifice and NetBus are not the only mechanisms which can be utilized to view a potential target's computer files. Sometimes, "friendly" programs like Netscape provide access for malevolent entities through program flaws.

Example—Dan Brumleve discovered problems in Netscape's implementation of Java. Naming the problem "Brown Orifice", Brumleve proved that an applet running on a Netscape browser transformed the target computer into a file server. He pointed out that these applets could be embedded in the background of any Web page, allowing viewing of a target's computer files without their knowledge. In addition, Brumleve demonstrated that the applet could be initiated through electronic mail messages read via Netscape Mail (Manjoo, 2000).

tional voyeurs. Like their traditional counterparts, these voyeurs are individuals whose motivations range from inquisitiveness to bravado to sensationalism. These individuals are very closely related to, but far outnumbered by, pure hackers or technological thrill seekers. Fortunately for law enforcement, these individuals are the most easily identified as they share the common affliction—braggadocio. Unlike the other categories which display a remarkable lack of consistency, pure hackers actually constitute a subculture—sharing their own jargon, rites of initiation, ethics, and lifestyles. Annual conferences, Web gatherings, and the like further solidify this marginal grouping. Traditionally, these individuals have proclaimed themselves to be seekers of knowledge, with an ethical obligation to report security holes to system administrators, and to reject any individuals who used their skills for nefarious purposes. Although some criminals have been found in their midst, history has revealed an unwillingness on the part of the hacker community to harbor these types of activities and to actually ostracize these individuals. Self-righteous proclamations aside, their activities do pose a threat to institutional security and personal privacy. In addition, the irrepressible urge to boast of their conquests may lead others to exploit these self-same vulnerabilities, as many hackers have packaged hacking programs for novices.

Perhaps the most overlooked danger to informational security are current and former employees, commonly referred to as **insiders**. Insiders are those individuals who have authorized or legitimate access to a computer system, but who exceed that authorization. While some insiders intentionally circumvent security measures for personal or financial gain, the major threat posed by institutional insiders resides in the unintentional. Far more breaches of institutional security result from careless log-in practices than do targeted attacks. Employees who post passwords in conspicuous places, allow others to shoulder surf, use common names for passwords, or disclose them to strangers pose a much greater risk to informational integrity. However, intentional actions undertaken by disgruntled or former employees also pose a serious problem for corporate or institutional administrators.

It must be noted that overlooking the danger posed by disgruntled or former employees is not a new phenomenon. Many employers seldom change their locks after someone resigns or is terminated, relying on backup or secondary mechanisms. Others fail to change security codes or, more likely, patterns of codes claiming that the expenses associated with retraining and the high rate of turnover make it impractical to change systemic practices. Many universities, for example, do not change codes for student records systems—relying on individual passwords and deleting user accounts upon termination.

Financial institutions are also responsible for inadequate security, failing to appreciate the damage that could be inflicted by someone who was formerly employed at a financial institution who knew the codes to system entries, password policies, and the intimate details of his/her former co-workers' lives. Even if this individual had been a loner, keeping to him/herself, they would still know the number of characters required in passwords. With a little brute force, social engineering, and/or a good cracking program, their access would virtually remain the same. In addition, these individuals would have knowledge such as schedules for system maintenance, etc. Even those individuals who are still employed pose a threat, as they may feel exploited. These individuals may receive personal (and financial) gratification from "getting over" on the company. In addition, these individuals might also pose a threat to their fellow employees with whom they are enamored or in competition.

Although the last two categories of hackers are not quite as prevalent as those previously discussed, they appear to be investigated at a much higher rate. Individuals in these categories are motivated by the potential for personal or political gain. *Criminals,* those who utilize computer technology to aggressively violate traditional criminal statutes for personal gain, are increasingly common. (Although any activity which involves unauthorized access violates Federal statutes thereby constitutes a criminal act, the bulk of literature tends to separate those individuals who violate traditional criminal statutes.)

Criminal hacking activities may be targeted at data which is valuable on its face (e.g., trade secrets, proprietary data, etc.) or directed at data (e.g., credit card data) which may be used to further other criminal activity. Unfortunately, many users recognize the potentiality for exploitation of valuable data and include at least a modicum of security, but fail to appreciate risks associated with other forms of data. In fact, the data targeted may appear to be totally benign or innocuous. In reality, the level of intrusion and the nature of the objective may pose risks ranging from physical security to operations security.

Exploitation of data associated with the physical security of an institution may represent a precursor to a traditional burglary. Uncovering access codes for alarms in an art museum may allow a sophisticated art thief to enter a secured area undetected. This same individual may also hack into operational plans, revealing scheduling of personnel, security policies, and the like to reveal a complete working schematic of the intended target. Personnel data may also be exploited by criminal syndicates. Japan's yakuza, experts at the practice of extortion (*sokaiya*), could significantly damage, if not destroy, an entire corporation by compromising personal information residing within its computer system.

A SAMPLING OF HACKING SITES

Some files which hackers have created and which are readily available (if you know where to look) include (partial file listed in The Hacker Crackdown):

06-11-91 Hacking Bank America **BANKAMER.ZIP**
06-11-91 Hacking Citibank **CITIBANK.ZIP**
06-11-91 How to Hack **HACK.ZIP**
06-11-91 Basics of Hacking **HACKBAS.ZIP**
06-11-91 Hackers Dictionary **HACKDICT.ZIP**
06-11-91 Hackers Handbook **HANDHAND.ZIP**

All of these are what they imply—other types of illicit files found on bulletin boards (and more recently on a variety of Web pages):

06-11-91 Anarchy Files **ANARCH.ZIP**
06-11-91 Anarchist Book **ANARCHST.ZIP**
06-11-91 How To Make Bombs **BOMB.ZIP**
06-11-91 Chlorine Bomb **CHLORINE.ZIP**
06-11-91 Anarchy Cook Book **COOKBOOK.ZIP**
06-11-91 Destroy Stuff **DESTROY.ZIP**
06-11-91 How to Pick Locks **LOCK.ZIP**
06-11-91 Pipe Bomb **PIPEBOMB.ZIP**
06-11-91 Revenge Tactics **REVENGE.ZIP**

Extortion and **Blackmail,** cash for action or inaction, can also be committed in more traditional ways using contemporary technology. In 2000, for example, two cases involving the theft of sensitive consumer information sent shock waves through the cyber-retail community and ripples of fear through the American public. The first of these attacks was directed at a well-known cyberstore which sold audio/video materials. A hacker, known as "Maxus", gained access to over 300,000 credit card numbers and threatened to release them across the world if

PROPRIETARY DATA AND TRADE SECRETS

Society fails to appreciate the plight of corporations which have experienced victimization, often championing the criminals who have compromised their security. In 1999, for example, DeCSS, a program written by a group of hackers to defeat the encryption used to protect copyrights of DVDs, proved to be one of the most popular downloads. While the author, Jon Johansen, 16, denied any criminal intent, claiming that the program was written due to the lack of DVD playback software for the Linux operating system, many individuals who downloaded the software echoed proclamations of innocence (Musgrove, 1999). In fact, First Amendment advocates also championed the program, claiming that this sort of posting (more specifically, linking data) is protected by the Constitution.

Although Hollywood depictions often portray hackers as super sleuths who conduct their invasions under the cover of darkness, today's hackers are more likely to commit such violations in open areas like computer stores or university centers. (Michael Newman/*PhotoEdit*)

his demand of $100,000 was not met. Calling his bluff, CD Universe called the FBI. Unfortunately, over 25,000 credit card numbers were compromised, and "Maxus" remains at large as of this writing (Kluger, 2000). A similar case, but one which was particularly troubling, occurred in September of the same year. This incident targeted the leading money transfer agency in the World, Western Union. Over 15,000 credit and debit card numbers were captured by intruders. (Although insiders claim that the act was undertaken for purely entertainment purposes, the breach was so significant that it caused the temporary closing of the company's Web site.) Thus, the threat to sensitive information or data is more real than imagined. It must be noted that the threat posed is not exclusive to professional hackers, organized criminal syndicates or outsiders. The introduction of previously mentioned back-door programs (i.e., NetBus, Deep Throat, Back Orifice, etc.) has also empowered novice users. (Imagine a scenario in which a prominent politician known for his conservative platform is confronted with evidence of his downloaded collection of sadomasochistic pornography.) In addition, the threat of computer contaminants, increasingly destructive, can be used to extort money from companies with valuable data.

CONTAMINANTS AND DESTRUCTION OF DATA

Industrial or corporate competition have also escalated to the malicious destruction of data. This **eco-terrorism** or **corporate warfare** is not unique, nor is it a new concept. Traditionally, other methods of destruction included attacks on physical structures (i.e., headquarters, research laboratories, etc.) or tangible objects (i.e., file cabinets, vials of chemicals, etc.). But just as the virtuality of cyberspace has altered traditional modes of communication, education, and commerce, it has transformed the competitive arena of big business. Indeed, the interconnectivity of technological devices which have become so prized across the globe have exponentially increased the vulnerability of those self-same corporations. Whereas the impact of a traditional mail bomb was limited to the physical area surrounding the packaging, the implications for e-mail bombs are limitless in their application and may include a complete dismantling of a company's informational infrastructure. Such occurrences are commonly referred to as *Denial of Service* (DOS) attacks.

The primary objective in a **denial of service attack** is to disable a large system without necessarily gaining access to it. While the most common way is mail-bombing (e.g., jamming a system's server with voluminous e-mail), other methods include the time-proven method of manipulation of phone switches or the more sophisticated method of low-level data transmission. These attacks have been directed at some of the Web's most popular portals, including *www.amazon.com, www.eBay.com,* and *www.Yahoo.com,* and are not limited to competitive motives. However, few of them have been political in nature. Thus, national infrastructures have remained relatively unscathed. However, these types of attacks pose a threat to national security as national infrastructures become increasingly reliant upon interconnectivity. Imagine the chaos that would result if the all of the electric utilities up and down the Eastern seaboard were shut down temporarily. (These sorts of implications will be explored later.) Unfortunately, this reliance also increases the vulnerability of individuals, corporations and governments to computer contaminants.

As discussed in Chapter Two, *malware* or *malicious programming code* refers to code that causes damage to computer systems. This broad based category includes: *back doors, Trojan horses, viruses,* and *worms.* All of these entities can be, and have been, employed by terrorists, hacktivists, corporate spies, criminals, and pleasure seekers. The range of their utilization includes blackmail, extortion, and espionage, while their payloads range in destruction from nuisance to devastation. Some viruses, for example, may simply insert, delete or scramble text within MS Word Documents (e.g., *wm97thu, Anna Kournikova,* etc.). Particularly destructive viruses like *Chernobyl* may attack by erasing a portion of the hard disk that makes it impossible to access the disk, even if booting from a floppy. They may also attack the file allocation table (FAT) of the first partition, making it impossible for the disk to assemble data logically.

Especially popular among hackers in the 1980s, the threat of malicious programming code created near hysteria among early computer users and spawned an entire industry. However, the creation of anti-virus and firewall programs has almost negated the unease experienced nearly two decades ago. Unfortunately, they have also led to a false sense of security among the American public, resulting in an apathetic approach to data security. In fact, malicious attacks or information theft are so dangerous that even computer giants like Apple and IBM have not been immune. In 1987, for example, Apple Computer reported that intruders may have reverse-engineered the secret code for its operating system, while a virus released in its electronic mail system caused organizational chaos by erasing all company voice-mail (Icove, et al., 1995). IBM suffered a similar fate, when a Trojan horse program affected IBM e-mail systems on five continents. Commonly known as the Christmas Trojan, the program was designed to react when individual users typed the word "Christmas." Ultimately, this incident resulted in a three-day shutdown.

Regardless of the level of scrutiny afforded to computer viruses or other contaminants, their threat remains genuine. In fact, virus creation and dissemination has become more pronounced with the inception of made-to-order virus and worm tool kits readily available via the Internet. The **VBS Worm Generator** (VBSWG 1.50b), for example, allows *script kiddies* (i.e., novice users with malicious intentions) to create viruses quickly and painlessly. Reportedly created in Buenos Aires, Argentina, VBSWG 1.50b creates VBS worms that infect Windows systems with MS VB5 run times or Windows Scripting Host 5.0. Unfortunately, this includes Windows 95 SE, 98 and 98 SE. Although other toolkits exist, this particular one has been directly responsible for a variety of recent viruses, including the popular *Anna Kournikova* virus, and is so specialized that users may name their own virus and select from a variety of payloads. It even allows users to choose manner of virus activation (i.e., timed, immediate, etc.).

Fortunately, Federal and state legislators have developed a variety of laws to punish those responsible for computer contaminants. Creating and distributing a computer virus may constitute a variety of state-level offenses including vandalism, trespass, harassment, destruction of property *and* a violation of a number of Federal laws, including the Computer Fraud and Abuse Act, etc. The New Jersey computer programmer who created the *Melissa* virus, for example, is currently facing charges of interception of public communications, theft of computer service, and conspiracy. He could receive a penalty of 40 years and almost $500,000 in fines. Although this figure pales in comparison to the millions in dam-

THE THREAT OF COMPUTER VIRUSES

Computer viruses can serve a variety of illegitimate purposes. Motivations can range from simple boredom to international terrorism, while payloads can be configured to be systemically destructive or act as covert information servers. The potential hazards of computer viruses have national security implications as informational warfare and global espionage are increasingly conducted via electronic media.

An evaluation of recent viruses reveals that we are not learning from our mistakes. In fact, three of the most infamous viruses in recent years (*Christma*, 1987; *Melissa*, 1999; *I LOVE YOU*, 2000) were actually variants of the same source code with similar methodology and payload (Cohen, 2001). Security experts suggest that this phenomenon may be attributed to an inadequate inoculation period, where users experience a heightened (but brief) awareness of data vulnerability. Thus, administrators must develop innovative training programs while continuously updating their virus protection.

ages experienced by compromised systems, it does illustrate a commitment on the part of the American government to aggressively pursue criminal charges against the initiators of computer contaminants irrespective of motivation or design. Unfortunately, this is not the case in many foreign countries, whose citizens have infected systems across the globe. Reonel Ramones and Onel de Guzman, for example, the creators of the *Love Bug* virus will not be prosecuted by the authorities in Manila due to the lack of applicable statutes, even though their virus affected approximately *45 million* computer users worldwide and caused *billions* of dollars in damages.

Data Piracy—Industrial Espionage and Terrorism

An additional criminal activity gaining in popularity involves the theft and trafficking of proprietary information. In fact, the increasing commercialization of knowledge is a precursor to this sort of activity. Although individuals could actively extort money from an organization whose data has been compromised, the financial gain realized in **data piracy** is through the actual sale of such information. Thus, the compromised data actually has value in and of itself. Such theft and sale of proprietary information is often committed by corporate employees. One employee at Gillette Company in Boston was caught using company equipment to solicit bids for the design specifications for Gillette's new Mach-3 razor (Andreano, 1999). However, it can also be committed by criminal outsiders, industry competitors, or even *government entities!* Such government agencies (and

Computer contaminants can cripple an entire network. They can be introduced into private systems and international ones. Robert Morris' Worm, for example, contaminated approximately 10 percent of all systems which were connected to the Internet at the time. (Michael J. Okoniewski/*AP/World Wide Photos*)

agents) engage in such behavior for personal gain and/or use patriotic arguments to justify their behavior. For example, the former head of the French Secret Service admitted on American television that his organization had planted electronic eavesdropping devices on Air France flights from New York to Paris. Information collected was then forwarded to the French corporation, French Mirage. This information enabled the company to undercut the bid of an American corporation. This multimillion dollar contract was directly attributed to the actions of their state-run intelligence service! This type of behavior, he argued, was necessary for smaller countries who wished to compete in today's global economy.

Theft of Information—Political Espionage

Technology has also escalated the potential for sophisticated attacks on a country's national security and public infrastructure. The most obvious, but not the most insidious, continues to be the theft of information. Like the corporate counterparts, government entities have not invested adequate resources to protect secrets technologically stored or created. In fact, many would argue that national security issues in general have become all but obscured since the end of the Cold War. Unfortunately, there appears to be no such apathy on the part of foreign governments. Indeed, the FBI estimates that at least 120 foreign governments are actively working intelligence operations currently targeting the United States (SEARCH, 2000). At the same time, the United States has seen an increase in trusted government agents charged with espionage (e.g., Robert Hansen). These threats are not only real, but are also increasingly sophisticated.

In 1998, while Benjamin Netanyahu was Israel's Prime Minister, intelligence agents infiltrated Telrad (subcontracted by Nortel, an American telecommunications conglomerate). By installing undetectable chips during the manufacturing process, agents were granted access to top secret and otherwise classified information. Such data included communications between President Clinton and senior staff officials within the National Security Council. This arrangement, which included weekly reports to Tel Aviv, was made possible due to a multimillion-dollar contract to replace communications equipment between Nortel, Telrad, and the Israeli Air Force. Curiously, contract specifications granted access to manufacturing areas by members of the Israeli Air Force *to protect government secrets!* As disconcerting as these activities may be, they are by no means the most insidious. In fact, a simpler, far more popular, method of technological espionage involves the physical theft of data storage containers (i.e., CPUs, diskettes, etc.).

Like most inventions created to increase the efficiency and effectiveness of corporate and government employees, the introduction of laptop computers was heralded as the solution to employee angst. Designed to facilitate home-based work environments, laptops were intended to empower overburdened workers, enabling them to work at home, on vacation, or at the dentist's office. However, their introduction has not been accomplished without a myriad of associated problems. In fact, their sheer portability, often seen as their greatest strength, is also their greatest weakness, making them prime targets for the burgeoning data black market. Neither corporate or government entities have been unscathed, and all areas of the globe have experienced this pattern of criminal activity. In London, for example, two government laptops filled with top secret or classified information were stolen from the same railway station over a period of two months; while during the Gulf War American officials were forced to tighten security measures after a laptop containing secrets of the Allies' war plans was stolen from an official car while the Wing Commander it was assigned to was car shopping. In fact, a variety of laptops have been stolen in recent times, usually as a result of employee carelessness (one was left in a taxi after a night of heavy drinking!). One location which has proven to be particularly popular among thieves are airports— a new variant of the classic briefcase switch. Simply replacing the targeted laptop with one of their own, thieves often escape detection and leave few clues for investigators. Another method which has proven successful involves a pair or team of thieves. While one thief stands at the end of the electronic scanner located at security checkpoints, another intentionally creates a diversion in front of the owner after the laptop has been placed on the moving belt. This method, however, poses greater risk to the perpetrator as the likelihood of detection increases. Regardless, both of these methods are only possible through an individual victim's carelessness. Thus, employers must address the vulnerability and subsequent security of laptops during training. Unfortunately, other incidents are a result of systemic vulnerabilities. These thefts, while just as costly, are more preventable once identified, as traditional methods of physical security may be employed. This lesson was recently learned by the State Department after an inventory search was initiated due to the theft of a laptop containing top-secret arms control data. This inventory revealed that more than 15 additional laptops were unaccounted for! Since this embarrassment and public relations disaster, the State Department has reportedly tightened security measures and established firm parameters of accountability for laptop users.

Data Manipulation—Political Terrorism

Recent events have forced the realization and recognition of the country's physical vulnerability to religious and/or political zealots. In the wake of the events of 11 September 2001, American citizens clamored for immediate retaliation against shadow targets. Unfortunately, such shadows have proven to be extremely elusive, and undeterred in their fanaticism. However, the disaster did awaken the American public and its corresponding government institutions to the dangers posed by terrorism—a danger long recognized by leaders from other areas of the globe. In fact, such hazards from extremists have existed for centuries.

Traditionally, terrorist actions involved physical actions directed at physical or human targets. Intending to create chaos, public disorder, and, ultimately, government instability, terrorist factions have long fantasized upon striking a mortal blow to their targets—temporarily shutting down the entire society and causing widespread fear. With the possible exception of the World Trade Center/Pentagon attacks of 2001, however, these sorts of "successes" have proven unobtainable, especially in First World countries. In fact, many individuals, academics, and institutions alike have declared that the positive environment (i.e., the rebirth of patriotism, community solidarity, and government resolve) born in the wake of the 9/11 tragedy , has all but negated any victory which Bin Laden's group may have originally claimed. Such American resiliency has astounded residents across the globe, but several experts have suggested that the phenomenon may be attributed primarily to the magnitude of human loss *and* the broadcasting of the entire event, including clean-up and rescue. They suggest that a pattern of smaller attacks may have been more successful in disrupting the targeted society, as the sheer magnitude of destruction all but anesthetized the American public, releasing a collective rage at those responsible. Thus, it may be argued that traditional notions (and methods) of terrorism, focusing on mass mayhem and physical destruction may be supplanted by a more sophisticated, subtler approach.

Similar to their counterparts involved in organized criminal activity, international terrorist groups are increasingly using advances in technology to increase their effectiveness and efficiency. They are using the Internet, for example, to formulate plans, spread propaganda, elicit funding, communicate, and terrorize their intended target. The Internet, in particular, is a wonderful tool for creating fear, because the potential for victimization increases. In addition, the threat feels more real to individuals who were not directly involved than in a traditional attack. The wide-scale, sustained panic that has resulted from a variety of recent computer viruses, for example, had far more impact on daily behavior and individual awareness than the events of 11 September 2001. Thus, a new day of terrorism which involves the theft or manipulation of data has dawned.

Cyberterrorism may be defined as a deliberate, politically or religiously motivated attack against data compilations, computer programs, and/or information systems which is intended to disrupt and/or deny service or acquire information which disrupts the social, physical or political infrastructure of a target. This general definition encompasses the complex myriad of possibilities involving the implementation of computer technology in terrorist activities. Like other activities involving the theft or manipulation of data, computers may be incidental to the activity or serve as the target or the instrument or all of the above. It is anticipated that most cyberterrorist acts will employ technology to target information systems, data, or the like. Thus, in this sort of activity, computers will be both targets and weapons. Such instrumentality is necessary to facilitate the acquisition of sensitive data, while the targeted device acts at best as an information server and, at worst, as a self-imploding weapon of mass destruction.

Such implementation may take various forms, including, but not limited to, hacking, Denial of Service attacks, and viruses or worms. Any of these forms could be successfully directed at critical national and/or international infrastructures causing electric blackouts, disrupted communications, and the like. While not nearly as sensational as traditional weapons of mass destruction, these targeted strikes could actually pose a greater danger to the American public, due to the interconnectivity and ultimate reliance on public switch telecommunications. Think of the devastation that could result from a simple (but sustained) electric blackout in Los Angeles. Water purification systems, telecommunications, 911

WEB OF HATE AND DESTRUCTION

One month after the Oklahoma City bombing, the Antiterrorism and Effective Death Penalty Act of 1996 (AEDPA), providing for the study of terrorist-type information, was enacted. Subsequent research conducted by the Department of Justice (1997) revealed a virtual plethora of bomb-making information in both traditional publishing venues (e.g., *Guerilla's Arsenal: Advanced Techniques for Making Explosives and Time Delay Bombs; Deadly Brew: Advanced Improvised Explosives; The Anarchist Cookbook; The Anarchist Arsenal,* etc.) and electronic media. The proliferation of electronically accessible information is especially troubling, as the sheer availability and affordability (i.e., *free*) creates a broader, less traditional audience which includes disgruntled teens and incarcerated felons. This information includes, but is not limited to, instructional sites for a variety of bombs (thermite, pipe, mail, etc.), and newsgroups and BBSs for exchanging information and soliciting advice.

emergency and central dispatch systems, fuel outlets, financial institutions, public GPS systems, etc. could all become useless, creating an untenable situation for public safety officials and health providers and destroying public trust and social integrity.

Imagine the loss of life that could result if hackers successfully penetrated and manipulated data sets located at major research centers or the Center for Disease Control. Surreptitiously altering a small portion of a formula for a vaccination, changing the labeling instructions for biological contaminants or systematically removing years of priceless research or patient records could result in tens of thousands of deaths. The introduction of a computer virus or worm could also wreak unforeseen havoc on public health, as officials across the globe have recently discovered. In Britain and Italy, for example, computer viruses wiped out vital information from lengthy hematology studies and one year's worth of AIDS research. While in the United States, one large hospital in the Northeast lost over 40 percent of its patient records due to a particularly destructive virus.

In addition to these highly focused attacks, terrorist organizations across the world are increasing in strength by propagandizing their radical rhetoric to a global audience. Like many domestic groups (e.g., Aryan Nations, White Aryan Resistance (WAR), Nation of Islam, etc.), international organizations have found a safe, virtual platform where they can spew their venomous dogma without fear of physical discovery or attack. These groups have also effectively used the Internet to solicit funds and recruit new members—streamlining the hate industry and reducing propaganda expenditures. In addition, groups such as Osama bin Laden's al Qaeda, Hezbollah, and Hamas are actively exchanging e-mail and utilizing strong encryption algorithms to support their organizations (Kerr, 2000b). (In fact, Ramzi Yousef, one of the designers of the first World Trade Center bombing, stored detailed plans to destroy U.S. airliners on encrypted files on his laptop computer.)

Other approaches include the launching of massive Denial of Service (DOS) attacks and defacement of Web sites against foreign governments (Kerr, 2000b).

These attacks are perpetrated by amateurs and professionals alike. The "Internet Black Tigers", a group allegedly affiliated with the Tamil Tigers, have repeatedly attacked official sites of numerous governments, while a variety of Chinese hacktivists announced their intention to launch massive DOS attacks against American financial and government sites in the wake of a crash involving a U.S. surveillance plane and a Chinese fighter. While American hackers vowed to fight back, the long-term effects of such activity are often trivialized by officials who claim that tightened site security will eliminate the successes of such actors. They fail to recognize the international conflicts or nuclear implications which may arise from the actions of cyberpunks. Unfortunately, hacking activities appear to be gaining in popularity as how-to information is freely distributed via the Internet.

Hackers' Secrets—How do they do it?

Whether the motivation is personal, economic or political, the methodology of hacking has remained remarkably unchanged over the past several decades. While many individuals struggle to understand, for example, how President Clinton's e-mail was compromised at least twice during his presidency; security experts point to White House employees as the likely culprit. Criminals usually prey on systemic vulnerabilities or employee weaknesses to steal or gain unauthorized access to privileged information. While the first may seem the first line of attack, research indicates that uninformed or careless employees pose the greatest threat. In fact, research indicates that data security and adequate training of personnel is a low priority for *all* levels of institutions, including government entities. Unfortunately, the lack of prioritization enables hackers to steal passwords and enter even the most complex systems almost at will.

Perhaps the easiest, and therefore the most popular, method for stealing passwords involves social engineering. Using deceptive practices, hackers employ traditional confidence scams to gain access to company computers or telephone systems. Most commonly acting as representatives for a vendor's security system or the company's IT section, hackers persuade employees to volunteer their user names, passwords, or both! Hackers may also gather personal information about an employee from the employee themselves or their co-workers, as many, many individuals personalize their passwords despite the advice of their supervisor or IT security administrator. Hometowns, birthdates, anniversaries, alma maters, school mascots, nicknames, social security numbers and maiden, children's, spouse's or pets' names are commonly used as passwords. (So, if Ellen Burnstein is single with two cats, chances are her password won't be hard to figure out.)

Either of these approaches exposes the potential hacker to little danger of exposure, and allows them to begin attempts at breaching security measures immediately. Remember: employees (even honest ones) are a company's biggest liability in terms of data security. Even if institutional security measures preclude personalized passwords, employees still pose a risk to data and system security due to their lack of regard (often due to naiveté) for its importance. Failing to appreciate the value of the data in their control, many employees will often post their passwords in conspicuous places—sometimes taping them to their computer monitors! (Ironically, this may be most common in situations where systems administrators are attempting to tighten system security by routinely changing passwords, requiring multiple or multi-level passwords, or preventing their personalization.) In other cases, employees will be susceptible to *shoulder-surfing* (i.e., literally watching over someone's shoulder as he or she inputs a password).

Employees who fail to follow proper security procedures for disposing of personal correspondence and company paperwork also pose a security risk to an institution's digital technology. Just like criminals of old would search trash containers for discarded credit card receipts, payroll records, and the like, hackers often resort to diving through corporate trash sites. Unfortunately, unwitting administrators and employees routinely dump sensitive information into the nearest trash receptacle. Information such as old technical manuals, internal phone lists, organizational charts and correspondence provide a wealth of information for the malicious hacker (SEARCH, 2000).

Finally, some hackers may employ more sophisticated approaches to gaining unauthorized access to "secured" data. One approach involves systemic vulnerabilities created by vendors in which remote access is allowed to perform routine maintenance, such as updating, on their systems. Hackers may target these backdoors in an attempt to gain superstar privileges. In addition, some successful hacking attacks may be attributed to a system administrator's negligence. Some system administrators, for example, never change the defaults in their networks once they are installed! By utilizing lists of default passwords, readily available on the net, unauthorized users are able to gain root access by simply using traditional network defaults.

CONCLUSIONS

If we had your skills in the 60s, the 80s would have never happened.
—Winn Schwartau, *Electrohippies*

Corporate and national security are becoming increasingly vulnerable to criminal acts. While computers have been instrumental in the creation of sophisticated defense and security mechanisms, they have also created unprecedented risks to national security on a variety of levels. First, computers act as the technical equivalent of storage warehouses—stockpiling information ranging from satellite locations to troop deployment to personal information of government personnel. Traditionally secure from all but the most dedicated of professionals, this information has long been an extremely valuable commodity. Their current vulnerability has not led to market devaluation. In fact, it is this very vulnerability that has proven irresistible to espionage agents, common criminals, and computer hackers alike (Icove, Seger, & VonStorch, 1995). Second, the increasing connectivity and interdependence of government and poorly regulated public infrastructures is creating a technological house of cards, in which the failure of one critical system could upset the precarious balancing of the entire techno-driven society. Third, the technical expertise necessary for information warfare has significantly declined due to the ready availability of instructional guidelines on the information superhighway. Fourth, the number of threat groups with sophisticated methodologies and advanced technology systems has exponentially increased. And, finally, there is the lack of recognition and government apathy which has been displayed towards protecting digital systems. Thus, the theft or manipulation of data may also lead to a new style of terrorism both here and abroad. Unfortunately, the United States has only recently revealed the physical vulnerability of our most prized institutions.

TERMS DISCUSSED IN THIS CHAPTER

black market dealers	Eco-terrorism	software piracy
cyberterrorism	extortion	shareware
data piracy	grey market dealers	VBS worm generator
denial of service (DOS) attack	hackers	wareZ
	insiders	

DISCUSSION QUESTIONS

1. What is software piracy? How pervasive is it, and how can it be eliminated?
2. How do contemporary hackers vary from their predecessors?
3. Discuss the six classifications of motive for contemporary computer intruders.
4. What does the term "theft of information" mean? Discuss the implications of such in terms of national security.
5. How has technology changed the face of terrorism? How may it be utilized in the future?

5

AVENUES FOR PROSECUTION AND GOVERNMENT EFFORTS

INTRODUCTION

As stated previously, the advent of computer crime has resulted in a myriad of problems for law enforcement administrators. The lack of resources available to small agencies, the traditional apathy toward non-violent crime, and the reluctance of legislative action have enabled many computer criminals to act with virtual impunity. While it is anticipated that an increase in technology-specific legislation and the modification of extant statutes is forthcoming, lawmakers should evaluate existing federal and state law for prosecutorial avenues currently available. This would empower local agencies and reduce demands on federal agencies.

Traditionally, state and local officials have been forced to rely exclusively on the expertise of better trained, better funded Federal agencies. Unfortunately, these agencies are incapable of addressing every call for assistance. In addition, they are often unwilling to expend resources on crimes which do not constitute threats to institutional security, the economic infrastructure, the exploitation of children, individual safety or violation of federal law. (It is unlikely, for example, that a federal agency would assist law enforcement in cases constituting misdemeanor offenses or those which appear to be minor in nature—e.g., installation of Back Orifice on a personal computer, a currently contained virus which destroyed two computers, etc.) Law-enforcement administrators should carefully evaluate state statutes. When used creatively, many can be directly applied to criminal activity involving computers. Remember, the method of execution is not an essential element in criminal law. Intent, action, and illegality are inherent in every case of larceny, for example. The method is irrelevant. Thus, an individual who utilizes a computer to steal money from a bank is just as culpable as the individual who resorts to physical theft. At the same time, criminal mischief or vandalism statutes may be utilized to prosecute an individual who remotely alters data. Investigators and administrators must be encouraged to look for the obvious! While there are a variety of statutes which have been enacted to specifically address technological crime, traditional statutes should be utilized where the former are lacking.

TRADITIONAL STATUTES

Title 18 of the United States Code has long been characterized as an invaluable resource for state and local legislators in development of state codes. As such, it can be used as a guideline for investigators seeking to apply non-technology-specific prohibitions generically to computer crime. In addition, Titles 15 and 17 may be useful.

Criminal Activity Statute	Applicable
Fraud and Embezzlement	
18 U.S.C. } 2314	Applies to goods known to be stolen or fraudulently obtained and worth more than $5,000 transported in Interstate commerce.
18 U.S.C. } 641	Embezzlement or theft of public money, property, or records.
18 U.S.C. } 2071	Prohibits concealment, removal or mutilation of public records.
18 U.S.C. } 1005 & 1006	Prohibits concealment, removal or mutilation of the records of banks or credit institutions. (Remote alteration or the like would clearly fall within these provisions.)
18 U.S.C. }	Prohibits false, fictitious, or fraudulent statements to a department or agency concerning a matter within the jurisdiction of the same *when something of value is involved.* (May be utilized if individuals misrepresent themselves to gain access to programs or pages.)
Terrorism or Espionage	
18 U.S.C. } 1905	Prohibits the disclosure of confidential information by a government employee.
18 U.S.C. } 793, 794, 795	Prohibits the gathering, transmission, or loss of defense information; prohibits the transmission or delivery of national defense information to a foreign government or agent; prohibits the sketching or photographing of defense installations. (May be utilized if individuals attach live feeds of military bases or the like or upload pictures or maps onto the Internet.)
Child Seduction	
18 U.S.C. } 2421	Prohibits the interstate transportation of minors for sexual activity.
Child Exploitation	
18 U.S.C. } 2251	Prohibits the sexual exploitation and other abuse of children.
Stalking	
18 U.S.C. } 2261	This amendment to Title 18 makes it a Federal crime to engage in repeated harassing or threatening behavior that places the victim in reasonable fear of death or bodily injury. Summarily stated, any person who travels (or causes to), uses (or causes to) the mail or any facility in interstate or foreign commerce, or enters or leaves

18 U.S.C. } 875(c)—
The Hobbs Act

(or causes to) Indian country is guilty of stalking if they place an individual in reasonable fear of death or harm to a loved one. *Whoever transmits in interstate or foreign commerce any communication containing any threat to kidnap any person or any threat to injure the person of another, shall be fined under this title or imprisoned not more than five years, or both.*

Forgery and Counterfeiting 18 U.S.C.} 471–509

Credit Card Fraud
15 U.S.C. 41 } 1644

Prohibits the use, attempt or conspiracy to fraudulently use credit cards in interstate or foreign commerce. In addition, it prohibits the transportation of such cards, receipt or concealment of goods and tickets purchased and money received through card transactions. (This statute could be used on individuals posting credit card numbers on BBS or on "carding"—hackers who use stolen credit card information to purchase goods or services.)

Extortion
18 U.S.C.} 1951

Copyright Infringement
17 U.S.C.} 102, 103

Provides definitional guidelines for protected information or material. In particular, it offers protection for "idea(s), procedure, process, system, method of operation, concept, principle, or discovery, regardless of the form in which it is described, explained, illustrated, or embodied in such work.

17 U.S.C.} 506

Prohibits the reproduction, preparation, distribution or public release of copyrighted material. This includes art, photographs, writings, etc. Probably one of the most common forms of theft on the Internet—where ideas are routinely misrepresented.

Software Piracy
15 U.S.C.} 1114

Prohibits the manufacturing of counterfeit products (may include software or hardware).

RICO
18 U.S.C.} 1961–1968

Racketeer influenced and corrupt organizations provides for the prosecution of individuals involved in a pattern of racketeering. It also provides for the punishment of offenders and the seizures of their assets.

Access Device Fraud
18 U.S.C.} 1029

Individuals may be prosecuted under this statute if they knowingly and with intent to defraud, produce, use, trafficking, or in some cases simply possess counterfeit and/or unauthorized access devices or device-making equipment. Such devices are broadly defined as cards, plates, codes, account numbers, electronic serial numbers, mobile identification number, personal identification number, or other means (Soma, et al., 1996). Although this statute was not directed towards computer-facilitated fraud, the courts have ruled that it may be used in cases where computer passwords are fraudulently obtained to steal things of value (*U.S. v. Fernandez*, No. 92 CR. 563 (RO), 1993 WL 88197 (S.D.N.Y. Mar. 25, 1993.) In addition, this statute could be used to prosecute phreakers using illegal boxes or electronic passwords used to access financial accounts, and the like. This section, never mentioning the word "computer," has been utilized by the Secret Service to prosecute those individuals who have stolen information or software from computers.

Illegal Wiretapping
18 U.S.C.} 119

A variety of laws at the state and Federal level make it illegal for individuals to unlawfully intercept electronic communications. This would include utilization of keyloggers or other functions included in back-door programs like NetBus or BackOrifice (since these programs also grant access to them). These would include provisions under Title 18 (18 U.S.C. {2511). In addition, 18 U.S.C.} 2701 prohibits the intentional acquisition of or alteration or destruction of stored communications. Thus, those individuals who intentionally access e-mail accounts not belonging to them may be prosecuted under this statute.

Although the above is not intended to serve as an exhaustive listing of all available statues, it is illustrative of the typologies of statutes applicable to criminal activity involving computers. Administrators and investigators should peruse their own state codes, and avail themselves of existing prosecutorial avenues. (Virtually all state resources, for example, prohibit the interception of electronic communications. These statutes could be used to creatively prosecute individuals who are utilizing Trojans to access other machines.) In addition, administrators must petition legislatures for relief, and familiarize themselves with computer-specific statutes which are emerging.

THE EVOLUTION OF COMPUTER-SPECIFIC STATUTES

While many state legislatures have been slow to enact computer-specific statutes, the United States Congress has reacted more quickly. Thus, measures enabling the prosecution of electronic fraud, hacking, and the theft of intellectual property may be found at the Federal level. Unfortunately, this legislation has been buffeted by a variety of legal challenges, the language characterized by jurists as vague and ambiguous. Such efforts can be traced back to 1977, when Senator Abraham Ribicoff (Connecticut) introduced the Federal Computer Systems Protection Act (FSCPA). Although the Act was eventually defeated, it created a climate ripe for future legislation.

Computer Fraud and Abuse Act of 1986

Originally known as the Counterfeit Access Device and Computer Fraud and Abuse Act of 1986, Section 1030 of Title 18 of the United States Code, quickly became the Federal government's main weapon in fighting computer crime. Known as the **"hacking statute,"** the act in its original form was very narrow in scope, making it a felony to knowingly:

MURPHY'S LAW

Ribicoff's actions stemmed from a computer scam conducted by Ian Murphy, the computer consultant for Universal Studios theatrical release *Sneakers* and a world class thief. Murphy began his consulting "career" as a thief who created dummy corporations to facilitate the transfer of thousands of dollars in computer equipment. Upon his conviction, his mother promptly petitioned Congressman Larry Coughlin to investigate the *leniency* of his sentence. (Apparently, she was outraged that her son was not being adequately punished.) Coughlin's response was to introduce legislation which eventually became known as the Counterfeit Access Device and Computer Fraud and Abuse Act of 1984 (Baker, 1993).

Access a computer without authorization, or in excess of authorization, in order to obtain classified United States defense or foreign relations information with the intent or reason to believe that such information would be used to harm the United States or to advantage a foreign nation. Second, the 1984 Act made it a misdemeanor knowingly to access a computer without authorization, in excess of authorization, in order to obtain information contained in a financial record of a financial institution or in a consumer file of a consumer reporting agency. Third, the 1984 Act made it a misdemeanor knowingly to access a computer without authorization, or in excess of authorization, in order to use, modify, destroy, or disclose information in, or prevent authorized use of, a computer operated for or on behalf of the United States if such conduct would affect the government's use of the computer. The 1984 Act also made it a crime to attempt or to conspire to commit any of the three acts described above (Andreano, 1999).

This legislation proved to be largely ineffective due to the ambiguity of the statutory language and an overemphasis on financial information. (Only one person was successfully prosecuted under the original provisions.) However, Congress strengthened the Act in 1986, taking great pains to clarify terms originally characterized as vague. **Federal Interest Computer,** for example, was expanded to include any computer *which is used in interstate or foreign commerce or communications*. This enabled Federal authorities to assume jurisdiction if a crime was committed via computer in a distant state. It also expanded the original language, broadening its scope to include all financial records not just those institutions and records found within the Right to Financial Privacy Act of 1978. In addition, the revisions expanded the criminal intent requirement from *knowingly* to *intentionally*. Thus, inadvertent intrusions would not be prosecutable. More succinctly, the new Act made it a misdemeanor to gain unauthorized access to financial information from any financial institution or credit reporting agency, any information in the possession of the government, or any private information where the defendant's conduct involved interstate or foreign commerce; and, a felony if the activity involved an expectation of gain or if the offense was in the furtherance of another crime. Finally, the 1986 revisions specifically targeted hackers by criminalizing password trafficking.[1]

As stated, these revisions proved to be invaluable to the investigation and prosecution of computer crime. Generally speaking, the current version of the Act (several subsequent revisions have taken place) protects computer(s) which are utilized in interstate commerce or communication, computers which involve the Federal interest, and any government computers. Actions included in this statute include theft, destruction, or corruption of sensitive information including, but not limited to, defense secrets, financial records, and passwords. In addition, the statute reduces traditional standards of *mens rea,* allowing the prosecution of individuals who behave with reckless disregard. (This would include the spread of computer viruses and back door programs like NetBus and Back Orifice.)

Ironically, one of the first individuals to be charged with a felony under this statute was Robert Morris, the infamous creator of the "Morris Worm," and son of the former chief scientist at the National Computer Security Center.[2]

This Act was also used to prosecute Herbert Zinn (a.k.a. Shadowhawk) and Kevin Mitnick. "Shadowhawk" was an 18-year-old high school dropout and hacker extraordinaire. Herbert Zinn, considered a juvenile at the time of his arrest, was sentenced to nine months and fined $10,000 for breaking into computers ranging from NATO to the United States Air Force. In addition, Zinn stole 52 AT&T programs valued at over $1 million. Provisions under the Act could have resulted in a prison term of 20 years for an adult charged with the same range of offenses. Unlike Zinn, Kevin Mitnick, one of the most infamous hackers in history, had a criminal history the length of which rivals that of many organized crime figures. His successful conviction under this Act was a result of his theft of programs valued at more than $1 million from Digital Equipment Corporation and the illegal manipulation of MCI service codes.

The Computer Fraud and Abuse Act has also been successfully used against employees who have exceeded their authorized access. In fact, the constitutionality of the Act has been affirmed in cases ranging from hackers to government employees. Perhaps the first (or best known) was *United States* v. *Rice,* in which an IRS employee accessed Service records to determine the scope the Service's case against his friend. As he was not in the criminal investigation decisions, Rice's actions constituted unauthorized access. His subsequent conviction was affirmed on appeal.

---

[1]Although challenged by Morris (*U.S.* v. *Morris,* 928 F.2d 504 (7thCir., 1991), the Court ruled that the Act did not require a demonstration that the defendant *intentionally* prevented authorized use, thereby causing loss.

[2]Since the earlier revisions, the Act has been amended on three different occasions. In 1988, protections were expanded to include all FDIC-insured institutions. The 1990 revisions focused primarily expanding traditional protections to include foreign banks. And, finally, the 1994 revision developed two levels of intent: 1) intentional; and, 2) reckless. In addition, it incorporated provisions for denial of service attacks and potential hard to systems or components.

Perhaps the most infamous of hackers is Kevin Mitnick, a poster child for the Electronic Frontier Foundation and other libertarian groups. (Bob
Jordan/AP/*World Wide Photos*)

As stated, the Computer Fraud and Abuse Act has been successfully utilized
to prosecute hackers. However, the Act does have significant limitations in that it
only involves those cases in which a computer data is a target. It does not include
other offenses committed via or in conjunction with computer technology, such
as child pornography.

EVOLVING CHILD PORNOGRAPHY STATUTES

Although a variety of laws have been enacted to combat the increase in technological crime, none are more emotionally charged than those dealing with child
pornography. Beginning in 1977, Congress has attempted to eliminate child
pornography. Originally criminalized at the Federal level with the Protection of
Children against Sexual Exploitation Act of 1977 (PCSE), Congress has periodically
revised legislation to protect children from sexual exploitation in keeping with
emerging legal doctrine. Unfortunately, the Court has not evaluated the constitu-

tionality of the most recent modifications. Instead, much of the extant case law reveals patterns of inconsistency among lower courts. In fact, virtually all of these cases rely on two Supreme Court decisions, whose interpretation of and application to emerging laws have been diverse.

In 1982, the Supreme Court evaluated free-speech challenges to child pornography and found them wanting (*New York* v. *Ferber,* 458 U.S. 747). Uncharacteristically emphatic, the Court ruled that child pornography was outside the scope of the First Amendment, and allowed states to enact blanket prohibitions against visualizations of children engaged in sexual situations. The Child Protection Act of 1984 (CPA) incorporated this decision. Although the Act lacked technological specificity, it was widely used against online offenders until the emergence of the Child Protection and Obscenity Act of 1988. While this Act officially prohibited the use of computers to transport, distribute, or receive such materials, it, and its successor, have been widely criticized by free-speech advocates. At the same time, the Court has remained resolutely silent.

Prior to the passage of the **Child Pornography Protection Act** (CPPA) in 1996, definitions of child pornography appeared to be nationally, if not universally, accepted. However, the incorporation of technology-specific language has resulted in a slew of constitutional challenges, and lower courts have displayed sharp disagreement. Perhaps the most controversial, and certainly the most attacked, provision of the revised Act involves the use of electronically altered photographs in depicting child pornography. Noting technological advancements, Congress recognized the possibility of creating child pornography out of innocent images. To prevent this, Congress expanded the definition of child pornography to include altered pictures of identifiable children, and depictions of what "appears to be" or "conveys the impression of" minors engaged in sexually explicit situations. (The latter includes wholly artificial images, entirely created through virtual, as opposed to actual, children.) While the First, Fourth and Eleventh Circuits have upheld the Act's constitutionality, the Ninth Circuit has consistently ruled that the language is vague. More importantly, the Ninth Circuit has ruled that the potential for virtual rather than actual victimization invalidates the Act's constitutionality by abridging the guarantees set forth by the First Amendment.

● GOVERNMENT INCENTIVES: COMMITTEES

While the courts have continued to interpret computer-specific legislation arbitrarily, government efforts have continued to create working groups and governmental committees to address emerging issues in technology. One of the first of these, the President's Working Group on Unlawful Conduct on the Internet, chaired by Attorney General Janet Reno, brought together individuals from all levels of the community, including representatives from the **business community** (Internet Alliance, the Computer Systems, the Computer Systems Policy Project, the Business Software Alliance), **government entities** (National Association of Attorneys General, the National District Attorneys Association, the National Asso-

COMPUTER FRAUD AND ABUSE ACT—18 U.S.C. } 1030

- Section 1030 expands the power of the Secret Service by specifying that "the United States Secret Service shall, in addition to any other agency having such authority, have the authority to investigate offenses under this section." However, due to Congress' refusal to remedy jurisdictional turf battles between the USSS and the FBI, authority is somewhat unclear.
- Section 1030 also prohibits simple access of full or part-time governmental computers—no damage must be done in order for this act to be violated.
- Section 1030(a)(4)—punishes those who use computers in schemes to defraud victims of property of more than $5,000.
- Section 1030(a)(5)—creates three separate offenses, two felonies and one misdemeanor (depends on intent and authority of the actor)—criminalizes the transmission of a program, information, code, or command, and as a result of such conduct, intentionally causes damage without authorization to a protected computer (felony); damage may include the availability or integrity of data, program, system or information that: 1) causes loss of more than $5,000 within a year to one or more persons; 2) modifies or impairs, or potentially modifies or impairs, the medical examination, diagnosis, treatment, or care of one or more persons; 3) causes physical injury to a person; or, 4) threatens public health 1030(e)(8).
- Section 1030(a)(5)—generally governs access without authority (outsiders).
- Section 1030(a)(5)(B)—individual who intentionally accesses a protected computer and, as a result of such conduct, recklessly causes damage is guilty of a felony.
- Section 1030(a)(5)(C)—individual who intentionally accesses a protected computer and, as a result of such conduct, causes damage is guilty of a misdemeanor when it cannot be shown that the damage caused was either intentional or reckless.
- Section 1030(a)(6)—prohibits trafficking in passwords, information or devices through which unauthorized access may result, if such trafficking affects interstate or foreign commerce or is a government computer—**aimed primarily at hackers, and underground hacking boards.**
- Section 1030(a)(7)—involves extortion through threats to damage a protected computer (this has been utilized against a variety of individuals who have threatened to exploit holes in security systems if their demands are not met).

ciation of Boards of Pharmacies, and the National League of Cities), and **civil liberty/non-profit advocacy organizations** (including the National Center for Missing and Exploited Children, the Center for Democracy and Technology and the Electronic Privacy Information Center).

This group was originally tasked with providing an analysis of legal and policy issues involving the Internet for criminal behavior. More specifically, they were charged to evaluate:

1. the extent to which existing Federal laws are sufficient to address unlawful conduct via the Internet (provide a framework for analyzing policy and legal responses;
2. the extent to which new technologies or legal authorities may be needed to investigate and prosecute Internet crime (i.e.,, the development of new tools and formulating training strategies);
3. the utility of education and "empowerment tools" to minimize the risks associated with this behavior (i.e., give teachers and parents the ability to teach their children proper usages) (DOJ, 2000).

Generally, the group developed a three-tiered approach:

1. **regulation** of Internet criminal activity in the spirit of traditional criminal law (i.e., consistent with statutory and constitutional mandates), stressing that technological crime should be treated the same as criminal activity which is not technologically advanced, ensuring privacy and protection of civil liberties;
2. **recognition** of special needs and challenges of investigating and prosecuting such activity, while emphasizing the need for tool development, enhanced training, and interagency (and international) cooperation;
3. **development** of specialized curricula including cyber-ethics and support for leadership within the private sector.

The group postulated that enhanced training of average users would decrease the risk that they would become involved in unlawful activity.

In addition, the group found that there were some laws in place which adequately addressed certain types of criminal activities, noting that traditional statutes which criminalize credit card fraud, gambling, identity theft, and the like may be used to address online or offline behavior. However, the group also recommended that many of these should be amended to specifically identify developing technologies and additional statutes or legislation should be enacted to address those activities peculiar to the Internet and computers. In particular, the group argued that mechanisms for tracing (and tracking) online offenders must be developed as the lack of current regulations allows ISPs to discard records at will, making it virtually impossible to identify originating information on dated activities or multi-jurisdictional cases. More specifically, they suggested that requirements attached to traditional telecommunications providers be applied to ISPs. (Imagine the chaos that would result if a bomb threat received via telephone was untraceable because the records were only kept for six hours.) As procedural guidelines require judicial oversight and articulated probable cause, digital evidence is often destroyed before judicial approval can be granted.

Finally, the group encouraged local agencies to establish a presence on the Net, introducing the community to the department and enabling citizens to make comments, suggestions, and (too often) complaints. Superficially, this presents an appearance of technological competence, to residents and criminals alike. More importantly, this establishes a link between the community and department, opening valuable lines of communication which could lead to an increase in anonymous tips, and ultimately improving organizational efficiency and effec-

> A satchel of dynamite and a truckload of fertilizer and diesel fuel are known terrorist tools, Today, the right command sent over a network to a power generation station's control computer could be just as devastating as a backpack full of explosives, and the perpetrator would be more difficult to identify and apprehend.
> (President's Commission on Critical Infrastructure Protection, *Critical Foundations.*)

tiveness. (Remember: the same anonymity that draws criminals to the Web, provides a level of comfort for tipsters who wish to remain anonymous.)

Unlike the President's Working Group on Unlawful Conduct on the Internet which focused on individual online crime, Presidential Decision Directive 63 (PDD63) was more global in scope, calling for a strategic plan to defend the nation against cyberattacks. This directive called for an investment of $1.46 billion in 2000 to defend the nation's critical infrastructures (i.e., power generation systems, banking and financial institutions, transportation networks, emergency services and telecommunications). In addition, the directive articulate the goal for a reliable, interconnected and secure information system infrastructure by 2003. This directive was also the centerpiece for the National Infrastructure Protection Center, a national agency which brings private industry and government resources together.

The National Infrastructure Protection Center (NIPC) is also responsible for the development of **Infragard,** an organization which attempts to bring local community leaders, corporate executives, and law enforcement agencies together to discuss potential threats. Other articulated objectives of the group include: protecting computer systems; education and training on vulnerabilities; access to an Alert Network with encryption furnished by the NIPC to report voluntarily actual or attempted illegal intrusions, disruptions, and vulnerabilities of information systems; and, finally, access to a secure information Web site reporting recent intrusions, research related to infrastructure protection, and the capability to communicate securely with other members. Unfortunately, many insiders report that InfraGard has not lived up to expectations. Anecdotal evidence suggests that the traditional distrust of the FBI by private industry may be interfering with the group's mission. However, other initiatives undertaken by the Federal government promise a variety of benefits to local agencies. For example, the designation of a prosecutor in each U.S. Attorney's Office to serve as a computer and telecommunications coordinator for that district has reduced the likelihood of duplicative efforts. In addition, *LawNet* (if implemented as designed) will further coordinate anti-cybercrime efforts between state and Federal agencies. Designed to be available 24 hours a day/7 days a week, LawNet attempts to articulate jurisdictional boundaries and procedures for multi-jurisdictional cases, which is especially prob-

OTHER GOVERNMENT INITIATIVES

Mid-80s—FCIC (Federal Computer Investigations Committee) comprised of local officers, state officials, and federal agents. However, some claim this is a shadow group, which has no membership role, no official place of residence, and no formal funding.

1989—CERT (Computer Emergency Response Team) was created in response to the Morris Worm. It is located at Carnegie Mellon University's Software Engineering Institute in Pittsburgh. CERT acts as an informational clearinghouse for public and private computer networks and assists entities which have been victimized.

1991—National Computer Crime Squad (FBI)—located in Tysons Corner, VA, part of the Washington Metro Field office of the FBI.

1995—DOJ: computer/telecommunications coordinator program which designates at least one Assistant U.S. Attorney—each of the 93 U.S. Attorney's offices have an in-house, high-tech expert.

October, 1996—Computer Crime Unit was removed from the General Litigation Section and elevated to a higher level, renamed Computer Crime and Intellectual Property Section.

November, 1997—Computer Crime Unit created within the General Litigation Section of the Justice Department (CCU).

lematic in online child pornography cases. (This effort has also been criticized for the ambiguity surrounding funding and allegations of Federal totalitarianism.)

Perhaps the most successful, and certainly the least controversial, of all Federally funded initiatives is **Innocent Images**. This initiative, founded in 1995, had investigated over 800 cases in which adults had traveled interstate to meet minors for illicit purposes, and more than 1850 cases of child pornography in a five-year period. Adequately funded, this project receives more than $10 million a year in Federal funds.

LAW ENFORCEMENT INITIATIVES

In the mid-80s two proactive investigative bulletin boards were created; the first, "Underground Tunnel", was created by Sgt. Robert Ansley in Austin, Texas. The second, known as "the Phone Company", was created in Phoenix, Arizona by Ken MacLeod of the Maricopa County Sheriff's Office. These boards, and those which emerged later, involved law-enforcement personnel who posed as hackers, and were primarily directed at prosecuting those individuals who shared code or loaded pirated software. Since this time, these boards have snowballed.

Over time, these boards granted legitimacy and authority to system operators, validating their authenticity based on the sheer longevity of their operation. This has provided an unexpected boon to law-enforcement initiatives, and has created a platform for additional programs in which keyword scanning and packet-capturing software has been effectively utilized against computer criminals. One such program, NetRadar, was used to identify threats prior to the Seattle demonstration protesting the World Trade Organization. These programs, however, are not without their critics.

Perhaps the most controversial tool in the FBI's investigative arsenal is the sniffing program, **Carnivore.** This program, designed to run in a Windows platform, claims to be a knockoff of commercial software and proprietary source code developed by the FBI. It is designed to "sniff" or "filter" e-mail on a particular network via a network card, routing evidence to a removable disk. According to the FBI, it is seldom used and is designed to be used in very rare instances where it is possible to demonstrate probable cause and state with particularity and specificity: 1) the offense; 2) place (telecommunications facility) where interception is to occur; 3) a description of the communications targeted for interception; and, 4) the identities of the perpetrators. Legally, the application must also include an explanation as to why this is necessary (i.e., other attempts to collect that type of evidence), and how other tools have proven inadequate. Thus, the FBI states that it is not an intelligence-gathering tool. Rather, it is designed to be a mechanism for evidence collection. Court orders are limited to 30 days, and termination of interception must take place once the objective is achieved. Court orders are often contingent upon weekly reports on the status of the investigation.

CARNIVORE ACCORDING TO THE FBI

In the face of sharp criticism by privacy advocates, the FBI has vehemently denied that Carnivore is designed to target innocent citizens. As a response, the FBI issued a formal statement to the United States House of Representatives, which stated that:

(Carnivore is) *a very specialized network analyzer or "sniffer" which runs as an application program on a normal personal computer under the Microsoft Windows operating system. It works by "sniffing" the proper portions of network packets and copying and storing only those packets which match a finely defined filter set programmed in conformity with the court order. This filter set can be extremely complex, and this provides the FBI with an ability to collect transmissions which comply with pen register court orders, trap and trace court order, Title III interceptions orders, etc.* (Kerr, 2000).

Carnivore does not search through the contents of every message and collect those that contain certain key words like "bomb" or "drugs." It selects messages based on criteria expressly set out in the court order, for example, messages transmitted to or from a particular account or to or from a particular user. If the device is placed at some point on the network where it cannot discriminate messages as set out in the court order, it simply lets all such messages pass by unrecorded. (Kerr, 2000).

Although the media has focused exclusively on Carnivore, the program is but one piece of a covert surveillance triad known as "DragonWare Suite." This suite is capable of "reconstructing the Web-surfing trail of someone under investigation." This suite also includes "Packeteer" and "Coolminer." In actuality, Carnivore is actually the end result of an evolution in **packet-sniffing** software. The common link in this evolution was initially called Omnivore, inarguably a more benign label. This original platform, designed as a sniffer of e-mail streams, had the capability to print out targeted e-mails and store other data on a removable drive. In fact, the FBI assured citizens that Carnivore represented a more efficient and strategic weapon, designed to surgically identify and intercept those communications specified by court order; it would ignore those which fell outside these specifications. Unfortunately, the government has acknowledged that these ideals are, as yet, unrealized. However, law enforcement *reactions* have not been as controversial.

Although Federal efforts have been attacked as overly intrusive, local efforts which include less invasive measures have been commended. (Unfortunately, such commendations have not resulted in job security.)[3] As in other areas of computer investigations, Chicago and Phoenix were two of the first local jurisdictions to actively pursue computer criminals. (Many of these enforcement efforts mimicked their criminal counterparts, springing up virtually overnight in an ad hoc manner.) Chicago was quite effective, but dipped off the radar screen after the scandals associated with the LoD crackdown. Phoenix, under the guidance of the ably equipped Gail Thackeray, gained notoriety among the hacker community. In May, 1990, Operation SunDevil was launched. This operation included 150 Secret Service agents, 40 seized computers, and 12 cities (Cincinnati, Los Angeles, Miami, Detroit, Tucson, Phoenix, Newark, San Diego, Richmond, San Francisco, Pittsburgh, and San Jose). Other cities, like New York City and Chicago, were also included in the sting. Because the thrust of the operation was computer seizure and not arrest, the hacker community was taken completely unaware. Unlike previous activities, the hacker community was taken completely aback. Luckily, this trend is continuing.

Although still hopelessly underfunded, many local jurisdictions have taken their cue from the early efforts in Phoenix and Chicago. In fact, roughly ⅔ of all agencies surveyed in an NIJ research project reported that they were involved in a Federal, state or local interagency task force. As expected, these task forces were most common in the Western region of the United States where the presence of high-tech corporations is much *en vogue*. (In fact, over half of the task forces identified were in this area.) Not surprisingly, the lowest number of such task forces was found in the Southeast, where local budgets and technological resources seem to be disproportionately low. Thus, a variety of professional associations have become the premier method of knowledge dissemination among computer

---

[3]Arizona Assistant Attorney General Gail Thackeray was well known for her expertise in prosecuting computer intrusions. Unfortunately, Thackeray was displaced in a political cleansing after the ousting of Steve Twist. The computer crime unit which had proven so successful was completely disbanded.

investigators. One of the most popular, the High Tech Computer Investigators Association (HTCIA) has regional chapters which come together annually. These regional chapters are bound by the same rules and covenants, but vary in expertise, personnel, and training. Members include representatives from both law enforcement and security communities, vendors, and some academics. Sponsorship is a prerequisite and defense attorneys or experts need not apply. **HTCIA** is a non-profit organization and is designed exclusively for training and informational purposes. Unfortunately, other professional associations have been developed or have evolved into self-serving entities.

The International Association for Computer Investigation Specialists (IACIS) has marketed itself as a non-profit, professional organization aimed at serving the law-enforcement community. However, its training platform and emphasis on accreditation has perverted the traditional goals, and many practitioners have become disillusioned. Unlike HTCIA, this organization offers a "certification" program, in which individuals are certified as "computer forensic experts." Although their training is not required for such certification, fees are required for the actual testing. Thus, individuals who are recognized across the country as computer forensic specialists are not formally recognized as such by **IACIS.** Unfortunately, the lack of nationally established criteria for expert certification undermines the credibility of such testing practices.

While a variety of other associations exist, IACIS and HTCIA are by far the most recognized and respected. Both have proven resilient to both criticism and skepticism. They have proven that a lack of resources, governmental interest, and public apathy may be overcome through determination and dedication. They have created an opportunity for professional training and practitioner communication, and provided a platform for political grandstanding and financial grubstaking. In addition, they have incorporated law-enforcement ethics and coordinated international efforts.

● INTERNATIONAL EFFORTS

We need to reach a consensus as to which computer and technology related activities should be criminalized, and then commit to taking appropriate domestic actions.
                    —Attorney General Janet Reno, 21 January 1997.

Although the 1990s have been characterized in the United States as the "Information Age," law enforcement communities have been slow to respond to the potential for cyber-criminality. However, an increasing recognition of the insidious nature of computer crime has reached global proportions. Both Japan and Britain, for example, have incorporated computer crime statutes into extant legislation. While Hong Kong has expanded their Telecommunications Ordinance to generally address cybercrime, Britain has created technology-specific initiatives targeting technological crime. The Regulation of Investigatory Powers Act (RIP), all but negating traditional notions of privacy in the United Kingdom, has allowed law-enforcement agencies to monitor and intercept Internet communications. It has also allowed government agencies free access to encryption keys, a much disputed issue in the United States. While these actions have been widely acclaimed as proactive measures to newly emerging criminal behavior, most countries have enacted reactionary laws. Cybercrime laws in the Philippines, for example, were only created after the creator of the Love Bug Virus walked free as a direct result of a deficit in technology-specific legislation.

Perhaps the first comprehensive international effort to combat criminal behavior created via computer began between 1983 and 1985 when an ad hoc committee discussed the *international harmonization of criminal laws in order to fight computer-related economic crime (www.ifs.univie.ac.at/~pr2gq1/rev4344. html)*. This committee, sponsored by OECD, also made suggestions as to a listing of offenses to which all member countries should agree. These suggestions included the criminalization of:

1. Any manipulation of data which is intended to commit illegal transfer of funds or other valuables.
2. Any manipulation of data intended to commit forgery.
3. Any manipulation intended to interfere with the functioning of a computer or other telecommunications system.
4. Any incident of software theft or software piracy.
5. Any unauthorized access or interception of another's computer with malicious intent.

In addition, the Select Committee of Experts on Computer-Related Crime of the Council of Europe, established after the OECD, included two lists. The first, proposing a number of items whose criminalization were optional, was overshadowed only by the second, which mandated the criminalization of other behavior. The first list, including optional revisions, included the criminalization of:

1. **The alteration of computer data or computer programs**—the alteration of computer data or computer programs without rights.
2. **The practice of computer espionage**—the acquisition by improper means or the disclosure, transfer or use of a trade or commercial secret without right or any other legal justification, with intent either to cause economic loss to the person entitled to the secret or to obtain an unlawful economic advantage for oneself or a third person.
3. **The unauthorized use of a computer**—the use of a computer system or network without right, that either: (i) is made with the acceptance of significant risk of loss being caused to the person entitled to use the system or harm to the system or its functioning, or (ii) is made with the intent to cause loss to the person entitled to use the system or harm to the system or its functioning, or (iii) causes loss to the person entitled to use the system or harm to the system or its functioning.
4. **The unauthorized use of a protected computer program**—the use without the right of a computer program which is protected by law and

which has been reproduced without right, with the intent, either to pro-
cure an unlawful economic gain for himself or for another person or to
cause harm to the holder of the right (United Nations, 2000: 23).

The second list, including mandatory offenses which should be criminalized by
all participating countries. Their categories, more broad in nature, included:

1. **Computer fraud**—the input, alteration, erasure or suppression of computer
   data or computer programs, or other interference with the course of data
   processing that influences the result of data processing, thereby causing economic or possessory loss of property of another person with the intent of
   procuring an unlawful economic gain for himself or for another person.
2. **Computer forgery**—the input, alteration, erasure or suppression of computer data or computer programs, or other interference with the course of
   data processing in a manner or under such conditions, as prescribed by national law, that it would constitute the offense of forgery if it had been committed with respect to a traditional object of such an offense.
3. **Damage to computer data or computer programs**—the erasure, damaging, deterioration or suppression of computer data or computer programs
   without right.
4. **Computer sabotage**—the input, alteration, erasure, or suppression of
   computer data or computer programs, or other interference with computer
   systems, with the intent to hinder the functioning of a computer or a
   telecommunications system.
5. **Unauthorized access**—the access without right to a computer system or
   network by infringing security measures.
6. **Unauthorized interception**—the interception, made without right and by
   technical means, or communications to, from and within a computer system or network.
7. **Unauthorized reproduction of a protected computer program**—the
   reproduction, distribution or communication to the public without right of
   a computer program which is protected by law.
8. **Unauthorized reproduction of a topography**—the reproduction without right of topography protected by law, of a semiconductor product, or
   the commercial exploitation or the importation for that purpose, done
   without right, of a topography or of a semiconductor product manufactured by using the topography (United Nations, 2000: 22).

Unfortunately, member countries have been slow to react to such international
mandates, citing jurisdictional sovereignty and American imperialism. Other efforts, highly supported by the United States, have been widely criticized. On 21
January 1997, Janet Reno urged the P8 Senior Experts' Group on Transnational
Crime to develop international laws and a *global legal support regime* (Reno,
1997). She encouraged countries to develop a global understanding with international cooperation firmly entrenched. These efforts would include the preservation of evidence which resided on foreign soil. However, this effort has been un-

duly criticized by smaller countries who are concerned about American imperialism.

Traditionally, several problems and troublesome questions have erupted concerning international procedures for the preservation of digital evidence. One of the most ambiguous areas involves the search and seizure of computer networks, as it is questionable whether, and to what extent, the right to search and seize a specific computer installation includes the right to search databases that are accessible by this installation but that are situated in other premises. The importance of such questions has reached astronomical proportions as more and more individuals and corporations are implementing offsite storage databases to protect proprietary information. Thus, pivotal questions include the international sovereignty over the stored data, and the accessibility of the information by investigating agencies. Thus, it is questionable whether and to what extent the right to search and seize a specific computer installation includes the right to search databases that are accessible by this installation but that are situated in other premises.

International entities have also been at odds regarding the level of privacy afforded certain types of data. Constitutional provisions in the United States, for example, apply elevated levels of security to those transmissions that include publishable material. The range of such protections may be characterized as a continuum, with totalitarian governments affording no protection to electronic communications, democratic societies providing security in compliance with strict due process, and libertarian societies which afford blanket protections to personal communications. However, virtually (no pun intended) all countries have recently passed guidelines on electronic monitoring of computer communications. Recent legislation in the United States regarding the use of electronic surveillance devices (i.e., ECPA) has extended protections originally reserved for aural communications to digital transmissions. (It must be noted that the FBI claims that traditional methods of electronic surveillance have been responsible for securing convictions of more than 25,000 individuals in 13 years (*www.fbi.gov/programs/carnivore/carnivore2.htm*). Similar efforts have also been undertaken in Denmark and Germany (United Nations, 2000).

CONCLUSIONS

Although recognition of the insidious nature of computer crime is increasing, much work remains to be completed on all levels of government. Legislation and the codification of computer criminality must keep abreast of emerging technology. Until such a time, investigators should look to traditional statutes to prosecute individuals committing traditional crimes via electronic means. In the United States, local agencies may find provisions under Title 18 particularly useful. Both local and Federal agencies should also implement traditional investigative methods until the constitutionality of emerging technologies are tested. Pen registers (used to identify outgoing numbers from a phone) and trap and trace devices (used to identify originating numbers of wire or electronic communications) combined with a solid investigation may be used successfully to identify harassing behavior without actually compromising the sanctity of the content of the communication.

Even in areas where state, local, and Federal government agencies have enacted regulations to specifically address online criminal behavior, some activity is sure to be overlooked. Thus, law enforcement officials must continue to evaluate the applicability of traditional legislation. The Federal Wire Fraud Act, for example, enables prosecutors to pursue individuals transferring funds, accessing bank computers, and the like. While most computer-specific legislation has tended to be enacted on the Federal level, state and local agencies may be able to implement generic statutes of enforcement. For example, although many states have not formally encoded electronic vandalism statutes, innovative departments may still pursue individuals responsible for computer worms or viruses through criminal mischief and destruction of property codes. In fact, local and state law enforcement officials should carefully evaluate local regulations and identify applicable statutes.

Effective international consortia must be established and global treatises implemented so that jurisdictional disputes do not compromise the interest of justice. Sovereignty and levels of privacy must be identified, and understandings of socio-legal interests achieved. Such efforts should not create an environment that impedes economic growth or stifles individual expression. In fact, the government must be ever-vigilant to the interests of society while taking measures to encourage economic growth consistent with an increasingly global marketplace.

TERMS DISCUSSED

carnivore	federal interest	infragard
Child PornographyPro-	computer	innocent images
tection Act	hacking statute	National Infrastructure
Computer Fraud	HTCIA	Protection Center
and Abuse Act	IACIS	packet sniffing

DISCUSSION QUESTIONS

1. What actions has the Federal government taken to legislate online behavior? How have these mandates evolved over time?
2. How may traditional statutes be applied to the contemporary phenomenon of computer crime?
3. What are some suggestions that you would make to local agencies?

APPLYING THE FIRST AMENDMENT TO COMPUTER-RELATED CRIME

6

INTRODUCTION AND GENERAL PRINCIPLES

As stated previously, the most common judicial challenges facing computer crime investigators include inconsistent interpretations and applications of the First, Fourth, and Fourteenth Amendments to emerging advancements in technology. Constitutional challenges have been issued, for example, in cases where traditional, non-technology-specific statutes have been utilized to combat the lethargy of legislative entities within a particular jurisdiction. Subsequent appellate decisions, based largely on non-technology-specific case law, have also come under attack with some displaying favoritism for law enforcement, others for civil rights, and still others, drifting aimlessly with no apparent consistency in rationale or legality (e.g., Ninth Circuit). Unfortunately, such legal capriciousness has not been alleviated even in those jurisdictions which have attempted to incorporate technological innovations into traditional criminal statutes, due to the lack of responsiveness of the Supreme Court. Thus, the very legislation which has been enacted to assist and guide law enforcement in the murky world of technology where all traditional boundaries of legality, reality, geography, and criminality are blurred have been all but negated by appellate courts unequipped for the sheer novelty of their language and the resulting ambiguities surrounding technological advancements. The resolute silence of the Supreme Court has exacerbated the problem, leaving the country rudderless with lower courts floundering—contradicting one another and creating a patchwork of constitutionality unintended by the framers.

Perhaps the most controversial legal issues involving the utilization of computer communication and technological innovations concern the First Amendment. Originally considered to be outside the scope or daily routines of patrol officers who were primarily concerned with issues arising from the Fourth and Fourteenth Amendments, First Amendment challenges have kept pace with technological advancements—providing no easy answers while presenting a myriad of legal conundrums. Such challenges include the inviolability of electronically published materials, the sanctity of electronic communications, the intersection of obscenity and community standards, and the necessary level of particularity and specificity in emerging legislative acts. While lower courts have tended towards consistency on the first two issues by reaffirming traditional case law, they have not even reached a semblance of consensus on the latter two.

OBSCENITY IN GENERAL

Defining obscenity has long been a concern among civilized societies. In the most generic sense, it is something not easily defined, but recognizable on sight, irrespective of medium. Traditionally, the Supreme Court has been the standard bearer for the line of demarcation between something simply perverse and that which is obscene—often making direct statements about specific materials, and sometimes, generalized proclamations about indecency. Although rare, such broad proclamations encompass a myriad of situations, and provide legal justification and academic rationale for their existence. For example, broad laws which prohibited depictions of minors in explicit or sexual situations were upheld due to the sheer indecency of such portrayals, *and* the increased potential for future victimization to generalized children due to their existence. However, the advent of electronic communications and sophisticated graphical programs has muddied the waters—making it possible for child pornographers to argue that computer-generated images (or *virtual* children) lack the requisite specified victim. Although few would agree that this argument has merit and most would willingly apply blanket prohibitions to any image, real or created, which exploited children, many challenges to recently emerging prohibitions have found a receptive audience among the judiciary. Thus, concrete notions of decency and pornography have not withheld the intangibility and virtuality of computer technology, and the Supreme Court remains resolutely mute.

TRADITIONAL NOTIONS OF DECENCY

Prior to the 1950s, traditional notions of decency and obscenity were governed by an obscenity statute originally developed in 1868 in **Regina v. Hicklin** (Doherty, 1999). This statute developed a level of obscenity which evaluated the alleged immorality of Catholic priests. To wit, it evaluated *whether the tendency of the matter charged . . . is to deprave and corrupt those whose minds are open to such immoral influences and into whose hands a publication of this sort may fall* (*United States* v. *Kennerley,* 209 F. 119, 120 (S.D.N.Y. 1913) as cited by Doherty, 1999). The vagueness and obscurity of this antiquated language remained largely in effect until 1957 when **Roth v. United States,** (354 U.S. 476) determined that obscene material was not constitutionally protected by the First Amendment. In its purest sense, *Roth* coupled the reasonable man with the community standard doctrine. Unfortunately, when abstractly applied, it appeared to cement a concept of national morality—creating a doctrine as unworkable as its predecessor.

The Supreme Court revisited the issue in 1973, establishing a three-pronged analysis of questionable materials and clarifying the sanctity of jurisdictional morality. While recognizing the difficult balance between the State's interest in protecting the *sensibilities of unwilling recipients* from exposure to pornographic materials and the *dangers of censorship inherent in unabashedly content-based laws,* the Court held that a work is obscene and not covered under the protections of the First Amendment, if: 1) an average person who is capable of applying contemporary community standards 2) determines that a work *depicts or describes, in a patently offensive way, sexual conduct specifically defined by the applicable state law:* 3) *taken as a whole, lacks serious literary, artistic, political, or scientific value* (***Miller* v. *California,*** 413 U.S. 15). Thus, the Court recognized the jurisdictional variability in standards of morality, and banished the notion of universal decency. However, the Court also reiterated premises originally specified in *Ginsberg* v. *New York* (390 U.S. 629), which recognized distinctions between certain categories of individuals. While stressing the need for individual consideration and cautioning against generalized or overbroad statutes, the Court ruled that minors and adults must be treated differently when definitions of constitutionally protected materials are at issue (i.e., minors' rights do not reach the standard of adults in questions of obscenity). Most importantly, the Court ruled that the state has a *compelling interest* in protecting the welfare of children, ruling that material which would not be considered for adults may still be considered as such by minors. Such interest is so compelling, in fact, that its consideration has affected all subsequent obscenity rulings by the Court, irrespective of medium.

Since *Miller,* the Supreme Court has been forced to consider technological advancements in media of communication, and their applicability to First Amendment protection, as well as to distinguish between *obscenity, indecency,* and *profanity.* Beginning with ***FCC* v. *Pacifica Foundation,*** 438 U.S. 726 (1978), the Court has ruled that new media of communication must be scrutinized as they are developed and that varying media result in varying protections. In *Pacifica,* for example, the Court basically diluted traditional First Amendment protections enjoyed by print media, and established new boundaries for free speech via television and radio broadcasts. In addition, it distinguished between obscene speech and indecent speech, ruling that "indecent" speech, even if it does not reach the level of obscenity, can not be broadcast during times when children may be presumed to be part of an audience. It further ruled that the broad-based nature of radio communication mandated a greater level of scrutiny because: 1) it was more accessible to children; 2) broadcasting invaded the home of individual citizens, thus creating a constant risk of exposure; and, 3) the scarcity of frequencies allowed government regulation. Thus, George Carlin's broadcast monologue, *Filthy,* which included references to excretory and sexual activities in an offensive manner, violated 18 U.S.C. 1464 and was not entitled to First Amendment protection, because of the content of the communication, the pervasiveness of the selected medium, and the subsequent accessibility to children.

The Court further reiterated these premises in *Sable Communications, Inc.* v. *FCC,* 492 U.S. 115 (1989) and *Turner Broadcasting System, Inc.* v. *FCC,* 518 U.S.

727 (1996), when it held that telephone communications and cable broadcasts, respectively, are afforded different degrees of First Amendment protection, comparable to their disparate accessibility to children. While reaffirming that obscene material is not sheltered by constitutional mandate, the Court held that telephone communications and cable television enjoy heightened levels of protection because they are not as pervasive or accessible as they require affirmative actions and do not reach captive audiences. The Court further afforded dial-up media greater First Amendment protection than their cable broadcast counterparts. However, the Court failed to establish an unequivocal standard of protection afforded to either medium. It simply ruled that protections afforded to cable communications were similar to those enjoyed by traditional print media. Finally, the Court restated the *compelling interest* in protecting children, but argued that a comprehensive ban of *indecent* communications would constitute an unacceptable infringement of free speech. As such, they upheld the constitutionality of the traditional statutes (see box), but cautioned against generalizing them. Unfortunately, these seminal rulings have not assisted contemporary law enforcement, as hoped. In fact, the application of traditional obscenity statutes remains convoluted and inconsistent at best; while emerging legislation has been largely ignored by the Supreme Court.

EMERGING STATUTES AND THE AVAILABILITY OF OBSCENE MATERIAL TO CHILDREN

As discussed, traditional statutes of obscenity, profanity, and indecency have been widely challenged by civil libertarians with varying results. Generally speaking, the Court, and government entities, have recognized varying degrees of jurisdictional tolerance for questionable materials, and considered disparate standards of community morality. However, all actors have unilaterally dismissed readily available obscene material *and* child pornography from active consideration of First Amendment challenges, recognizing both a compelling government interest in protecting children from harm (*Ginsberg* v. *New York*, 390 U.S. 629, 639 (1968);

TRADITIONAL STATUTES

18 U.S.C. { 1460—crime to possess obscene material with intent to distribute

18 U.S.C. { 1462—crime to distribute or receive obscene material through a common carrier in interstate or foreign commerce

18 U.S.C. { 1464—crime to broadcast obscene, profane, or indecent language

18 U.S.C. { 1465 and 1466—crime to knowingly transport or engage in the business of selling obscene, lewd or filthy material through interstate commerce. (This statute was first successfully applied to the Internet in *U.S.* v. *Thomas*, (74 F.3d. 701 (1996)—which held that using a computer to transmit pornographic material violated this statute.

FCC v. *Pacifica Found,* 438 U.S. 726, 749-50; *Santosky* v. *Kramer,* 455 U.S. 745, 766, (1982) and a subsequent interest in prosecuting those individuals who promote the sexual exploitation of children (***New York* v. *Ferber,*** 458 U.S. at 761; and ***Osborne* v. *Ohio,*** 495 U.S. 13, 109-11 (1990). As such, Federal and state bodies have acted consistently to supplant traditional standards and formally encode those interests in legislation which would withstand the onslaught of emerging technologies.

The first act specifically aimed at protecting families and children from online sexually explicit materials was incorporated into the **Telecommunications Reform Act of 1996.** Introduced by Senator James Exon (D-Neb), it was *designed to regulate the previously untamed frontier of cyberspace.* Criminalizing the harassment, stalking, annoyance, or abuse of any individual in an electronic medium, the act further criminalized any obscene communication to a minor recipient or the transmission of any communication that depicted or described sexual or excretory activities or organs that were *prima facially* offensive. Touted by law enforcement officials as a valuable weapon in the protection of children, the act was quickly dealt a mortal blow in jurisprudential circles. Challenged by a diverse grouping of nonprofit organizations, educational societies, and business communities, the act was immediately struck down by the U.S. District Court for the Eastern District of Pennsylvania. Applying a strict scrutiny analysis, the court invalidated the law on two grounds: overbreadth and vagueness. Essentially, the court ruled that the breadth of the law would unconstitutionally abridge adult expression of free speech, *and* that the law failed to establish a line of demarcation separating valuable materials and those criminal in nature. This decision was affirmed by the Supreme Court which invalidated sections 47 U.S. C. 223(a) and 223(d) and held that *the interest in encouraging freedom of expression in a democratic society outweighs any theoretical but unproven benefit of censorship* (at 2346-2347). The Supreme Court further likened the Internet to a marketplace of ideas, and suggested that it was entitled to the highest level of First Amendment protections so that the free flow of ideas and the exchange of information would continue undeterred. Arguing that an absolute right to free speech is a noble idea worth pursuing, but one which is not necessarily possible, the Court compared Internet communications to traditional notions of telephonic communications, in which individuals must take affirmative actions to access obscene material via the Net. Emphasizing that their research revealed a minimal risk to children of exposure to obscene material by simply *surfing the Net,* the Court upheld the District Court's ruling, applying the highest standard of First Amendment protection to the Internet. In essence, they ruled that although the government's interest was legitimate, the means taken (i.e., the Communicat Decency Act) threatened to *torch a large segment of the Internet community* (*Reno* v. *ACLU,* 117 S.Ct. at 2336) and that the characteristics of scarcity and invasiveness which are predicates of standards applied to broadcast media are lacking in Internet communications. The Court based their ruling on the reasoning that the Internet did not: invade an individual's home, have a history of extensive government regulation, and has no scarcity of available frequencies. Thus, the limitations on broadcast media do not apply to the Internet even though commercial speech is not as protected, and communications media like radio and television enjoy far less protection than their print media counterparts. In addition, it ruled that the compelling government interest in protecting children was outweighed by the broadness and vagueness of the CDA as it suppressed an overbroad area of protected speech when a less restrictive area or provision could have been enacted. Finally, the Court ruled that the statute should have incorporated or addressed all three prongs of *Miller*, instead of just one.

DEFINING CHILD PORNOGRAPHY

Like issues relating to the accessibility of obscenity to children on the Internet, depictions of **child pornography** or the exploitation of children have been hotly debated by civil libertarians and law enforcement officials. Unlike debates regarding accessibility or pervasiveness of obscenity, however, traditional classifications of child pornography have remained virtually absolute in most cases. Forsaking Court categorizations of **obscenity, indecency,** or *profanity*, the majority of legislative and judicial entities have upheld even the vaguest or most obscure of all child pornography definitions, citing the potential harm to children. However, a minority of courts have tended to be more liberal in their application of the First Amendment, and even the most nobly designed statutes have been successfully challenged.

Beginning with the **Protection of Children Against Sexual Exploitation Act of 1977** (Pub. L. No. 95-225, 92 Stat. 7 (1977) (codified as amended at 18 U.S.C.SS 2251–2253), communities have attempted to prohibit visual depictions of child pornography, while lower courts have grappled with the constitutionality of such legislation. As a result, the intersection of legislative intent and jurisprudential interpretation has resulted in continuous renovations of extant laws, whereby prohibitive statutes have been revamped in keeping with the current judicial climate. The *Protection of Children Against Sexual Exploitation Act of 1977*, for example, was directly guided by the principles originally established in *Miller*. Applying the three-pronged obscenity test, the act expressly prohibited those explicit depictions of children which did not have redeeming social value. In keeping with *Miller*, it also did not require scienter on the part of the violator as to the age of the individuals depicted. This omission proved to be the act's Achilles heel, as the Ninth Circuit ruled, and the Supreme Court upheld, that *the First Amendment mandates that a statute prohibiting the distribution, shipping or receipt of child pornography require knowledge of the minority of the performers as an elements of the crime it defines* (*U.S.* v. *Thomas*—893 F.2d 1066 (Ninth Circuit), cert denied, 498 U.S. 826, 111 S.Ct 80 (1990); *U.S.* v. *X-Citement Video, Inc.* (982 F.2d 1285, Ninth Circuit 1992). Thus, the act, in and of itself, was invalidated. As a result of these deficiencies and the Supreme Court's ruling in *Ferber*, Congress enacted the **Child Protection Act of 1984** (Pub. L. No. 98-292, 98 Stat. 204 (1984)—codified as amended at 18 U.S.C. (2251–2253). This act eliminated the obscenity requirement established in *Miller*.

LIVERPOOL
JOHN MOORES UNIVERSITY
AVRIL ROBARTS LRC
TEL. 0151 231 4022

However, the Court did recognize a specific state interest in enacting legislation prohibiting child pornography.

APPLYING CASE LAW TO CHILD PORNOGRAPHY STATUTES

As stated, child pornography definitions have been the result of the intersection of jurisdictional mandates and constitutional interpretations. While the Court has been loathe to issue blanket prohibitions involving child pornography at the Federal level, it has upheld such prohibitions at the state level. Thus, law-enforcement officials may find more success in combating child pornography with state resources. Without question, the single most important decision regarding state prohibitions of child pornography may be found in *New York* v. *Ferber,* (458 U.S. 747, 102 S.Ct. 3348, 73 L.Ed. 2d 1113 (1982). In *Ferber,* a bookstore proprietor, convicted for selling films depicting young boys masturbating, argued that a New York statute prohibiting the promotion of sexual performances by children under the age of 16 through the distribution of materials depicting such activity was unconstitutionally overbroad. Ferber argued that because the statute also prohibited the distribution of materials, such as medical and/or educational books, which *deal with adolescent sex in a realistic but non-obscene manner* [458 U.S. 747, 753], it failed to establish a level of obscenity consistent with *Miller.* The Supreme Court, however, held that states are granted more leeway in the regulation of pornographic depictions of children than in regulation of obscenity (756) because:

1. the use of children as subjects of pornographic materials is harmful to the physiological, emotional, and mental health of the child;
2. the standard of *Miller* v. *California,* 413 U.S. 15, for determining what is legally obscene is not a satisfactory solution to the child pornography problem;
3. the advertising and selling of child pornography provide an economic motive for and are thus an integral part of the production of such materials, an activity illegal throughout the nation;
4. the value of permitting live performances and photographic reproductions of children engaged in lewd exhibitions is exceedingly modest, if not de minimis;
5. recognizing and classifying child pornography as a category of material outside the First Amendment's protection is not incompatible with this Court's decisions dealing with what speech is unprotected. When a definable class of material, such as that covered by [458 U.S. 747, 748] the New York statute, bears so heavily and pervasively on the welfare of children engaged in its production, the balance of competing interests in clearly struck, and it is permissible to consider these materials as without the First Amendment's protection. Pp. 756–764.

In a clear departure from normal procedure, the Court specifically relied on statistics and opinions gathered from sources ranging from scholars to law-

NOTABLE QUOTES FROM *FERBER*:

The prevention of sexual exploitation and abuse of children constitutes a government objective of surpassing importance.

The legislative judgment, as well as the judgment found in the relevant literature, is that the use of children as subjects of pornographic materials is harmful to the physiological, emotional, and mental health of the child.

The distribution of photographs and films depicting sexual activity by juveniles is intrinsically related to the sexual abuse of children in at least two ways. First, the materials produced are a permanent record of the children's participation and the harm to the child is exacerbated by their circulation. Second, the distribution network for child pornography must be closed if the production of material which requires the sexual exploitation of children is to be effectively controlled . . .

There is no serious contention that the legislature was unjustified in believing that it is difficult, if [458 U.S. 747, 760] not impossible, to halt the exploitation of children by pursuing only those who produce the photographs and movies. While the production of pornographic materials is a low-profile, clandestine industry, the need to market the resulting products requires a visible apparatus of distribution.

The most expeditious if not the only practical method of law enforcement may be to dry up the market for this material by imposing severe criminal penalties on persons selling, advertising, or otherwise promoting the product.

The *Miller* Standard, like all general definitions of what may be banned as obscene, does not reflect the State's particular and more compelling interest in prosecuting those who promote the sexual exploitation of children. Thus, the question under the *Miller* test of whether a work, taken as a whole, appeals to the prurient interest of the average person bears no connection to the issue of whether a child has been physically or psychologically harmed in the production of the work.

It is irrelevant to the child who has been abused whether or not the material . . . has a literary, artistic, political or social value. It is not rare that a content-based classification of speech has been accepted because it may be appropriately generalized that within the confines of the given classification, the evil to be restricted so overwhelmingly outweighs [458 U.S. 747, 764] the expressive interests, if any, at stake, that no process of case-by-case adjudication is required. When a definable class of material, such as that covered *(in this case)* bears so heavily and pervasively on the welfare of children engaged in its production, we think the balance of competing interests is clearly struck and that it is permissible to consider these materials as without the protection of the First Amendment.

enforcement practitioners to child psychologists. Noting that the Federal Government and 47 states had enacted statutes to prohibit the production of child pornography, the Court emphatically stated that child pornography was a national problem. Through the extrapolation of the potential harm to real children resulting from virtual images, the Court squarely placed child pornography outside the umbrella of free speech guaranteed by the Constitution, noting that any literary, artistic, political, scientific value of child porn does not ameliorate potential harm to children. However, the Court also cautioned against overgeneralization of their ruling, unwittingly setting the scene for a new round of challenges.

In an effort to balance the interests of children and the Constitution, the Court suggested alternatives to child involvement in the production and distribution of child pornography. To wit, *if it were necessary for literary or artistic value, a person over the statutory age who perhaps looked younger could be utilized.* ***Simulation outside of the prohibition of the statute could provide another alternative.*** (Unfortunately, this language has become the focal point in current debates involving simulated child pornography.) In addition, the Court argued that any legislation must be evaluated independently, as the First Amendment does require specificity in an elemental application. Thus, it ruled that the behavior proscribed and the level of scienter must be clearly articulated, although it failed to provide thresholds for each. In fact, no formal level of scienter existed until 1990.

In *Osborne* v. *Ohio,* (495 U.S. 103, 115, 110 S.Ct. 1691, 1699 109 L.Ed. 2d 98) the Court finally established a standard of scienter that had been lacking in *Ferber.* More specifically, the Court stated that traditional definitions of *recklessness plainly satisfied the requirement laid down in* Ferber. This important demarcation was once again supported by the potential harm to children generated by the existence of child pornography. The Supreme Court reiterated premises originally articulated in *Ferber,* and declared that Ohio may constitutionally proscribe *the possession and viewing of child pornography* as it was enacted *on the basis of its compelling interests in protecting the physical and psychological well-being of minors and in destroying the market for the exploitative use of children by penalizing those who possess and view the offending materials.* In addition, the Court noted that the Ohio statute *encourages possessors to destroy such materials, which permanently record the victim's abuse and thus may haunt him for years to come . . . and which, available evidence suggests, may be used by pedophiles to seduce other children.* Although the Court did vacate *Osborne's* conviction on a legal technicality, it was a major victory for law enforcement as it failed to strike down the statute in question, noting that the constitutionality of statutes determined to be overbroad is still upheld if a court restricts its application and the court's interpretation is known to practitioners. In addition, it rejected petitioner's interpretation and application of *Stanley* v. *Georgia,* 394 U.S. 557 (1969) which prohibited a state from limiting the *private* possession of obscene material, arguing that later decisions like *Ferber* had spoken to the narrowness of *Stanley* (i.e., that child pornography is not the same as traditional materials deemed to be obscene). To wit, *the difference here is obvious: The State does not rely on a paternalistic in-*

terest in regulating Osborne's mind. Rather, Ohio has enacted 2907.323(A)(3) in order to protect the victims of child pornography; it hopes to destroy a market for the exploitative use of children. Once again recognizing the potential harm, the Court ruled that the legislative judgment, as well as the judgment found in relevant literature, is that the use of children as subjects of pornographic materials is harmful to the physiological, emotional, and mental health of the child. That judgment, we think, easily passes muster under the First Amendment (*Ferber,* 458 U.S. at 756–758). It is also surely reasonable for the State to conclude that it will decrease the production of child pornography if it penalizes those who possess and view the product (495 U.S. 103,110) thereby decreasing demand. In *Ferber,* where we upheld a New York statute outlawing the distribution of child pornography, we found a similar argument persuasive: "the advertising and selling of child pornography provide an economic motive for and are thus an integral part of the production of such materials, an activity illegal throughout the Nation. 'It rarely has been suggested that the constitutional freedom for speech and press extends its immunity to speech or writing used an integral part of conduct in violation of a valid criminal statute.'" Id., at 761–762, quoting *Giboney* v. *Empire Storage & Ice Co.,* 336 U.S. 490, 498 (1949).

Thus, both *Ferber* and *Osborne* recognized the state's compelling interest in protecting children from harm. While even the most commonsensical application of technology-specific legislation would appear to be constitutionally supported in light of these rulings, lower courts have failed to reach consensus on emerging legislation at both the state and federal levels.

● TECHNOLOGY-SPECIFIC LEGISLATION—CONTENTION IN THE COURTS

In an effort to tighten prohibitions of child pornography on the Federal level, Congress replaced the *Protection of Children Against Sexual Exploitation of 1977* with the *Child Protection Act of 1984* (CPA). Dismissing the traditional obscenity standard found in *Ferber,* the Court also dismissed the requirement that the production or distribution of the material be for the purpose of sale, thereby formally recognizing that a large portion of pornographic trafficking was for sexual gratification. This act was also amended to include prohibitions of:

1. the production or use of advertisements for child pornography (*Child Sexual Abuse and Pornography Act of 1986,* Public Law No. 99–628, 100 Stat. 3510 (1986) codified as amended at 18 U.S.C. { 2251);
2. the use of a computer to transport, distribute, or receive child pornography (*Child Protection and Obscenity Enforcement Act of 1988,* Public Law No. 100–690, 102 Stat. 4181 (1988) codified as amended at 18 U.S.C. { 2251A–2252); and,
3. the possession of three or more pieces of child pornography (*Child Protection Restoration and Penalties Enhancement Act of 1990,* Public Law

No. 101-647, { 301, 104 Stat. 4789 (1990) codified as amended at 18 U.S.C. S 2252(a)(4)).

In fact, there have been more than a handful of amendments made to the original Act banning child pornography. However, all of these amendments have concentrated on the utilization of real children in the production and distribution of such materials.

In 1996, Congress, anticipating an explosion of explicit material on emerging media like the Internet, again revisited the problem of child pornography. The *Child Pornography Prevention Act of 1996,* departing from traditional legal reasoning, was enacted to prohibit virtual child pornography, arguing in part, that the very existence of child pornography, real or not, increases child molestation and pedophilia. To wit, the law specifically forbade *any visual depiction, including any photography, film, video, picture, or computer or computer-generated image or picture, whether made or produced by electronic, mechanical, or other means, of sexually explicit conduct.* This verbiage, considered by many to be vague and ambiguous, has resulted in a myriad of constitutional challenges across the country.

Generally speaking, the *Child Pornography Prevention Act of 1996* (CPPA), expanded the Child Pornography Act to include the production and distribution of computer-generated or other mechanically altered images of minors engaging in explicit conduct. Unlike the original CPA and the preceding amendments, which were drafted after definitive ruling by the Court, the CPPA *preceded* any discussion of simulated child pornography. Rather, relying on the extrapolation of potential harm to children by pedophiles aroused by such images, the act assumed that the lack of an actual victim is irrelevant as actual or real victimization may occur via a communication of no social significance and which fails to further the interest of free thinking. Indeed, it would appear to many that the risk of child victimization is not diminished by the fact that no actual children were victimized as the viewer is largely unaware of the true nature of the scene depicted. Unfortunately, the lower courts remain sharply divided, and the Supreme Court has remained resolutely mute on the applicability of *Ferber* and *Osborne* to emerging legislation.

At issue among the lower courts is the generalized language of the CPPA which prohibits material that **appears to be** or **conveys the impression of** child pornography. While the First, Fourth, and Eleventh Circuits have upheld the constitutionality of the act, denying it was overbroad or vague (*United States* v. *Hilton,* 167 F.3d 61 (First Circuit, 1999); and (*United States* v. *Mento,* (#99-4813) (Fourth, 2000); (*United States* v. *Acheson,* 195 F.3d 645 (Eleventh Circuit, 1999), the Ninth Circuit (California) has ruled conversely (**The Free Speech Coalition v. Reno** (9th Circuit, 1999)—(198 F.3d 1083, Ninth Circuit 1999) #97-16536). In *United States* v. *Mento,* (#99-4813) (Fourth, 2000), the Petitioner argued that the act was unconstitutional as it unfairly abridged the First Amendment as it is aimed at inhibiting the expression of child pornography itself as opposed to the secondary effect of such expression. While the Fourth Circuit agreed that the act's ban of child pornography *unquestionably constitutes a content-based regulation* which is not rendered content-neutral by its intent to control the secondary effects of the material in question, it ruled that those same regulations withstand strict scrutiny because they are narrowly tailored to serve a compelling government interest. To wit, *Mento* interprets Ferber *too narrowly*. Ferber *necessarily dealt only with depictions of actual children long before virtual pornography became an issue . . . [it] in no way stands for the proposition that permissible governmental interests in the realm of child pornography would be forever restricted to the harm suffered by identifiable children participating in its production.* In addition, the court ruled that the Court's earlier decisions in *Ferber* and *Osborne* clearly stated a compelling government interest in protecting *all* children from potential exploitation resulting from child pornography—***not*** just those involved in the actual production. Finally, the court ruled that there is no difference between the harm posed by actual vs. virtual child pornography, arguing that child molesters viewing images of child pornography receive sexual gratification if those images *appear to be* minors. Thus, no compelling government interest would be served with the removal of the words *appears to be* as without them, proof of age of those individuals presented would be required to overcome reasonable doubt. Unfortunately, the Ninth Circuit is not in agreement with this interpretation, and the constitutionality of the CPPA is still undecided.

In 1997, the Ninth Circuit, in keeping with their traditional zealousness in matters relating to the First Amendment, struck down the bulk of the Child Pornography Prevention Act (*Free Speech Coalition* v. *Reno*, #97-16536– *www.findlaw.com*). More specifically, the court held that the CPPA was unconstitutional *to the extent that it proscribe[d] computer images that [did not] involve the use of real children in their production or dissemination* [4]. Thus, sections 2556(8)(B) and 2556(8)(D) were deemed unconstitutional by the court, who reasoned that content-based restrictions on free speech are presumptively unconstitutional in the absence of a *compelling interest* by the government in prohibiting images of non-real children. The court denied the adequacy of the extant literature in establishing the potential harm posed by this sort of material. In addition, the court declared the language of the act vague, arguing that it did *not give the person of ordinary intelligence a reasonable opportunity to know what [was] prohibited, and fail[ed] to provide explicit standards for those who must apply it, with the attendant dangers of arbitrary and discriminatory application* [12]. Finally, the court rejected the notion of generalized victims in keeping with earlier decisions (*U.S.* v. *Boos*, #96-50404, *www.findlaw.com*).

In *Boos*, the court reasoned that individual victims were more salient than societal interests. Interestingly, Boos, a child pornographer who exchanged pornographic images and erotic fantasies of children via the Internet, argued that his sentencing was inaccurate as his crimes represented the victimization of society, not of the individuals depicted Ruling that Congress intended to protect *real* children from *actual,* not expected, exploitation, the court denied his claim, and affirmed the upward sentencing departure based on the number of images found. Thus, the Ninth Circuit has clearly established a standard of evaluation which protects large portions of child pornography activities, in direct contradiction to other circuits across the country. Fortunately, or not, the Supreme Court has decided to rule upon the constitutionality of the CPPA. They are scheduled to hear *Free Speech Coalition* v. *Reno* this session.

CONCLUSIONS

Technology-specific legislation, enacted to combat the growing problem of computer-related criminal behavior, has been greeted with a myriad of legal challenges. Although many legal issues have emerged, a large majority of such cases involve the First, Fourth, and Fourteenth Amendments, and virtually all of the challenges to child pornography legislation have questioned the parameters of the First Amendment. In the most basic sense, the First Amendment protects an individual's right to free expression from interference from government entities. More succinctly, any content-based restriction of the free flow on information is expressly prohibited, and when regulation of speech is necessary, it must be accomplished in the least restrictive manner possible. While few would argue that the guarantees found within the Amendment warrant substantial lessening, many may support some sort of blanket prohibition of materials which might be threatening to children.

The Supreme Court has repeatedly recognized a compelling government interest in the protection of children (e.g., *New York* v. *Ferber, Osborne* v. *Ohio, FCC* v. *Pacifica, Globe Newspaper Co.* v. *Superior Court,* 457 U.S. 596, 607) stating that *"a democratic society rests, for its continuance, upon the healthy, well-rounded growth of young people into full maturity as citizens"* (*Prince* v. *Massachusetts,* 321 U.S. 158, 168 (1944). In addition, it has recognized the insidious nature of child pornography, and held that such material is outside the scope of protections provided by the First Amendment. However, the introduction of emerging legislation which attempts to address technologically generated or altered images has come under fire by civil libertarians, and the Supreme Court has not yet ruled on the constitutionality of such prohibitions. As a result, jurisdictional application of Federal legislation is contradictory.

TERMS DISCUSSED

child pornography
Child Pornography
  Prevention Act
Child Protection Act
FCC v. *Pacifica Foundation*
indecency

Miller v. *California*
New York v. *Ferber*
obscenity
Osborne v. *Ohio*
Protection of Children
  Against Sexual Ex-
  plottion Act of 1977

Roth v. *United States*
telecommunications
  Reform Act of 1996
The Free Speech Coalition v. *Reno*

DISCUSSION QUESTIONS

1. Provide a historical analysis of the legal concepts of *indecency* and *obscenity* within the United States. You should pay particular attention to the decisions rendered in *Ferber*

and *Osborne*. What is the current climate of the Court, and what are your predictions for the future of indecency and obscenity in cyberspace?

2. Fully discuss the jurisprudential inconsistency in the application of child pornography laws across the country. What are the advantages and the disadvantages to a conservative application of the law? To a liberal application? Which is most consistent with your own view?

3. What appears to be the primary issue debated in the application of the Child Pornography Prevention Act of 1996? What is the latest ruling by the Supreme Court regarding this matter?

THE FOURTH AMENDMENT

1

INTRODUCTION

Possibly excepting the First Amendment, the Fourth Amendment has been considered to include the most important constitutional protection against governmental intrusion into personal matters (Winick, 1994). Generally speaking, the Fourth Amendment provides protection against unreasonable searches and seizures conducted by government officials. As such, searches must be predicated on **probable cause**—a legal term used to denote that a reasonable person would conclude that: 1) a crime has been committed, 2) evidence of that crime exists, and 3) evidence presently exists at the place to be searched. Only in extreme situations is this determination made by individuals other than magistrates.

The Fourth Amendment protects people, not places. It protects both tangible and intangible items, extending even to oral communications. Thus, physical intrusion is not necessary to establish a constitutional violation. (*Warden* v. *Hayden*, 387 U.S. 294, 304; *Katz* v. *United States*). Thus, a judicial order must be obtained to conduct limited electronic surveillance. The Fourth Amendment only applies to government searches and seizures. It does not apply to searches and seizures conducted by private parties unless they are acting with the knowledge of and under the supervision or direction of law enforcement.

HISTORY OF THE FOURTH AMENDMENT

Fearful of the tyranny inherent in England's system, the forefathers of the United States saw fit to introduce checks and balances in the American judicial system. The division of Federal powers into three distinct branches: executive, judicial, and legislative. The Constitution itself, specifically providing for the sovereignty of individual states, proved to be the most resilient. In fact, the first ten amendments to the document (the Bill of Rights) added the specificity that the original Constitution failed to articulate. Such amendments were necessary to solidify the sanctity and security of the American home and the privacy of its citizens, one of the greatest concerns, due to the abuses of power practiced by government officials in England where it was common practice to invade and search a home without any semblance of due process.

One of the greatest debates surrounding the Constitution involves the role of the Fourth Amendment. On the one hand, conservative approaches, fearing that those government officials least responsible to the electorate would become too powerful, hesitate to view the Constitution as a living document. The notion that judges who are granted lifetime tenure will create policies or make decisions based upon individual notions of constitutional scope make these individuals uncomfortable. Those on the opposing side make the argument that the Constitution is designed to serve as a guide for limiting government powers, not a limitation (Tuerkheimer, 1993).

An evaluation of the past century reveals that the second notion has taken root in the rulings of the Supreme Court. While many of these decisions have undermined the ability of the government to control the decisions of individual citizens (*Griswold* v. *Connecticut* struck down a prohibition on contraceptives; *Roe* v. *Wade* struck down a prohibition of abortions), others have seemed to increase the ability of government to intrude upon the personal privacy afforded to those same individuals. More specifically, the same Justices who upheld reproductive rights have expanded the rights of government officials to electronically monitor American citizens. Beginning with *Olmstead* v. *U.S.,* (U.S. 277 [1928]), the Supreme Court has evaluated the level of protection afforded to individuals in electronic communications.

The *Olmstead* decision ruled that the sanctity afforded to a private home did not include telephone communications made within that home. Their implication was clear—the Fourth Amendment protected places, not people. Almost four decades later, a different Court would reverse the decision in its entirety. (*Katz* v. *United States* (U.S. 389 [1967]). Indeed, the *Katz* ruling appeared to grant American citizens more protection under the Fourth Amendment than ever before. *Katz* ruled that "the Fourth Amendment protects people, not places . . . what [a person] seeks to preserve as private, even in an area accessible to the public, may be constitutionally protected." Thus, those communications which are held on public telephones may be granted protection if individuals have a reasonable expectation of privacy or take measures to make their communication private. The Court further ordered that future wiretaps be granted only after adequate judicial review is undertaken and approval granted. Consequently, all Federal and state domestic wiretaps require a court order predicated on an articulation of probable cause. Since these seminal rulings, advances in technology have far outpaced legislative proceedings and judicial rulings. In fact, the sluggish nature of the judicial system is all but antithetical to the activity surrounding computer, wireless, and communication technology. Thus, the rule of law must be found in emerging case law and in the general principles of the exclusionary rule.

First enunciated in *Weeks* v. *U.S.,* (232 U.S. 383, [1914]), the **exclusionary rule** stated that if government agents engage in unlawful searches or seizures, than all fruits of that action could not be used in subsequent prosecutions. Such "fruits of the poisonous tree" not only included evidence collected in tainted searches, but *any* information or evidence obtained in later activities if such were predicated on the original search. In essence, this rule was necessary because the self-restraint of the police did not provide adequate protection against violations of the Fourth Amendment. It was intended to prevent governmental abuse of search and seizure powers. As such, the courts have traditionally excluded any evidence seized in violation of the Fourth Amendment. However, more recent case law has limited the exclusionary rule to those actions that deter *future* constitutional violations, not to punish past actions (*U.S.* v. *Leon,* 468 U.S. 897 ([1984]). Unfortunately, the Supreme Court has remained resolutely silent on issues of digital evidence and the amount of privacy afforded to wireless communications. Therefore, the exclusionary rule has been used sparingly in computer crime cases, and the most pressing consideration is the legislative and judicial articulation of the limitations of the **expectation of privacy** in cyberspace.

THE EXPECTATION OF PRIVACY AND ELECTRONIC SURVEILLANCE

Although not specifically verbalized in the text of the U.S. Constitution, legislative bodies have attempted to extend an "expectation of privacy" to American citizens in specific situations (see text box). Virtually all of these statutes, however, have been challenged, and the Supreme Court has been left to establish objective measures of privacy. Generally speaking, they have ruled that the Fourth Amendment, prohibiting unreasonable searches and **seizures,** cannot be translated into a general constitutional right to privacy. In fact, they have noted that other provisions of the Constitution protect personal privacy from other forms of governmental invasion, such as the First Amendment's imposing limitations upon governmental abridgment of freedom to associate and privacy in one's association, the Third Amendment's prohibiting the nonconsensual peacetime quartering of soldiers, and to some extent, the Fifth Amendment's reflecting the Constitution's concern for the right of each individual to a private enclave where he may lead a private life, whereas the protection of a person's general right to privacy is, like the protection of his property and of his very life, left largely to the law of the individual states. This "right" to privacy is moderated only by the expectation of such privacy, which is not a generalized notion but based on case characteristics.

Certain characteristics may erode expectations of privacy. For example, those things knowingly divulged to third parties are not subject to Fourth amendment protection, (*Lewis* v. *United States,* 385 U.S. 206, 210; *United States* v. *Lee,* 274 U.S. 559, 563.), but those things he/she seeks to keep private, even in an area accessible to the public, may be (*Rios* v. *United States,* 364 U.S. 253; *Ex parte Jackson,* 96 U.S. 727, 733). Unfortunately, the issue of what constitutes disclosure is all but unclear. For example, a bank depositor has no claim under the Fourth Amendment because "the depositor takes the risk in revealing his affairs to another, that the information will be conveyed by that person to that government" (*United States* v. *Miller,* 425 U.S. 435, 443 [1976]).

Many people are concerned that with the advent of information-driven technology that even the limited expectation of privacy currently recognized will be eroded. They argue that the degree of information that is necessary to live in cyber-worlds will all but negate privacy in the United States if it is not protected in some fashion. Medical records, financial information, and personal details disclosed under a façade of anonymity or confidentiality via emerging communication mediums, for example, may be surveyed by government officials. Thus, char-

LEGISLATING PRIVACY

Federal Wiretap Act, 18 U.S.C. { 2511 and the Stored Communications Act—derivatives of the original Wiretap law enacted in 1968. Both were included in the **Electronic Communications Privacy Act of 1986** and sought to establish federal privacy protections and standards in light of advances in computer and telecommunications technologies.

Wiretap Act—protects against unauthorized "interception" of electronic communications 18 U.S.C. { 2511.

Stored Communications Act—protects against unauthorized access to electronic communications while in electronic storage 18 U.S.C. { 2701.

CALEA (Communications Assistance for Law Enforcement Act of 1994) also known as Digital Telephony Act (47 U.S.C. 1002)—1994 Amendments to the Federal Wiretap Act extended protection to cordless and cellular calls. Mandates that new technology does not interfere with and do not impede some LE interception. Prohibited telephone carriers from developing technology which impedes law enforcement investigations (i.e., electronic interception). In addition, Congress required carriers to configure their systems to ensure the privacy and security of communications not authorized to be intercepted.

Title III of the Omnibus Crime Control and Safe Streets Act of 1968—was enacted by Congress in response to the rulings by the Supreme Court. It delineated specific requirements for wiretapping. It stated that wiretaps were only permissible if issued upon a ruling of probable cause by a court official. It also required that all other investigative techniques were exhausted, and that precautions were taken to ensure that "innocent" conversations were excluded from analysis. It further outlined punishments for violations, and required disclosure of such surveillance upon cessation of activity.

Foreign Intelligence Surveillance Act (FISA—1978)—Congressional act which regulated wiretapping in national security cases. Much broader than Title III, it allows more invasive searches with a lower probable-cause threshold. The most important differences include: 1) no requirements to disclose the contents of or even the presence of the surveillance, unless the government seeks to introduce them in a criminal prosecution; 2) affords no protection for individuals who are not permanent residents or citizens of the United States; 3) does not necessarily require *criminal* activity—rather, it allows surveillance for individuals who are believed to be engaged in clandestine intelligence activities on behalf of a foreign power.

Comprehensive Crime Control Act (1984)—Congress extends to the United States Secret Service jurisdictional powers over credit card fraud and computer crime.

acteristics and the constancy of interpretation vary, especially in regard to electronic surveillance.

ELECTRONIC SURVEILLANCE AND THE RIGHT TO PRIVACY

Due to the resolute silence of the Supreme Court, the issue of electronic surveillance and the application of traditional statutes have been somewhat haphazard. Like conventional wiretap standards, the legality of this issue has been tested much more in the private sector, where employers routinely attempt to control the activities of their employees.

Certain companies routinely place employees under electronic surveillance, arguing that it is necessary to improve efficiency and productivity. It has been reported that airline personnel are instructed (and their performance evaluated) to complete reservations within two minutes, while directory assistance operators are expected to maintain a 29-second average call length (Tuerkheimer, 1993). Interestingly, private wiretaps are prohibited, but restraints on private interception of e-mail and network communications have not been extended. Recent court decisions do not indicate that individual privacy protections are likely to emerge. In fact, there has been a tendency by courts to imply that the expectation of privacy is more limited with the introduction of computers and cyberspace. Thus, employers and law enforcement have been granted greater leeway in monitoring electronic communications. Systems administrators, in particular, are increasingly authorized to monitor employee communications. Such authorization has increased the reliance of law enforcement on workplace surveillance.

PRIVATE V. PUBLIC-SECTOR SEARCHES

Traditional expectations of privacy within the work area have varied based on contextual elements of each case. However, public employers are much more limited in their actions than are their private counterparts. Generally speaking, purely personal items which have no connection to the employment relationship are not subject to standards for a workplace search. However, other factors which are considered include:

1. whether the items or areas to be searched have been set aside for the employee's exclusive or personal use;
2. whether the employee has been given permission to store personal information within the area;
3. whether the employee has been advised that the system may be accessed by others;
4. whether there has been a history of searches or inspections of the area; and,
5. whether there is a clearly articulated policy which identifies common areas vs. private areas (Soma, et al., 1996).

Public employers are directly bound by the rulings originally articulated in *Ortega*. This three-pronged approach determines:

1. whether the employee's expectation of privacy was consistent with the operational realities of the workplace (i.e., the exclusivity of the workspace, accessibility to workplace by others, nature of employee's duties, knowledge of search procedures or practices, and reason for search;
2. whether the invasion of the employee's Fourth Amendment protections was reasonable when balanced against governmental interest in the intrusion (reasonable suspicion is sufficient in investigations involving work-related employee misconduct); and,
3. whether the search was reasonable at inception, and was the subsequent scope of the search related to the original justification of the search (Coacher, 1999).

In essence, *Ortega* ruled that while employees may have a reasonable expectation of privacy against workplace intrusions by law-enforcement personnel, when supervisory personnel are responsible for the intrusion "operational realities of the workplace . . . may make some employees' expectations of privacy unreasonable" (*Ortega*). Thus, *Ortega* may be characterized as a scale that weighs the individual employees expectation of privacy against government interest (i.e., supervision, control, and efficient operation of the workplace). Under these general considerations articulated in the **Ortega doctrine,** employers who fail to warn employees of systems monitoring or allow employees access to electronic mail for personal reasons as well, may lose some of their monitoring powers over employees due to an elevated expectation of privacy.

● APPLICATION OF ORTEGA TO E-MAIL: THE CASES OF *SIMONS* AND *MONROE*

Although the legal landscape is far from clear, two cases appear to apply the *Ortega* doctrine to electronic mail. In *U.S.* v. *Simons,* an employee of the Foreign Bureau of Information Services (branch of the CIA) was indicted for violation of child pornography statutes after a systems administrator discovered that over 1,000 pornographic images had been downloaded. During trial, Simons moved to suppress, arguing that he had a reasonable expectation of privacy on his individual workstation. Court disagreed, stating that the systems administrator was simply monitoring usage of network resources by employees and used the word "sex" to identify inappropriate activity. The Court further stated that even if the employee had an expectation of privacy, the system administrator's actions including viewing the employee's work-station computer and copying the hard drive were both justified at their inception and reasonable in scope. Thus, systems administrators may scan networks to identify non-work-related activity.

A further case, *United States* v. *Monroe* (50 M.J. 550 (A.F.C.C.A. 1999) allowed administrators to search non-delivered messages stored on an employee server for system maintenance. This particular case involved a system administrator who opened several messages stored on the server prior to their arrival at the destination mailbox (messages were placed here indefinitely if they were too large or were defective). The system administrator opened several of these messages, because of the amount of storage that these messages required and the danger that they posed to the stability of the system. Upon discovering that they were addressed to the accused and were from newsgroups with sexually explicit names, the administrators accessed the accused's e-mail account, searching through messages sent from the user to the originator of the 59 e-mail messages. Deciding that these messages were not sent to the user inadvertently, and, in fact, represented a consensual exchange, administrators then released the information to the commander, and copied the image files and printouts of two e-mail messages from the accused to the newsgroup. They also copied to disk a memo from themselves for the record detailing their discovery of the files. This information was used by the Air Force Office of Special Investigations (AFOSI) to obtain search authorization for searching and seizing all computer-related items. Defendant argued that he had an expectation of privacy and that while he consented to monitoring, he did not **consent** to being investigated. Court disagreed, stating that he had no reasonable expectation of privacy in files lodged in the government server. They further noted that there was no reasonable expectation of privacy in the e-mail box in regards to supervisory oversight, as the system was properly bannered with a warning indicating that use of the system conferred consent to monitoring. Thus, employers may protect themselves through warning banners, negating future contentions of privacy.

Both *Simons* and *Monroe* indicated the court's reluctance to extend rights of privacy to proprietary government equipment. In each case, it was determined that systems administrators may monitor employee communications and actually search computers attached to networks, as there is no expectation of privacy. Indeed, both courts likened these types of maintenance searches to private searches and, therefore, permissible. Summarily, government employees using government computers have no expectation of privacy from systems administrators acting within the scope of their duties. (These duties may include maintaining security through routine systems protection monitoring, system management, prevention of unauthorized access, verification of security procedures, survivability and operational security. To maintain security, these individuals routinely engage in systems protection monitoring.) This is not to suggest, however, that other forms of privacy are not constitutionally protected, but must be tested by the degree to which they exceed the scope of the private search.

While systems-protection monitoring may constitute a legitimate workplace search, monitoring electronic mail by law enforcement must be based on consent of one or more parties to the communication *or* authorized by court order, warrant, or special probable cause circumstances (Coacher, 1999). Thus, law enforcement has traditionally relied on system administrators to report unlawful intrusion and other sorts of criminal activity. However, system administrators may not gather the amount of information necessary for a criminal prosecution, as they are not necessarily concerned with the content of the suspect communication. As such, law enforcement has looked to (and prayed for) broad interpretations of the ECPA, PPA, CALEA, and the Fourth Amendment.

THE ELECTRONIC COMMUNICATIONS PRIVACY ACT AND THE PRIVACY PROTECTION ACT OF 1980

In order to provide a framework for the protection and privacy of electronic data, legislators have passed several pieces of legislation including the Privacy Protection Act, the Electronic Communications Privacy Act, and the Communications Assistance for Law Enforcement Act. Coupled with the Fourth Amendment, this legislation has also attempted to address the issues of searching and seizing digital evidence. Although the Court has not specifically ruled upon limitations surrounding these issues or expectations of privacy within computer systems or products, lower courts have afforded some insight (albeit contradictory) into the application of legal doctrines to electronic communications. On its surface, the Electronic Communications Privacy Act **(ECPA)** applies specifically to computer searches, while the Privacy Protection Act attaches the same significance to electronic bulletin boards and other on-line computer systems. Both statutes broaden traditional constitutional protections found within the Fourth Amendment.

Electronic Communications Privacy Act of 1986

The Electronic Communications Privacy Act (1986) extended provisions originally found in Title III of the Omnibus Crime Control and Safe Streets Act of 1968 to include non-aural electronic communications, including electronic mail. It also extended Title III to wireless communications. Theoretically, it was designed to ensure the privacy of American citizens, as Congress argued that privacy may be inadvertently eroded with the advent of technology. They argued that lack of privacy within technological exchanges would deter further development: a situation they wished to avoid as it would impede electronic commerce. However, they also identified the potential for criminal activity. Thus, they provided penalties for individuals who knowingly intercepted wireless and electronic communications, while providing avenues of surveillance for law enforcement officials (Dempsey, 1997). Unlike protections provided by the Fourth Amendment, these statutory prohibitions apply to all individuals, not just those acting on behalf of the government (Winick, 1994). Theoretically, then, the ECPA was formulated in such a way that it necessarily conferred an expectation of privacy to emerging mediums of communication and stored messages.

Three Titles Under ECPA

Although the first two are the most relevant to forensic computer investigations, there are three titles found under the Electronic Communications Privacy Act. The first, updated Title III of the Omnibus Crime Control and Safe Streets Act of 1968;

the second provided protection for stored electronic communications (limited to systems affecting interstate or foreign commerce); and the third governs the use of trap and trace devices. Generally speaking, the ECPA is most applicable to un-read electronic mail. Once the communication has been fully transmitted, the Fourth Amendment applies (Soma, et al., 1996). These titles, designed to work to-gether, are actually somewhat vague and ambiguous. Theoretically modeled after the Federal Wiretap Act, the ECPA is a congressional attempt to broaden expec-tations of privacy with emerging technologies while providing avenues for inter-ceptions. In essence, the ECPA protects against unauthorized access, disclosure or interception by the government, individuals, and third parties while providing po-tentially harsh civil penalties.

Title I of the Act outlines statutory procedures for intercepting wire, oral, and electronic communications. Prior to the passage of the ECPA, only those audio communications sent by a common carrier which could be heard and understood by the human ear were protected by traditional wiretap statutes. In effect, the ECPA extended these protections to inaudible, digital, and other electronic com-munications (i.e., those transmitted through copper wire, coaxial or fiber optic ca-bles, microwave, or radio transmissions). In addition, the ECPA removed the com-mon carrier requirement, while providing protection for nontraditional forms of communication (i.e., video, text, computer data, etc.). However, there are several ambiguities found within the statute that give some scholars pause.

One failing of the ECPA for law-enforcement purposes is one that has not yet been heard by the courts. The ECPA's statutory protections are only extended to those communications which affect interstate or foreign commerce. While the Internet appears to fall squarely within this realm, other types of systems may not. Thus, questions arise in cases involving company intranets or other systems which do not physically cross state lines. An additional failing involves the omission of an articulated exclusionary rule for evidence collected in violation of the statute. While the ECPA provides monetary compensation to those who are violated, it does not specifically provide for the suppression of the fruits of the violation. However, attorneys may rely on traditional mechanisms for relief. First, many vi-olations of the ECPA also constitute violations of the Fourth Amendment. As such, the exclusionary rule may apply. In addition, attorneys may petition for "declara-tory relief" in the form of a suppression order, as provided by the ECPA. (Interestingly, an automatic exclusion is provided in traditional wire-tap statutes. It is unclear why this omission exists.)

This statute also prohibits the manufacturing, possessing, or selling of inter-ception devices (including software)—with one important exception. Govern-ment agents are exempt from this provision, although they must secure a court order to intercept the contents of a communication. However, they are not pro-hibited from identifying the *existence* or *presence* of such communication. Thus, law enforcement officers may identify connections between computers and mon-itor the recipients and sources of an individual's electronic mail. In laymen's terms, investigators can covertly survey Joe Public, but they can not listen to his conversation. An additional exception, applicable to system administrators, en-ables sysops to take actions necessary to maintain or manage an electronic mail

THE REINS ON ELECTRONIC SURVEILLANCE

1. **Title III and ECPA**—provide law enforcement with the capability of electronically monitoring targeted communications:

   a. **By design**—electronic surveillance should be used judiciously, and only in those situations where they are deemed necessary.

   b. **Authorization**—can only be made by a Federal district court judge, *not* Federal magistrates like traditional search warrant applications. Very important—is supposed to elevate the judicial oversight and the privacy protections afforded American citizens.

2. **Requirements under TITLE III**

   a. Must be authorized by a Federal District Court Judge.

   b. Must demonstrate probable cause which specifies, with particularily, the offenses being committed, the telecommunications facility (or place) from which the targeted communication is to be intercepted, a description of those communications, and the identities of the perpetrators.

   c. Must identify previous attempts at evidence collection, and articulate why less intrusive methods have proven unsuccessful. This may include unacceptable levels of danger.

   d. Generally limited to 30 days, although extensions may be granted.

   e. Progress Reports issued on a regular basis (7–10 days).

   f. Surveillance must be terminated if the objectives are met prior to the 30-day period.

   g. Must be recorded for evidence integrity, and sealed under the supervision of a Federal district judge.

   h. Upon surveillance termination, targeted subjects must be notified of the previous surveillance and given an inventory of the communications catalogued.

   i. Service providers must cooperate with authorities with valid court orders. However, they are also bound by the same provisions as law enforcement. That is, they may be held liable for violations of this Act.

   j. **Emergency provisions**—Attorney General, Deputy or the Associate Attorney General may, if authorized, initiate electronic surveillance of wire or electronic communications without a court order, if an application for such order is made within 48 hours of surveillance initiation (Kerr, 2000).

3. **Punishments available under TITLE III**—any party to an illegal interception may be charged with a Federal offense punishable by imprisonment up to 5 years, a fine, or both. Also, those individual victims may seek compensation through civil proceedings.

system. This does not, however, grant them the authority to read e-mails or communications. Rather, it has been interpreted to mean that routine communications which do not pose a threat to the system are private. At the same time, the court has upheld the admissibility of criminal evidence which was obtained when system administrators monitored messages which were excessive in size, slowing the system. Other exceptions have been made when one of the parties to the communication issued consent and when banners which informed users of the possibility of monitoring were included on systems.

Title II—(often referred to as the **Stored Communications Act**—provides protection to stored communications. In essence, this is designed to protect those communications not in transmission which have been stored or saved in some way. More specifically, this Title prohibits access to a facility through which an electronic communication service is provided, to obtain, alter, or restrict or prevent authorized access to a communication held in electronic storage. This rule also prohibits electronic communication providers from disclosing the contents of a communication held in such storage, and also prohibits said providers from disclosing any contextual information included in a message carried or maintained by the provider. As in all things, however, there are some exceptions that may be helpful to law enforcement. The first allows such disclosure if permission is granted by any party to the communication or the subscriber. The second allows disclosure of such information to law enforcement if it inadvertently comes to the attention of the system administrator and if it pertains to the commission of a crime. (On its face, it would appear that those communications that are stored on a server prior to downloading by the recipient would be protected. The courts, however, have handed down rulings inconsistent with this supposition.) Finally, Title III addresses pen registers and trap and trace devices.

These titles, designed to work together, are actually somewhat vague and ambiguous. Theoretically modeled after the Federal Wiretap Act, the ECPA is a congressional attempt to broaden expectations of privacy with emerging technologies while providing avenues for interceptions. In essence, the ECPA protects against unauthorized access, disclosure or interception by the government, individuals, and third parties while providing potentially harsh civil penalties. It also provides for the backup preservation of electronic files when notice to the subscriber would cause destruction (Soma, et al., 1996). More specifically, the act requires a subpoena or court order compelling the system administrator to make copies. It further stipulates that due notice be given to the subscriber (i.e., suspect) within three days of copying. The suspect then has 14 days to file a motion to suppress or to vacate the court order before the government can access said copies.

Privacy Protection Act

The Privacy Protection Act of 1980 (PPA), codified under 42 U.S.C. } 2000, made it unlawful for local, state or Federal law enforcement authorities to search or seize those materials which may be publishable. In essence, it attempted to expand the scope of the 1968 wiretap act to include electronic bulletin boards, specifically protecting "work product" (i.e., mental impressions, conclusions, opinions, or

IMPORTANT DEFINITIONS FOUND WITHIN THE ECPA

1 "Wire communication"—any aural transfer made in whole or in part through the use of facilities for the transmission of communications by the aid of wire, cable or other like connection between the point of origin and the point of reception (including the use of such connection in a switching station) furnished or operated by any person engaged in providing or operating such facilities for the transmission of interstate or foreign communications or communications affecting interstate or foreign commerce and **such term includes any electronic storage of such communication.**

4 "Intercept"—the aural or other acquisition of the contents of any wire, electronic, or oral communication through the use of any electronic, mechanical, or other device.

8 "Contents"—when used with respect to any wire, oral, or electronic communications, includes any information concerning the substance, purport, or meaning of that communication.

12 "Electronic communication"—means any transfer of signs, signals, writing, images, sounds, data, or intelligence of any nature transmitted in whole or in part by a wire, radio, electromagnetic, photo-electronic or photo-optical system that affects interstate or foreign commerce, but does not include:

    a. any wire or oral communications
    b. any communication made through a tone-only paging device;
    c. any communication from a tracking device
    d. electronic funds transfer information stored by a financial institution in a communications system used for the electronic storage and transfer of funds

14 electronic communications system—means any wire, radio, electromagnetic, photo-optical or photo-electronic facilities for the transmission of electronic communications, and any computer facilities or related electronic equipment for the electronic storage of such communication.

theories of the person who prepared, produced, authored, or created such material) and "documentary materials" (i.e., materials upon which information is recorded, and includes . . . mechanically, magnetically, or electronically recorded cards, tapes, or discs). However, it has been criticized by various courts and numerous citizen groups for its vagueness, ambiguity, and the overbroad scope of its content. Interestingly, the PPA does not preclude admitting evidence seized in violation of this act. Rather, it specifically provides civil remedies for victims of government abuse (Winick, 1994).

Victims may include publishers, authors, editors, newspapers, or individuals/companies involved in the dissemination of information. This includes those individuals who act as system operators for electronic bulletin boards or news-

THE CASE OF STEVE JACKSON GAMES, INC.

Perhaps the most notorious of all court cases involved a small company in Texas which produced game-playing software and published game-playing manuals. They also ran a bulletin board system in which numerous members posted messages and sent and received electronic mail. SJG came to the attention of the Secret Service when it became known that co-sysop had illegally downloaded a sensitive 911 document by hacking into a Bell South computer. Arguing that the easy accessibility threatened emergency communications, the Secret Service raided SJG and seized three computers, 300 disks, and a variety of other equipment.

Illuminati, SJG's BBS, was effectively shut down. The Secret Service then read messages stored on the board, and deleted others at will. SJG argued that the government had violated provisions found within the Federal Wiretap Act and Title I of the ECPA. In a seminal ruling, the court ruled that e-mails are only subject to interception during actual transmission and the Federal Wiretap Act did not apply to e-mail in electronic storage. In addition, the court ruled that Title I of the ECPA is not applicable to the unauthorized access of electronic messages stored in a service provider computer.

However, the court did find that the Secret Service had violated the requirements of Title II of the ECPA (18 U.S.C. } 2703). The court also declined to extend a "good faith" defense for the agents' reliance on the warrants. This case proved to be a public relations disaster for the U.S. Secret Service. Long characterized as the most professional of the Federal agencies, the USSS has long been immune from the scandals which have plagued other agencies. However, the fallout of this particular case includes an increasingly suspicious and hostile audience of computer users.

groups. Under this statute, all information which is compiled for purposes of public distribution may not be seized without probable cause. This does not suggest, however, that officers are prohibited from evaluating this type of information. Rather, investigators *may* prevent allegations of abuse if drives are imaged and returned or if subpoenas are issued upon probable cause. In other cases, departmental policy may dictate on-site searches (not recommended) or rapid investigation and subsequent return. In addition, this material may be seized if there is reason to believe that advance notice would result in destruction, alteration, or concealment of such materials or if the documents have not been produced as required by a court order. Summarily, higher levels of scrutiny are afforded to computers which are operating electronic bulletin boards or are part of a network. However, the messages which are transmitted and received from BBS communications are afforded virtually (no pun intended) no protection. Reasoning that messages are posted in **plain view,** courts have ruled that expectations of privacy are all but nonexistent. Thus, investigators may monitor or actively survey an activity occurring in these cyber-exchanges with one important exception. Private bulletin boards or those not accessible to the general public do carry an elevated expectation of privacy.

Much like traditional vice investigations, officers may develop pseudonyms and alter-identities to engage in online exchanges. When done so through legitimate venues and when other investigative techniques would not be productive, investigators may act as observers without necessarily revealing themselves. (Remember: individuals who intentionally disclose information to unknown parties (as individuals on bulletin boards most assuredly are) run the risk of encountering law-enforcement officers). However, the sanctity of the messages themselves must be maintained. This applies not only to sysops, but to individual users as well. Thus, law-enforcement officers must exercise due care when searching computers due to the relative ease with which a BBS can be created and operated. As additional privacy has been afforded to them, investigators should endeavor to identify any potential BBS operated by the suspect or maintained on a targeted system.

Defining Interception under ECPA and the PPA

Like traditional wiretap statutes, the ECPA and the PPA both hinge on the actual *interception* of a communication. Under the original Wiretap Act, a communication was "intercepted" if the acquisition of the communication was contemporaneous with the transmission of information from sender to recipient. This is consistent with the current meaning, yet some privacy advocates question the applicability of traditional standards. Currently, acquisition must occur "before arrival". Some argue that messages in storage which have been sent but not yet opened by the recipient have not been "received". Thus, looking at these stored communications would represent an interception. However, the courts have not agreed, interpreting *interception* to include any act which allows individuals to view an electronic message while it is in actual transmission (*U.S. v. Meriwether,* 917 F.2d 955, 960 (Sixth Cir., 1990); **Steve Jackson Games,** *Inc.* v. *U.S. Secret Service, et al.,* 36 F. 3d 457, 463 (Fifth Cir., 1994); *U.S. v. Reyes,* 922 F. 2d Supp. 818, 836 (S.D.N.Y. 1996). Privacy advocates have expressed hope that this trend may change, as a recent case winding its way through the courts directly contradicts this.[1]

Communications Assistance for Law Enforcement Act

In an attempt to further articulate the need for greater latitude in electronic surveillance and to incorporate wireless communication and emerging communications media, the Federal government developed an initiative known as the Com-

---

[1]*Fraser* v. *Nationwide Mutual Insurance* (decided March, 2001) United States District Court for the Eastern District of Pennsylvania. # 98-CV-6726—has suggested otherwise; . . . *the meaning of interception does not change when the communication is indirect, passing through storage in the course of transmission for sender to recipient . . . in an e-mail communication system, as in a voice-mail communication system, a message passes through intermediate storage in the course of transmission . . . retrieval of a message from storage while it is in the course of transmission is "interception" under the Wiretap Act: retrieval of a message from storage after transmission is complete is not "interception" under the Act.* (page 8 of 21, *www.paed.uscourts.gov/documents/opinions/ 01D0255P.HTM*)

munications Assistance for Law Enforcement Act (CALEA). This act, also debated in the appellate court system, required that the manufacturers of telecommunications equipment and service providers develop systems which provide the capability for surveillance of telephone and cellular communications, advanced paging, satellite-based systems, and specialized mobile radio. The act also required the delivery of "packet-mode communications" by these providers to law enforcement without a warrant.

Theoretically, this Act amended certain provisions found within the ECPA to *heighten* privacy protection. (Remember: the ECPA attempted to balance three competing interests: law enforcement needs, privacy, and technological innovation (Dempsey, 1997).) With the CALEA, Congress explicitly declared that the surveillance requirements of the Act should be narrowly interpreted, and not expand, but maintain, traditional levels of government surveillance. In addition, they required carriers to develop secure systems which ensured the privacy of communications not authorized to be intercepted. They further prohibited the government in general, and the FBI in particular, from dictating network or equipment design standards. In fact, the FBI initially supported the Act and its relevant limitations for law enforcement. In August 1994, Director Louis Freeh assured Congress, and the American people, that CALEA was not intended to further erode privacy expectations, declaring:

> *Without question . . . court-authorized electronic surveillance is a critical law enforcement and public safety tool. I think we have reached a remarkable compromise and achievement in preserving that tool as it has existed since 1968 . . . We believe that the legislation, as introduced this past Tuesday, offers the strongest investigative assurances that the authority which Congress gave us in 1968 will continue unimpeded by technology.* (Digital Telephony Hearings, supra note 9, at 112–113).

However, Freeh's earlier statements, made on behalf of the FBI, are not consistent with recent actions by the Bureau. In fact, the FBI has consistently argued that they, in addition to the entire law-enforcement community, are unfairly restricted by the provisions established by Congress. In particular, they argue that CALEA requires cellular phone companies and other wireless providers to have location tracking capability built into their configurations. They have loosely interpreted CALEA's provisions, and argued that interception of conference calls which include judicially approved, targeted communications may continue even if the target is no longer a party to the communication (Dempsey, 1997). Finally, the government has argued that mere pen register orders sufficiently provide the authority to obtain signaling information and communication content. They argue that the delivery of the entire communication is necessary because of the difficulties associated with distinguishing signal and content in communications which involve packet switching protocols (Dempsey, 1997). In addition, the Bureau has argued that carriers should be required to ensure that encrypted communications be decipherable even if the individual user holds the key. Once again, this directly contradicts the act's original provisions.

Challenges to the CALEA

In direct contravention of their earlier assurances before Congress, the FBI, claiming to represent the entire law-enforcement community, has attempted to extend the original provisions established under the Federal Wiretap Act. Once zealously guarded by the Court and Congress, these privacy protections have been slowly eroded. The Clinton administration, for example, in its proposed anti-terrorism statute, asked Congress to permit roving wiretaps, lessening the sanctions on illegal wiretaps, and creating exemptions to the Foreign Intelligence Surveillance Act, which eliminated much of the privacy protection originally included. Although they were largely defeated in this effort, the Justice Department has been successful in challenges to the CALEA and the ECPA. In cooperation with the FCC, for example, requirements that cellular phones be traceable and that information on digits dialed during a communication (i.e., account numbers, credit card numbers, etc.) be recoverable have been established, directly contradicting those provisions in the CALEA which extended privacy to cellular communications and prohibited the government from interfering with the development of technology. In addition, the Justice Department's effort to require disclosure of communication content along with addressing or signaling data from telecommunication providers using "packet switching" technology has all but negated the original provisions established by the Federal Wiretap Act.

Current State of Privacy

Although law-enforcement officials are quick to point out that wiretapping and electronic surveillance are reserved for the most serious of cases, statistics suggest otherwise. Between 1968 and 1996, the list of offenses for which wiretapping is permitted has more than tripled. In addition, the number of Federal, state, and local law-enforcement wiretaps is steadily increasing, and unsuccessful wiretap applications are all but nonexistent (Dempsey, 1997). Finally, the short duration requirement first articulated in *Katz* has been so eroded as to become defunct (the longest wiretap issued in 1996 lasted over fourteen months).

Challenges to Warranted Searches

In the most general sense, the Fourth Amendment to the U.S. Constitution requires that all warrants particularly describe the place to be searched, the items to be seized, and applicable justifications to prevent *general, exploratory rummaging in a person's belonging* (*Coolidge* v. *New Hampshire,* 403 U.S. 443, 467, 29 L.Ed. 2d 564, 91 S.Ct. 2022 (1971). Although courts have responded differently, the current climate indicates that warrants must be adequately narrow so that individual officers may reasonably infer the limits of the search. In addition, this **particularity** must be so specified that unrelated items remain immune from search and/or seizure. Unfortunately, the particularity requirement may prove somewhat burdensome for officers investigating computer-related crime due to characteristics unique to computers.

Unlike traditional cases in which warrants are issued for very specific items in very specific locations, computer searches involve potentially voluminous amounts of criminal evidence. Conversely, they may contain very small amounts of evidence hidden within a virtual warehouse of information. Thus, they may be characterized as the proverbial needle in a haystack. In addition, enhancements in technology allow suspects to hide criminal evidence in plain sight much more effectively than they once did. Although many legal analysts have likened these types of searches to file-cabinet searches, this analogy is sorely lacking. Investigators looking for child pornography in a file cabinet, for example, may simply glance through files, quickly dismissing text documents. Unfortunately, such practices are not adequate in computer searches. Suspects may change file extensions, use steganography or encryption programs, or employ a variety of other simple methods to hide incriminating information from investigators. Thus, a debate on the particularity and **specificity** necessary for voluminous computer searches rages on.

Particularity

Traditional case law has established that the Fourth Amendment expressly prohibits exploratory searches, requiring searches to be "tailored to its justifications" (*Maryland* v. *Garrison,* 480 U.S. 79, 84). Thus, search warrants that include searches for "all records" have generally been considered to lack particularity. (*Naugle* v. *Witney,* 755 F.Supp. 1504). However, court decisions regarding computer searches have varied not only across jurisdiction, but within them as well. The Ninth Circuit, notoriously unfriendly to law enforcement, have uncharacteristically supported LE interests by suggesting that computer searches may not be held to the same standard of specificity demanded in traditional cases (*U.S.* v. *Gomez-Soto,* 723 F.2d 649 Ninth Cir.); and by upholding the seizure of an entire computer system (hardware, software, and storage media) because *the affidavit in the case established probable cause to believe Lacy's entire computer system was likely to evidence criminal activity* (*U.S.* v. *Lacy,* 119 F.3d 742, 745 (Ninth Cir. 1997). These views were supported in large part by two rulings in the Tenth Circuit which ruled that the sheer volume and variety of stored information precludes specificity. In other words, warrants can "not be expected to describe with exactitude the precise form the records might take" (798 F.2d 380, 383 (Tenth Cir. 1986). The Tenth Circuit reiterated this perspective in *U.S.* v. *Simpson,* (152 F.2d 1241 (Tenth Cir. 1998) where they argued that warrants authorized broad searches of computers and computer equipment including individual files, so **secondary warrants** were not necessary, and in *U.S.* v. *Campos* (Tenth Circuit)—upheld a warrant which authorized the seizure of computer equipment:

> which may be, or [is] used to visually depict child pornography, child erotica, information pertaining to the sexual activity with children or the distribution, possession, or receipt of child pornography, child erotica, or information pertaining to an interest in child pornography or child erotica.

It further affirmed the government's original contention that child pornographers often hide contraband, stating that:

. . . he often stores it in random order with deceptive file names. This requires searching authorities to examine all the stored data to determine whether it is included in the warrant. This sorting process can take weeks or months, depending on the volume of data stored, and it would be impractical to attempt this kind of data search on site. . . searching computer systems for criminal evidence is a highly technical process requiring expert skill and a properly controlled environment . . . it is difficult to know before a search which expert should analyze the system and its data . . . the controlled environment of a laboratory is essential to its complete analysis.

All of these rulings seemed to trumpet victory for the law-enforcement community. However, both the Ninth and the Tenth Circuit have issued rulings which appear to be diametrically opposed to these cases.

In 1995, the Ninth Circuit ruled invalid a warrant which allowed the seizure of *virtually every document and computer file*. The Court further ruled that the warrant failed to separate criminal vs. non-criminal documents and to specify how they related to specific criminal activity (*U.S.* v. *Kow,* F.3d 423,427 (Ninth Cir., 1995). Although this would appear to directly contradict their earlier rulings, it is consistent with the inconstancy found within juridical circuits. The Tenth Circuit has also issued rulings which contravene previous holdings. In *U.S.* v. *Carey* (172 F.3d 1268; 1999 U.S. App. LEXIS 7197; 1999 Colo. J. C.A.R. 2287), the Tenth Circuit denied a general warrant that was directed at drug paraphernalia, in which officers searched JPEG files and found child pornography—although government claimed that their finds were "inadvertent" and therefore legal under the "plain view" doctrine, the Court ruled that the contents of the file were not in plain view.

Although the courts have been anything but consistent, most courts have granted greater latitude in computer searches and seizures. *U.S.* v. *Hay* (2000 WL 1576880 (Ninth Cir, 2000) upheld the seizure expressly stating that digital evidence can be stored virtually anywhere. Thus, it is necessary to look at all of the possibilities. They also ruled that it was proper and necessary to seize the computer system, as forensic analysis is not always possible at the scene. This ruling is consistent with *United States* v. *Kufrovich* (997 F.Supp. 246 (D. Con. 1997) which argued that criminal evidence may be hidden or outside the practicality of on-site searches. The issue before the court involved the validity of a broad-based warrant accompanied with an appendix suggesting that on-site searches are not practical and may sacrifice the effectiveness of data recovery. They have also consistently ruled that when the computer is actually an instrument of the crime, warrants require less particularity. *Davis* v. *Gracey,* [111 F.3d 1472, 1480 (Tenth Cir. 1997)] and *U.S.* v. *Kimbrough* [69 F.3d 723, 727 (Fifth Cir. 1995)], for example, ruled that the seizure of a computer and all of its associated storage, printing, and viewing devices in a child pornography case was permissible as those items represented an instrumentality of the crime.

The courts have also been willing to accept broad seizures of storage media. *U.S.* v. *Sassani,* [1998 WL 98875 (Fourth Cir. March 4) (Per curium) (unpublished decision), cert. denied, 119 S.Ct. 276 (1998)] upheld the seizure of 382 floppies. In addition, the courts have consistently upheld that individual items on a diskette may be counted singularly. This is extremely important to child pornography cases in which sentencing is based on number of images. Thus, defendants who argue that the diskettes, not the actual graphics files, should be counted as containers will be unsuccessful (*U.S.* v. *Perreault* [Ninth Circuit], 1999, #9930087). In addition, *U.S.* v. *Lyons,* 992 F.2d 1029 (Tenth Cir. 1993) held that there was no expectation of privacy on a stolen computer (this involved a case where an employee had stolen a computer from his employer, Unisys, and also software programs. FBI agents located the stolen computer through a valid warrant. Subsequent warrantless search of the stolen computer revealed the proprietary software. He argued that the search was not permissible.) Thus, when possible, investigators should attempt to seize entire computer systems so that adequate investigation may occur. Supporting documentation such as the appendix in *Kufrovich* is also highly recommended until the Supreme Court hears a similar case. However, in cases where seizure of an entire computer is not possible or legally impermissible, proper imaging (discussed in Chapter 8) of drives will enable investigators to conduct a thorough investigation. In addition, investigators should seek secondary warrants whenever they are in doubt as to the scope of the original warrant so as to avoid challenges based on **overbreadth.**

Seizure of Evidence

For purposes of the Fourth Amendment, the reasonable actions that are less intrusive than a traditional arrest depends on a balance between the public interest and the individual's right to personal security free from arbitrary interference by law officers, and consideration of the constitutionality of such seizures involves a weighing of the gravity of the public concerns served by the seizure, the degree to which the seizure advances the public interest, and the severity of the interference with individual liberty. (Rawlings v. Kentucky, *448 U.S. 98; 100 S.Ct. 2556; 1980 U.S. Lexis 142; 65 L.Ed.2d 633.)*

The Fourth Amendment's mandate of reasonableness does not require the agent to spend days at the site viewing the computer screens to determine precisely which documents may be copied within the scope of the warrant, so long as a review procedure promptly after seizure safeguards against the government's retention and use of computer-generated documents known to lie beyond a reasonable interpretation of the warrant's scope (United States v. Gawrysiak, *972 F. Supp. 853, 866 (D.N.J. 1997).*

Similar to the rulings regarding particularity challenges, the courts have been reluctant to rule adversely to police interests on challenges of overbreadth of equipment seizure. In cases in two different districts, courts have ruled that officers may search any container which they reasonably believed could contain criminal evidence (*U.S.* v. *Musson,* 650 F.Supp. 525 (D.Colo. 1986) and *U.S.* v. *Sissler,* 966 F.2d 1455 (W.D. Mich 1991). *Sissler,* more importantly, argued that officers were not required to give deference to descriptive labels, and that items could be seized and transported to a place where careful analysis could be conducted. Basically, the Court has ruled that *the requirement that warrants shall*

*particularly describe the things to be seized makes general searches under (**13)
then impossible and prevents the seizure of one thing under a warrant describing
another. As to what is to be taken, nothing is left to the discretion of the officer executing the warrant,* Marron v. U.S., 275 U.S. 192, 196, 72 L.Ed. 231, 48 S.Ct. 74
(1927). This holding was applied to technology specific warrants in *Center Art
Galleries—Hawaii, Inc.* v. *U.S.,* [875 F.2d 747 (Ninth Cir. 1989)] where they invalidated a warrant as *overbroad because it allowed virtually unrestricted seizure of
items without describing the specific crimes suspected* (2000 WL 1576880, 6).
Finally, *U.S.* v. *Tamura,* [694 F.2d 591, 595-96 (Ninth Cir. 1982)] cautioned investigators to obtain secondary warrants when specified and unspecified documents
were seized wholesale. Specifically ruling that further approval of a magistrate is
necessary. In addition, the search and search and seizure of *encrypted* files may
only be acceptable if the warrant specifies such. (In consent searches, encrypted,
or otherwise protected files, may heighten expectations of privacy.) If encrypted
files are seizable, but are not accessible due to unknown keys or passwords, investigators may wish to seek a subpoena to compel individuals to reveal the same.
When seeking such action, investigators should liken the situation to traditional
investigations where a key was necessary to search items which were included in
a warrant (i.e., safes, etc.). In addition, courts have upheld the search and seizure
of deleted or erased files, likening them to pieces of a shredded ransom note (*U.S.*
v. *Upham,* 168 F. 3d 535, 537).

Another consideration often discussed in challenges to seizing evidence includes the intermingling (often called "commingling") of personal or irrelevant information with potential evidence. These challenges have often been predicated
on voluminous searches of text or database documents which include nonevi-
dentiary materials. Although the courts have not ruled on this specific issue in
computer cases,[2] investigators may avoid challenges by using software which
searches for specific text or keywords within documents.[3] By carefully documenting the software packages used and the keywords searched for, investigators
can argue that they acted with due regard for the privacy of the individual.
Another safeguard may include securing an additional warrant (which specifically
addresses the documents in question) to search for this information. It is absolutely critical for investigators to be cognizant of the potential hazards involved
in these types of cases and plan their strategies accordingly. For example, preliminary warrants should specifically include all materials which may include
criminal evidence that are to be seized. Investigators may argue that removal of
all computer media is necessary to prevent contamination and destruction of potential evidence. Once in the custody of law enforcement, application for an ad-

---

In *Davis, et.al* v. *Gracey, et. al* (#95-6245 111 F.3d 1472, 1997 U.S. App. Lexis 7903 (1997, Tenth Cir)—
court ruled that *the fact that a given object may be used for multiple purposes, one licit and one illicit,
does not invalidate the seizure of the object when supported by probable cause and a valid warrant.*
[3]In *Steve Jackson Games, Inc.* v. *United States,* the court recognized the capabilities of text-searching
software. With a mind towards limiting invasive actions, a good rule of thumb for investigators is to
utilize these programs in every case. Not only will this practice insulate investigators from allegations
of misconduct, it also enables investigators to expedite their case findings—limiting the investigation
to relevant information.

ditional warrant can only strengthen the case against judicial challenges. Indeed, the broadness traditionally afforded to computer searches may be extremely curtailed once exigent dangers are removed.

Due to the lack of specificity contained within current statutes and criminal codes, emerging legal dogma has consistently included storage devices such as diskettes—floppies, zips, etc. Several cases have been consistent with *United States* v. *Ross* (456 U.S. 798, 820-22 (1992). In *New York* v. *Loone,* 630 N.Y. S.2d 483 (Monroe Cy. Ct. 1995) the court ruled that agents did not require a second warrant for computer media. According to the court, the initial warrant, clearly specifying the search and seizure of *any and all computers, keyboards, Central Processing Units, external drives and/or internal drives, external and internal storage devices such as magnetic tapes and/or disks or diskettes* (Ibid at 878) was sufficient to search the information included within the computer media. More specifically, the court ruled that *Ross* allows officers to search the entire area in which criminal evidence may reasonably be found even if various points of entry emerge.

Third Party Origination

While the scope of the Fourth Amendment is unclear in searches conducted by law enforcement, no protection exists for those searches conducted by third parties acting independently absent direction from the government. This issue is increasingly common as more and more cases are brought to the attention of law enforcement via computer repair technicians and network administrators. As always, the admissability of information collected in an investigation by a **third party** hinges on whether the third party was constructively acting as an agent of the government. Courts have repeatedly ruled that files which are open to the public negate any expectation of privacy, and that relinquishing computers to a third party reduces or eliminates an expectation of privacy. This includes computer hardware and any communications or shared files.

In *United States* v. *Pervaz* [118 F.3d 1 (First Cir, 1997)] the court evaluated the admissibility of information gathered by a cellular telephone company after being alerted by authorities that they were being victimized. The court ruled that *the extent of the government's role in instigating or participating in the search, its intent and the degree of control it exercises over the search and the private party, and the extent to which the private party aims primarily to help the government or to serve its own interests* (at 6). In this case, the court ruled that the company's actions were primarily motivated by its wish to identify those individuals guilty of defrauding their consumers, as opposed to helping the government. In addition, the fact that the government was not informed of the company's intention to undertake action to ascertain the culprit's identities was indicative of the lack of control exercised by the government in this situation. Clearly, this case involved individuals or entities that were acting independently of government instruction. Such was not the case, however, in *United States* v. *Hall* [142 F.3d 988 (Seventh Cir. 1998)], where a computer technician copied files from a computer he was repairing under the direction of law enforcement. In this particular case, the technician inadvertently discovered several images of child pornography, phoned the authorities, and copied the files which they specified. Although the court recognized that the authorities acted inappropriately, they upheld the conviction on the grounds that the actual warrant was predicated on items found prior to law enforcement instruction. In this case, the court also evaluated the argument that the ruse to allow time for warrant preparation perpetrated by said repairman under the direction of law enforcement was violative of the Fourth Amendment. Citing *United States* v. *Mayomi,* 873 F. 2d 1049 (Seventh Circuit, 1989), the court ruled that the one-day delay was not unreasonable because it was brief and based on adequate suspicion (at 994).

Other Arguments Used in Warranted Searches

Particularity and overbreadth are not the only challenges that have been levied against law enforcement searches. Traditional challenges like staleness of evidence and insufficient probable cause have also found their way into this new realm. However, the courts have not issued generalized rulings. Rather, they have tailored their interpretations to case characteristics. In *U.S.* v. *Hay,* 2000 WL 1576880 (Ninth Cir. Wash), the court upheld the search and seizure of an entire computer system which was predicated on information that was several months old. The defendant argued that the warrant was stale as it was based on a transfer of child pornography six months previously. The Court disagreed, citing *Lacy.* The Court affirmed the expert (i.e., police) opinion that collectors of child porn tend to keep images for an extended period and that computer depictions, in particular, are easily stored. Thus, it was reasonable to believe that the images were still there. (Lacy's affidavit was predicated on a transfer of data that was ten months old.)

In *U.S.* v. *Lacy* [119 F.3d 742 (Ninth Cir. 1997)], an individual downloaded six image files from a Danish bulletin board known for trafficking in child pornography. Although the defendant argued that this activity was not sufficient to establish probable cause that he received and possessed computerized visual depictions of child pornography, the court disagreed. However, the Ninth Circuit had previously ruled that a warrant application (supported through affidavit) predicated on assumptions as to how "child molesters," "pedophiles," and "child pornography collectors" behave did not establish probable cause to search for items other than the specific photographs ordered by the defendant in a sting operation. Thus, the legal waters remain murky.

Warrantless Searches

Regardless of case characteristics, there are certain categorical situations in which the courts have ruled that no warrant is required. As in non-computer cases, circumstances which may indicate potential harm to human life, the destruction of relevant evidence, and other characteristics which may frustrate legitimate law enforcement efforts may allow officers to seize evidence in the absence of a warrant. While some of these "warrantless searches" are deemed necessary for the protection of human life and criminal evidence, others are based on an independent waiver of the Fourth Amendment.

Consent

Some searches may involve individuals who have voluntarily waived their Fourth Amendment rights. Consent searches are admissible without a warrant if consent is given voluntarily by an individual who has the proper authority over the area to be searched and is legally capable of granting such access [*Schneckloth* v. *Bustamonte,* 412U.S. 218 (1973)]. Under these guidelines, consent may be given by a third party if that third party has a shared interest or authority over the equipment [*United States* v. *Matlock,* 415 U.S. 164 (1974)]. However, the subsequent search must be limited to that area of the consenting third party's common authority [*United States* v. *Block,* 590 F.2d 5335 (Fourth Cir. 1978)]. In computer cases, the presence of encryption or security mechanisms may negate the concept of common authority unless that person giving consent had previously been given the unlocking capability by the owner. Networked computers may also be immune from consent searches, as system operators may have access to most, but not all, files. The same is true with family members. Thus, the most important characteristics in determining the validity (and legality) of consent are physical control and limited access. In other words, if a computer is shared by family members, and the suspect member has taken pains to prevent common access (i.e., encryption, steganography, etc.), others may not be able to give consent. Investigators must also evaluate the totality of the circumstances in any particular situation to determine the validity and the *scope* of the consent being offered.

In legal terms, the **totality of the circumstances** would include a compilation of age, education, intelligence, physical, and mental conditions of the person granting consent. It also includes whether the individual was incarcerated and had been notified of his or her right regarding consent. If a child's computer is the intended search target, parents may give consent if the child is under 18. Over the age of 18, the totality of the circumstances would include factors such as the dependency of the child, the location of the computer, and the like. The *scope of consent* also hinges on the totality of the circumstances. It is rarely holistic and all-encompassing. Rather, it hinges on the breadth of the reasonable understanding of the grantor. *Government agents may not obtain consent to search on the representation that they intend to look only for certain specified items and subsequently use that consent as a license to conduct a general exploratory search.* (*United States* v. *Dichiarinte, 445 F.2d 126* (Seventh Cir. 1971) at 129-30. Finally, the courts have made it clear that the burden to prove that the search was within the scope of the consent lies with the government [*United States* v. *Schaefer,* 87 F. 3d 562, 569 (First Cir. 1996)].

Exigent Circumstances and Emergency Situations

The courts have ruled that actions which are undertaken to protect or preserve human life are acceptable even if they would not be so in non-emergency situations [(*Mincey* v. *Arizona, 437* U.S. 385, 392-93 (1978); [*U.S.* v. *Doe,* 61 F.3d 107, 110-111 (First Cir. 1995)]. Thus, officers are not precluded from making warrantless entries if they reasonably believe that an individual(s) is in need of immediate aid. Upon entry, contraband or criminal evidence which is in plain view may be seized. Keep in mind that reasonable seizures do not automatically warrant

A CASE FOR CONSENT—A CAUTION FOR INVESTIGATORS

U.S. v. *Turner http://laws.findlaw.com/1st/981258.html*—suppressed evidence of child pornography after it was found in a consensual search by an individual who was identified as a suspect in the sexual assault of his neighbor. Facts of the case—Defendant was charged with one count of child pornography after officers found child porn on his computer. At the time, the investigators were investigating the sexual assault of his neighbor. Upon noticing blood on his window sill and throughout the house, investigators suspected Turner and obtained his permission to search his house for items involving the sexual assault of his neighbor. Subsequently, the defendant waited outside while the investigators initiated a comprehensive search. Upon seeing a screen saver on his computer screen of a naked woman that resembled the victim, the investigator searched his hard drive for last documents accessed and picture files. He found photographs of adult women in bondage type situations. After phoning the district attorney, the officer copied adult pornography over to a floppy. In addition, the officer extended his search to "My Computer" and opened files which had names that suggested child pornography (ex. "G-Images", "young with breasts" etc.). The officer subsequently found images which appeared to be child pornography. The district court suppressed the evidence saying that names suggesting child pornography were unrelated to the charges. The Circuit Court affirmed, yet expanded.

Rulings:

1. Although the defendant agreed to a general search for evidence of the assault, it was not reasonable to assume that the investigators would look in places where evidence of the assault could not be contained. Thus, the search was exploratory—which is not permissible. Citing *Florida* v. *Jimeno*, 500 U.S. 248, 251 (1991), the court argued that "the scope of a [consensual] search is generally defined by its expressed object."

2. Officers exceed the scope of the consent search. His consent was based on the understanding that they were looking for "any signs the suspect had been inside [the apartment] . . ." "any signs a suspect had left behind." The court stated that "it obviously would have been impossible to abandon physical evidence of this sort in a personal computer hard drive, and bizarre to suppose—nor has the government suggested—that the suspected intruder stopped to enter incriminating evidence into the Turner computer.

3. Also "an objective observer, witnessing in context the pre-consent exchange between Turner and the investigating detectives, reasonably would construe "evidence of the assault itself" to mean physical evidence linked to the crime scene, rather than documentary or photographic evidence."

subsequent searches. In other words, officers may (and should) seize a computer where evidence is at risk, but should seek judicial approval before undertaking a search of its contents (Levin, 1995).

Once again, the totality of the circumstances will determine the presence and duration of exigent searches and seizures. In determination of the applicability, the courts have found several factors which should be evaluated. These include:

1. the degree of urgency involved;
2. the amount of time necessary to obtain a warrant;
3. whether the evidence is about to be removed or destroyed;
4. the danger or possibility thereof at the site;
5. information which suggests that the possessors of said material are aware of the officer's intention to secure it;
6. the ready destructability of said contraband.

These characteristics may prove especially salient in situations in which computers are involved as digital evidence is particularly fragile. Remember: warrantless seizure is limited to the length of the exigency. Once the urgency is passed, warrants must be obtained.

When specifically applied to computer cases, the courts have ruled that seizure of computer hardware may be conducted under this doctrine, but the subsequent search of hardware may necessitate a warrant. In *U.S. v. David* [756 F.Supp. 1385, 1392 (D.Nev. 1991)], the court held that while the officer's seizure of suspect's computer memo book was reasonable in light of the defendant's action of deleting files, the subsequent search and re-access was not reasonable, as there was adequate time to secure a search warrant. In this case, the court analogized the computer with a container arguing that the authorization for a warrantless seizure does not necessarily grant authorization for a search of such item (*Texas v. Brown*, 460 U.S. 730, 750 (1983). One of the determining factors, of course, would be the ever-resilient "expectation of privacy." If, for example, the circumstance surrounding such computer suggests security, a warrant will be required.

Incident to Arrest

Traditionally, those situations in which an officer's safety may be compromised allow for searches without a warrant. The search of an individual and his/her immediate vicinity upon arrest has been determined reasonable as it is necessary to ensure the safety of the officer and those around him/her. (*United States v. Robinson*, 414 U.S. 218, 234-36 (1973). While this includes the seizure of those items within the arrestee's possession and immediately within reach, it may not include further search of these items. Thus, the search of a laptop, palmtop or electronic organizer for data is prohibited by the Electronic Communications Privacy Act of 1986. Thus, investigators should secure a warrant before proceeding. Although originally intended to protect officers from armed suspects, *Robinson* has been applied to pagers, and the courts have consistently ruled that investigators may access the memory at the time of arrest (*U.S. v. Reyes*, 922 F. Supp. 818, 833

(S.D.N.Y. 1996). This permission has not been extended to personal computers, laptops, and Personal Digital Assistants (PDA). However, the court did validate the seizure of a zip disk found in the car of an arrested suspect, but failed to rule on the constitutionality of the subsequent search [*Cf. United* v. *Tank*, 200 F.3d 627, 632 (Ninth cir. 2000)]. Once again, investigators must be cautioned that issues of search and seizure are separate! Thus, the subsequent search of items seized may not be justified, irrespective of the legality of the seizure.

Plain View

Things which are obviously evidence of a crime can be collected when the officer is acting in a lawful manner; items which are unobstructed may be seized. In addition, those things which are criminal contraband may be seized. *However,* investigators *cannot* broaden the scope of the original search based on new evidence. Instead, investigators should obtain a secondary warrant prior to further investigation (*U.S.* v. *Carey,* 172 F.3d 1268, 1273 (Tenth Circuit, 1999). However, the courts have been reluctant to extend plain view to the contents of an entire computer citing *Coolidge* which argued that *the plain view doctrine may not be used to extend a general exploratory search from one object to another until something incriminating at last emerges* [*Coolidge* v. *New Hampshire,* 403 U.S. 443, 465; 29 L.Ed. 2d 564, 91 S.Ct. 2022 (1971)].

The most notable computer-specific case involving plain view, *U.S.* v. *Carey,* [172 F.3d 1268; 1999 U.S. App. LEXIS 7197; 1999 Colo. J.C.A.R. 2287] was extremely narrow in scope and was not intended to be the final word on the matter. The facts of the case preclude any such generalization. In this case, the original thrust of the search specifically targeted evidence of drug trafficking. While searching through computer files, the investigator, by his own admission, noticed a large number of JPEG files containing sexually explicit names. He then opened a variety of these images, and ascertained that they were child pornography. Once the first image was viewed, the detective changed the direction of his search to include child pornography, thus, subsequent "findings" were not inadvertent, but intentional. He then opened a variety of these images, ascertained that they were child pornography, and "changed the focus of his search." Government likened the search to a file cabinet, but the court rejected this, stating that it was the content of the files, not the files themselves which were seized. In addition, the Court pointed out that the files were not in "plain view" as they were in closed files. However, the Court was quick to point out that this ruling did not address the particularity necessary in all computer cases—just this one. In addition, in the concurring opinion, a Justice points out that the defendant's testimony made it impossible to uphold an argument of plain view. Indeed, had the officer not made his intentions clear, the evidence may not have been dismissed (i.e., it is reasonable that criminals hide evidence, and it may be necessary to ascertain the contents).

Since *Carey,* courts have upheld plain view discoveries on the computer when stating that the actions of the agent were consistent with the terms of the original warrant. The court ruled against an argument by the defendant that the searching of JPEGs was not consistent with searching for hacking activities. The Court ruled that the officer's practice of systematically searching documents without regard to file names or suffixes was reasonable, as potential evidence could be hidden anywhere in the defendant's files (i.e., the officer does not have to assume that file extensions adequately characterize the contents of the file) [*U.S.* v. *Gray,* 78 F. Supp.2d 524 (D. VA 1999). Thus, law enforcement should take note:

1. focus on the original search warrant. If contraband is found in pursuit of items covered under the original warrant, get a secondary warrant!
2. Automated or SOP which are conducted in every case (i.e., text string, thumbnail of graphics, viewing of subdirectories, etc.) may support an officer's contention that files outside the scope of the original warrant were inadvertently discovered during routine procedures.

Border Searches

The Supreme Court has recognized a special exception to the warrant requirement for searches occurring at the country's international borders, ruling that warrantless searches at the border are acceptable on their face [(*United States* v. *Ramsey,* 431 U.S. 606 (1977)]. Probable cause and reasonable suspicion are not necessary for routine searches. However, reasonable suspicion must be present for more intrusive searches. The Court has ruled that borders may be less tangible than traditionally thought—extending the power of border searches to include areas several miles from the actual border (*Almeida-Sanchez* v. *United States,* 413 U.S. 266 (1973)). While case law applying this doctrine to cyberspace boundaries is not yet available, we can certainly anticipate future occurrences.

Other Warrantless Searches

Traditionally, automobiles, field interrogations, and inventory searches have also been areas in which searches were conducted without the necessity of a warrant. However, they are not exactly applicable to computer-related evidence. Inventory searches, for example, are designed to protect the rights of the arrestee by detailing his or her personal property. As computer files are not discoverable under plain view, the presence of a floppy in a detainee's shirt pocket is all but meaningless without specific probable cause. The same applies to automobiles and field interrogations.

OTHER LEGAL CONSIDERATIONS

Vicinage

Although the courts have not ruled specifically on questions of jurisdiction and sovereignty, past Supreme Court cases may indicate an issue which may arise. (i.e., contemporary crimes transcend traditional boundaries). In *Johnson* v. *U.S.* [351 U.S. 215, 219-221 (1956)] the Court ruled that the *requirement of venue states the public policy that fixes the situs of the trial in the vicinage of the crime, rather than the residence of the accused.* This premise was reaffirmed by *Travis* v. *U.S.* [346 U.S. 631, 633-634 (1961)] which ruled that the locality of the offense, not the personal presence of the offender, is the constitutional basis for venue. If this premise is not revisited (and reversed), then prosecution of computer crime committed on the Internet will be all but impossible.

Undercover Techniques

Although the courts have issued contradictory rulings in many areas, most are in agreement regarding the appropriateness of traditional investigative techniques. In *United States* v. *Charbonneau,* 979 F.Supp.1177 (S.D. Ohio 1997), the court ruled that real time, online conversations observed by an agent in a chat room did not require a warrant as there is no expectation of privacy in virtual areas where others visit. They argued that people conversing in chat rooms run the risk of talking to an undercover agent. Elaborating on *Hoffa* v. *U.S.* 385 U.S. 293 (1966) the court ruled that senders of electronic mail run the same risk as those using the Postal Service in that they might be mailing it to an undercover agent. Thus, there is no Fourth Amendment protection which applies to chatroom conversations.

Sentencing Guidelines

Although a variety of cases have involved departures from sentencing guidelines, most involve the definition of "items." This is increasingly important as child pornography statutes are specifically tied to the number of items. Unfortunately, courts have proven no more consistent in this area, than others we have previously discussed. While some courts have ruled that individual diskettes represent one item, others have ruled that *a graphic file is the container used for compiling and storing visual depictions in a computer qualifies as an item* (*U.S.* v. *Wind,* 128 F.3d 1276 (Eighth Cir. 1997). And *U.S.* v. *Hall,* 142 F.3d 988 (Seventh Cir. 1998) rejected an argument that a computer disk regardless of disk content should be counted singularly, further ruling that computer files are the equivalent of items under sentencing guidelines. Courts have also ruled that hard disks do not consitute a singular item under the sentencing guidelines (*U.S.* v. *Fellows,* 157 F.3d 1197–(Ninth Circuit, 1998).

A two-level sentencing enhancement for using a computer to obtain or possess child pornography was added to the Sentencing Guidelines in U.S.S.G. } 2G2 4(b)(3) primarily as a deterrent against the presumed anonymity of the Internet. It also recognized the particular difficulties of detection and prosecution of cyberspace child porn. Unfortunately, the trend across the judicial landscape is to depart downward! Thus, many child pornographers receive sentences far less than those which are provided for under law. Curiously, the courts have granted such departures for reasons ranging from the lack of a direct impact on the supply of child pornography on the web to good behavior on the part of a child pornographer who failed to further act out sexual deviations.

● CONCLUSIONS

Because the Supreme Court has remained resolutely mute on the convergence of technology and the expectation of privacy , no constitutional framework has been established. Thus, a lack of uniformity in legal application of constitutional standards exists. Many of these concerns focus almost exclusively on the Fourth Amendment, while others involve the Exclusionary Rule. The lack of physicality of data origination poses jurisdictional questions and the lack of cooperation among local and Federal agencies further compounds the issue. The lack of a clear ruling by the Court on computer warrants further leads to an over-reliance on Federal resources, which leads to claims of imperialism and loss of state sovereignty. Thus, it is essential that the Court issue clear edicts on the issues discussed throughout this chapter. Otherwise, claims of disproportionate or jurisdictional inconsistency are well founded.

TERMS DISCUSSED

consent	particularity	Steve Jackson Games
ECPA	plain view	Stored Communications
Exclusionary rule	probable cause	Act
expectation of privacy	seizure	third party
incident to arrest	secondary warrant	totality of the circum-
Ortega doctrine	specificity	stances
overbreadth		

DISCUSSION QUESTIONS

1. Briefly discuss the evolution of the Fourth Amendment in regard to physical searches.
2. What do you believe is a good balance of individual privacy and governmental interest?
3. How has electronic surveillance changed since the 1950s? Have technological advancements lessened or increased expectations of privacy? Why or why not?
4. How has *Ortega* been applied to electronic mail?
5. What is the ECPA and why was it designed?
6. Why are traditional definitions of "interception" problematic when applying them to electronic communications?
7. What are some examples of warrantless searches and in what circumstances may they be conducted?

8

FORENSIC TERMINOLOGY AND COMPUTER INVESTIGATIONS

● FORENSIC COMPUTER SCIENCE—AN EMERGING DISCIPLINE

As stated, the introduction of computer technology has heralded the approach of a new wave of illegitimate behavior and multiplied the avenues of criminal procurement. The utilization of technology has also changed the investigative playing field, and necessitated the development of contemporary forensic techniques. More succinctly, the digitalization of information and the increasing interconnectivity of society require a corresponding ability to retrieve data inadvertently lost, as well as that which has been intentionally misplaced. While such abilities clearly serve the law enforcement mission, they may also be utilized by corporate entities and individual citizens to ensure the continuity of public services, private interests and government stability (see text box).

Private interests aside, forensic computer science is critical to the successful disposition of computer-related cases. Empirical methodologies serve a variety of

WHO BENEFITS FROM FORENSIC COMPUTER SCIENCE?

Prosecutors—variety of crime where incriminating documents can be found ranging from homicide to financial fraud to child pornography.

Civil litigators—personal and business records which relate to fraud, divorce, discrimination, and harassment.

Insurance companies—mitigate costs by using discovered computer evidence of possible fraud in accident, arson, and workman's comp cases.

Corporations—ascertain evidence relating to sexual harassment, embezzlement, theft, or misappropriation of trade secrets and other internal/confidential information.

Law enforcement officials—for pre-search warrant preparations and post-seizure handling of computer equipment.

Individuals—support of claims of wrongful termination, sexual harassment, or age discrimination.

ENCRYPTION—A NEW NIGHTMARE FOR INVESTIGATORS

Recent paranoia about government intrusion fanned by civil libertarians has increased many computer user's awareness of data security. As such, many are now employing encryption technology, both manual and automated. The possibilities for manual encryption are virtually endless. For example, users can encrypt their own data by simply adding or subtracting a constant in hexadecimal mode or by switching nibbles (i.e., splitting bytes down the middle and transposing the two). Luckily, most users are either unaware of such potential or are too lazy. Thus, they often rely on encryption options found within many popular software packages, such as WordPerfect™, Excel™, Lotus™, Microsoft Word™ and PKZIP™ files. Subsequent files, relying on algorithmic computations, *may* be defeated with forensic packages. However, some users employ more sophisticated encryption strategies, such as *BestCrypt*™ and *PGP*™, which may store passwords up to 128 characters!

BestCrypt™, a popular program among pornographers, uses Blowfish, Twofish, and Gost2814789 encryption (256 bit) to encrypt the entire drive and may prove impenetrable through traditional methods. In addition, this program, and others like it, also has a variety of options quite detrimental to computer investigations, including: 1) hot keys—all virtual drives automatically close if hot key combination is pressed; 2) timeout option—all virtual drives close automatically after a specified period of inactivity; and 3) container guard—prevents a users from accidentally deleting encrypted containers. In addition, this particular program allows users to employ their own encryption algorithms, making it virtually impossible for investigators to manually crack.

law-enforcement functions and provide the accountability necessary in a democratic society. In the most general sense, computer forensics provides a mechanism for the investigation of computer-related criminal activity consistent with constitutional mandates. To wit, privileged information is protected and the integrity of potential evidence is maintained by: 1) maintaining a chain of custody; 2) ensuring that viruses are not introduced to a suspect machine during analysis; and 3) ensuring that evidence or potential evidence remains in an unaltered state (i.e., not destroyed, damaged, or otherwise manipulated during the investigative process). In addition, it enhances the likelihood of timely processing—necessary to protect departments from civil litigation claiming unreasonable interruption of business operations. More specifically, it establishes procedures for the recovery, preservation, and analysis of digital evidence.

Computer forensic science protects digital evidence from possible alterations, damage, data corruption or infection by design or carelessness. By providing mechanisms for evidence duplication, it enables the creation of forensically sound images useful for data analysis. As such, it prevents allegations of corruption or misconduct on the part of investigators, all but guaranteeing evidentiary introduction in court. It also uncovers all relevant files on suspect systems, including

LIVERPOOL JOHN MOORES UNIVERSITY
LEARNING SERVICES

overt, hidden, password-protected, slack, swap, encrypted, and some deleted files. In addition, computer forensics assists in information dissemination as printouts may illustrate an overall analysis of the subject computer such as system layout, file structures, data and authorship information, documentation of any data manipulation, and any other relevant computer system information manipulation.

TRADITIONAL PROBLEMS IN COMPUTER INVESTIGATIONS

The ability to retrieve electronic data is increasingly important in both criminal and civil investigations. Electronic data recovery should not be reserved for instances where the instrumentality of computer technology has been demonstrated. In fact, digital evidence has been utilized in cases ranging from homicide to software piracy. However, the importance of computer forensic capabilities has not been univeralsally recognized, and is, in fact, in debate in departments across the country. Traditionally, this reluctance was attributed to *cyberphobia,* or the fear of new technology. Such fear of innovation is consistent with, but not unique

Uncovering Digital Evidence—Like other types of criminals, individuals engaged in computer-related criminal activity often attempt to obscure evidence of their involvement. Investigators should remember that their activities are consistent with their non-technological counterparts, and search for clues underneath objects just as they would at a traditional crime scene. Luckily for investigators, computer criminals often lack criminal sophistication, and are unable to destroy the remnants of their activities. Below is a list of manipulated files which may be found in a criminal investigation in which forensic analysis may prove critical.

Overt files—those things which are not hidden, deleted, encrypted, or intentionally or unintentionally covert.

Hidden files—files which are manipulated (often intentionally) to cover the contents of the original file. Common practices used by suspect users include altering file extensions and the like.

Password-protected files—files which are protected from non-authorized users with password programs.

Slack space, free or unallocated space, and swap files—free space is that part of the disk which the computer has not yet overwritten with data (i.e., space that is currently unused but a possible repository of previous data). Slack space is the area of the disk located between the end of the current file data and the end of the last assigned disk cluster of that file. Swap files include those which are temporarily placed on the computer when applications run out of space.

to, the police subculture or its adminsitration. Indeed, administrators across the world experience sedentary apathy (i.e., atrophy), and are hesitant to employ new technologies. In addition, law-enforcement administrators, grappling with the emerging socio-legal culture of political correctness and multiculturalism, express dissatisfaction with the changing nature of police work, and perceive computer forensics as unnecessary constraints on budgets already stretched to the limit.

Inadequate Resources
The lack of adequate resources necessary for the procurement of forensic software and training is not alien to state and local agencies. Long characterized by dwindling budgets and increased responsibilities, local police agencies have been forced to compete amongst themselves for the proverbial scraps throuwn from state and Federal tables. As expected, small or rural agencies lack the competitive edge present in larger, more sophisticated agencies, which often have individuals or units assigned exclusively to grant writing. Although not equivalent to rocket science, the successful preparation and submission of grant proposals does require a certain knack. Such idiosyncrasies are often discussed at annual meetings which small agencies fail to attend due to lack of resources. Thus, the vicious cycle continues whereby the least equipped agencies are the least abvle to secure external funding for necessary equipment or training. Even those agencies currently favored by funding entities struggle to justify the exponential costs associated with computer forensics.

As the forensic analysis of computer technology becomes *en vogue* across the country, training programs have increasingly targeted large, well-funded corporate entities. Although most reserve a selected number of seats and offer "discounts" to law-enforcement officers, many are still priced outside the resources of the law-enforcement community, routinely garnishing as much as $2,000 per person (e.g., NTI—New Technologies, Inc.; Litton/TASC; etc.) and providing individualized, renewable licenses. In an effort to combat disproportionate opportunities and the rising cost of training, Federal agencies such as the Federal Bureau of Investigation (FBI) and the Federal Law Enforcement Training Center (FLETC) have developed similar courses. Ostensibly, these courses are "free" to qualified law-enforcement personnel. However, the number of attendees is limited, and certain organizations appear to receive preferential treatment. Even those programs which do not display bureaucratic nepotism often lack significant representation of smaller agencies. In fact, many agencies are unable to avail themselves of the "free" training often found at the Federal level, as they cannot afford the loss of personnel (e.g., one person from a ten-person department represents 10 percent of their entire organization!). However, the creation of non-profit training and research centers (e.g., the National White Collar Crime Center (NWCCC) is a step in the right direction.

Lack of Communication and Cooperation among Agencies
Because of the competition inherent among local governments, law enforcement has long been typified by a lack of cooperation and communication between bordering agencies. Although agencies have often been forced to develop formal

With funds generated from state and federal grants, South Carolina's State Law Enforcement Division (SLED) was able to secure a new facility for their computer crime unit and purchase new equipment. Unfortunately, this is not the norm in many agencies. (Courtesy of *SLED*)

partnerships by legislative entities threatening to withhold allocated financing, such shotgun alliances have not been characterized by spirited collaboration. Rather, these relationships may be likened to arranged marriages, with neither party entirely fulfilled but both sedated with counterproductive complacency. Fortunately, computer forensic professionals have overcome jurisidictional competition, developing listservs and practitioner associations (e.g., HTCIA, etc.) which share information and encourage cooperation among investigators.

Over-Reliance on Automated Programs and Self-Proclaimed Experts

The lack of resources and the flux of technology coupled with technological ignorance has resulted in an overemphasis on automated recovery programs and self-proclaimed experts (discussed later). As we will discuss later, automated forensic programs are essential tools in a computer crime fighter's toolbox, and are extremely useful in routine investigations. However, they are not the end-all, be-all to computer forensic science. In fact, the familiarity and utilization of automated programs may result in a situation where investigators know just enough to make them potentially hazardous to the very investigation to which they are dedicated. Couple this with this their informal anointment as "departmental computer expert" and a situation dangerous to litigation erupts. Fortunately for law enforcement, defense attorneys have accepted such "expertise" at face value, but this trend is sure to evaporate.

Lack of Reporting

Although rarely impeached in judicial proceedings, the expertise of law enforcement personnel is often challenged privately. Perceived largely as incompetent, law enforcement officials have unsuccessfully encouraged victims of computer-related crime to report their victimization. Such perceptions have only been exacerbated by corporate advisors who routinely discourage formal notification. Rosenblatt (1995: 23), for example, argues that *victims should not report a case to law enforcement unless they are willing to cooperate in subsequent prosecution,* and advises clients to contact local authorities prior to invoking federal powers as they are more malleable. Strongly suggesting that local agencies are more appropriately situated to investigate business computer cases, he warns that Federal entities *will not investigate cases which do not involve large losses* (Rosenblatt, 1995: 24). Unfortunately, such advice is speculative at best. Anecdotal evidence suggests that local law enforcement is grossly lacking in adequate resources. Thus, even the most dedicated of agencies may lack the necessary wherewithal to properly conduct such investigations. Further admonitions contained therein suggest that Rosenblatt's book is only appropriate for self-serving corporate interests, and may, in fact, be counterproductive, if not blatantly detrimental, to formal criminal inquiries.

Evidence Corruption

As a result of the problems discussed above, many computer investigations have been conducted in a less than perfect manner. Often relying on officers versed in popular software programs identified as "departmental computer experts" or non-sworn computer "experts" whose primary role is to identify all obvious files on a hard drive, many cases have been lost before they even got to court. Unfortunately, these investigators do not adequately understand computer structure and the civilian "experts" do not understand nor appreciate the legal complexities of evidence preservation and custodial documentation (i.e., investigators are evidence-oriented and computer specialists are computer-oriented).

Thus, evidence is often overlooked, corrupted or destroyed entirely. Some networked computers, for example, have been seized and simply disconnected without saving dialogue or documenting configuration, resulting in an inability by the investigator to reconfigure a seized system in court (may overcome this by using a "fox

THREE CARDINAL RULES OF COMPUTER INVESTIGATIONS

1. Always work from an image, leaving the original intact.
2. Document, document, document.
3. Maintain chain of custody.

and hound" cable locator). While other cases have been lost by a failure to search hidden files or slack space. Thus, it is essential that recognized standards of forensic computer science be developed through the interaction of LE and the corporate community. In the interim, all investigations should be conducted in keeping with the three cardinal rules of computer forensic science: 1) always work from an image; 2) document, document, document; and 3) maintain the chain of custody.

COMPUTER FORENSIC SCIENCE AND DISK STRUCTURE

Traditional problems associated with the investigation of computer-related crime notwithstanding, computer forensic science can only be initiated by individuals with at least a basic understanding of computer structure.[1] Although few users in-

Tracks, Cylinders, and Sectors

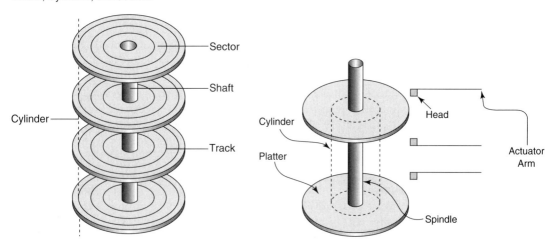

Illustration of a Cylinder: Physically, a drive is usually composed of a number of rotating platters. Each platter is divided concentrically into tracks. In turn, tracks are divided into sectors, which are further divided into bytes. Finally, read/write heads are contained on either side of the platters.

Head—Each platter has one head per side. These heads are very close to the surface of the platter, and allow reading of and writing to the platter. Heads are numbered sequentially from zero.

Tracks—the concentric bands dividing each platter. Tracks are numbered sequentially beginning with zero.

Cylinder—the set of tracks located in the same position on every platter in the same head position. Unlike physical disk units, cylinders are intangible units. Simply put, they are a cross-section of a disk. (Imagine using a hole puncher on a perfectly positioned stack of paper. The resulting hole would be a visible representation of an empty sector.) Each double-sided floppy has two tracks. The same track is on all stacked platters. The set of corresponding tracks on a magnetic disk that lie the same distance from the disk's edge. Taken together, these tracks form a cylindrical shape. For a hard drive, a cylinder usually includes several tracks on each side of each disk platter.

---

[1]This is not intended to be a comprehensive introduction to computer science. Rather, the following should provide the reader with a brief look at the components of a computer system which are most relevant to computer investigations. It is intended to simply familiarize the reader with common terms used in computer investigations.

tellectualize the contents and layout of their computer system, investigators must be aware of both the physical and logical structure, disk management, and memory storage. In a most basic sense, computers are comprised of three primary components: hardware, software, and firmware.

A *computer* may be defined as a device capable of storing, transmitting or manipulating data through mathematical and logical processes or operations (Kovacich and Boni, 2000). *Static memory* is that area on hard and/or floppy disks in which data and programs are stored; while **volatile memory** is that area of a computer which holds during processing and is erased when power is shut down. **Semi-permanent storage** refers to that area of a disk that is not dependent upon a power source for its continued maintenance, and which may be changed under the appropriate operating conditions (i.e., storage devices, floppy and fixed disks, magnetic tapes, etc.). This area is where the majority of the work and storage is conducted, and where most processed data is stored. Thus, it is extremely important in computer forensics. *Computer storage* is the holding of data in an electromagnetic form for access by a computer processor. *Primary storage* is data in RAM and other built-in devices. **Secondary storage** is data on hard disk, tapes, and other external devices. *Floppy disks* or *diskettes* are single circular disks with concentric tracks which are turned by spindles under one or more heads. **CD-ROMs** have a single track, spiraling from the disk edge towards the center, which may only be written to once (CDs write data from the *center* out, and music from the *outside* in; while **CD-RWs** act as traditional disk drives which may be written to more than once. *Hard/fixed disks* are one or more disks comprised of one or more heads which are often fixed inside a sealed enclosure (may have more than two sides if the disk consists of more than one platter).

Disk Structure and Data Storage

On all disks in DOS-based systems, certain structural rules exist in which physical drives are loaded first, logical drives second, and drivers third. **Physical drives** refer to devices and data at the electronic or machine level, while *logical drives* (most important in computer forensics) are allocated parts of a physical drive that are designated and managed as independent units.

RAM VS. ROM—COMPUTER MEMORY

Random Access Memory (RAM) is that volatile memory which is used to store programs and data that are being accessed by the user. Also referred to as *main memory,* data contained in RAM is lost when computers are powered down. Traditionally reserved for hard drives, RAM is now found in other computer hardware like printers to allow storage and formatting of pages queued for printing so that other computer functions are not delayed.

Read-Only Memory (ROM) is that memory built into the operating system which can be accessed, but not altered, such as that which contains programs necessary for the booting process.

STORAGE EQUIVALENCE

Techno terms			Visual Comparison
Nibble	= 1/2 a byte	= 4 bits	A single
Byte	= 1 byte	= 8 bits	character
	= 2 bytes	= 16 bits	A word
Double Word	= 4 bytes	= 32 bits	
Kilobyte	= 1,024 bytes	= 2^{10} bytes	1000 characters; One-half page of text
Megabyte	= 1,048,576 bytes	= 2^{20} bytes	Small novel; 5 MB— Shakespeare's work
Gigabyte	= 1,073,741,823 bytes	= 2^{30} bytes	Truck full of paper
Terabyte	= 1,099,511,627,776 bytes	= 2^{40} bytes	Text on 50,000 trees 10 TB— Library of Congress

The smallest forms of data storage are represented by *binary digits* or **bits.** Based on a principle of two, bits may be likened to on/off switches. Collections of bits are interpreted by the computer and are reported to users as characters, words, etc., and are basically transformed into a format most appropriate for non-mechanical, human consumption. In essence, this process identifies a standard association between particular binary patterns and characters so that compatibility between systems and system components are ensured. The most common set of associations is the *American Standard Character for Information Interchange* or **ASCII** (Appendix A). This code defines characters for the first 128 binary values (i.e., 0 to 127). The first 32 of these are used as non-printing control characters which were designed to control data communications equipment and computer printers and displays (Sammes & Jenkinson, 2000). Extended ASCII code has since been developed by IBM, and provides particular character symbols to binary values 128 through 255.[2]

Computers interpret data in a variety of ways. In a binary system, interpretative rules are associated with a base of two with integers represented by zeroes and ones. In a **hexadecimal** system, on the other hand, interpretative rules are associated with a base of 16 with integers ranging from 0 to 9 and A to F. In a binary system, the range of whole numbers that can be represented by a single byte is 0 to 255. Thus, it is often necessary to use two bytes to represent whole numbers, and four bytes where greater levels of precision are required[3] (Sammes & Jenkinson, 2000). Hexadecimal interpretations provide data analysts with a more compact method of listing and evaluating long binary sequences, as the interpretative scheme has a base of 16 and 16 digit symbols. Investigators should routinely evaluate files with a hexadecimal viewer, as some programs (Microsoft products, in particular) reuse memory blocks without modification. Although this does not allow viewing of these blocks in normal mode, hexadecimal views may reveal the content of these blocks.

Irrespective of interpretative scheme, data is stored in disks in fixed units. **Sectors,** the smallest physical storage unit on a disk, are arc-shaped portions of one of the disk tracks. Although the operating system determines the size of each sector, magnetic disks formatted for U.S. versions of Windows contain a standard 512 bytes (Symantec, 1997). Beginning at 1, sectors are numbered sequentially on a track-by-track basis. **Clusters,** also known as **file allocation units,** are comprised of one or more adjacent sectors, and represent the basic allocation units of magnetic disk storage. Although size varies with disk size, clusters represent the minimum space allocated to an individual *file* in DOS. Basically, clusters make it easier for operating systems to manage files, although some allocated space re-

---

[2]Though it is the most common, it must be noted that ASCII is not the only set of associations in use. Windows systems, for example, use the Windows ANSI code, while electronic organizers and personal information managers use a particularized modified version of ASCII. In addition, a two-byte code known as Unicode is increasing in popularity.

[3]For a comprehensive explanation of interpretative schemes, including Little Endian and Big Endian, floating decimal points, and the like, see Sammes, Tony and Jenkinson, Brian (2000). *Forensic Computing: A Practitioner's Guide,* Springer-Verlag: London.

mains unused in most cases. (Remember: space is allocated to files in specified units. Thus, a file will always be allocated at least one cluster even if it is only nine bytes.) Files, composed of one or more clusters, are the smallest unit that enables distinguishing one set of data from another, and may be looked at logically or physically for forensic purposes. The **logical file size,** for example, refers to the exact size of a file in bytes. In contrast, the **physical file size** refers to the actual amount of space that the file occupies on a disk. Such distinction is necessary in comprehensive investigations as it allows for the discovery of information found within that portion of unused space between the *logical end of a file* and the *physical end of a cluster* (i.e., **file slack**). (Although this concept may seem complex, it may be likened to a table in a restaurant in which a couple is seated at a table for four. Although the extra two chairs are empty, they constructively belong to those individuals until they are finished with their meal.) For example, two clusters will be allocated for a physical file of 2016 bytes. The excess space, or file slack[4], may contain the remnants of older files or other evidence, including passwords, old directory structures, or miscellaneous information stored in memory. (This is extremely important for investigative purposes, as most individuals who intentionally delete files in the hopes of hiding them from investigators do not realize that these remnants may include critical evidence.) *Compressed files* are those files which have been algorithmically compressed to save space.

The next level of data storage on a hard drive is known as a *partition.* Disk partitions are portions of fixed disks that the operating system identifies as a single unit (maximum of four). Letter designations are given to these entities that can be formatted for different file and operating systems.To increase the system's fault tolerance or speed file access, Windows NT and other operating systems may treat multiple partitions on different physical disk drives as a single disk volume (identified by a single drive letter). Every bootable hard disk includes one disk partition for any operating system it stores that may be used to start the computer. To allow the operating system to treat a single hard disk as multiple logical disks, the hard disk may have an "extended partition" that can be subdivided into a maximum of 23 additional logical disks. In other words, every hard disk drive has a primary partition or extended partitions, with one requirement. The partition of the "boot" drive where the operating system resides *must* be bootable. (Programs like Microsoft's FDISK or Norton's GDISK prepare a hard disk for use by creating partitions and logical disks. Partitioning creates a master boot record and **partition table** for the hard disk. Floppy disks do not require partitioning.)

Data Location

Once investigators can articulate the structure of fixed disk and identify the units of data, it is necessary to understand how to locate specific data contained therein for forensic purposes. On DOS-based systems, *File Allocation Tables* (**FAT**) are es-

---

[4]*File swap,* also important in forensic investigations, is that data which is stored on hard disk drive due to limited virtual memory (i.e., when working, if there is not enough space for all applications, data may be "swapped" in order to make room).

MASTER BOOT SECTOR/RECORD/PARITION TABLE

http://www.pcguide.com/ref/hdd/file/structMBR-c.html

Master Boot Record (MBR)

When you turn on your PC, the processor has to begin processing. However, your system memory is empty, and the processor doesn't have anything to execute, or really even know where it is. To ensure that the PC can always boot regardless of which BIOS is in the machine, chip makers and BIOS manufacturers arrange so that the processor, once turned on, always starts executing at the same place, FFFF0h.

In a similar manner, every hard disk must have a consistent "starting point" where key information is stored about the disk, such as how many partitions it has, what sort of partitions they are, etc. There also needs to be somewhere that the BIOS can load the *initial boot program* that starts the process of loading the operating system. The place where this information is stored is called the *master boot record (MBR)*. It is also sometimes called the *master boot sector* or even just the boot sector. (Though the master boot sector should not be confused with *volume boot sectors,* which are different.)

The master boot record is always located at cylinder 0, head 0, and sector 1, the first sector on the disk. This is the consistent "starting point" that the disk always uses. When the BIOS boots the machine, it will look here for instructions and information on how to boot the disk and load the operating system. The master boot record contains the following structures:

Master Partition Table: This small table contains the descriptions of the partitions that are contained on the hard disk. There is only room in the master partition table for the information describing four partitions. Therefore, a hard disk can have only four true partitions, also called primary partitions. Any additional partitions are logical partitions that are linked to one of the primary partitions. One of the partitions is marked as active, indicating that it is the one that the computer should use for booting up.

Master Boot Code: The master boot record contains the small initial boot program that the BIOS loads and executes to start the boot process. This program eventually transfers control to the boot program stored on whichever partition is used for booting the PC.

pecially important in this respect as they provide the mechanism for data configuration on a given medium. (This is not the same housekeeping strategy as NTFS under NT). Generally speaking, the FAT is the system used to identify and locate files on a disk. The 12-, 16-, and 32-bit designations used by DOS indicate how many bits the FAT uses to identify where on the disk (appropriate cluster numbers) a file resides. Literally speaking, every number contained within the FAT identifies a particular cluster. Information contained therein identifies: if the cluster is "bad" or available; if the end of a file is contained within; and points to the next cluster attached to a file. Originally created to manage space on floppies

(FAT12), the system was later extended to manage fixed/hard disks with FAT16 and was employed in DOS and older Windows systems. However, the system proved to be cumbersome, and failed to manage data economically. (As an example, if a partition size was 2GB, each cluster would be 32K. Thus, a file requiring 4K would result in 28K of slack space (32K − 4K = 28K). To remedy this waste, FAT32 was developed. Currently in use by most Microsoft products, except Windows NTFS, FAT32 is a more robust system which manages space more efficiently by utilizing smaller cluster sizes. Thus, less space is wasted, making data management faster and more efficient. (Unfortunately, this is bad news for investigators, because it reduces the slack space in which evidence is often found.) Generally speaking, the emergence of FAT32 is advantageous to users in two primary areas: 1) FAT32 systems can reallocate and change the size of the root directory; 2) FAT32 drives contain a copy of the boot record(s), which may make the system less prone to failure. There is no limit as to how large the root directory can be or where it can be located.

Partition Table

Like the FAT, the partition table describes every logical volume on a disk. In addition, it identifies corresponding locations, indicates which partition is bootable (only one partition may be bootable at a time), and contains the **Master Boot Record.**[5] Traditionally standard, newly improved software packages (e.g., Partition Magic, etc.) enable the manipulation of partition by even the least sophisticated user. This knowledge is extremely important in forensic investigations, as it enables users to hide entire partitions. Investigators unaware of this fact may be confused to see that the logical drive size is contrary to identified characteristics. Partition data is stored at physical: cylinder = 0; head = 0; sector = 1.

Data Management—Operating Instructions

The **boot sector** of a computer is located at the very first sector of the physical disk, or *absolute sector 0*. (Under WIN98, there are actually three boot sectors making up the entity.) It contains code that enables the computer to find the partition table and the operating system (Similarly, the first sector of every partition is referred to as the *partition boot sector*). The *Basic Input Output System* **(BIOS)** is a number of machine code routines stored in ROM which includes a variety of commands including those necessary for reading physical disks by sector. These commands are executed upon system booting. The first of these to be executed is referred to as the *bootstrap loader.*

---

[5]Some technical documents refer to the first sector on the disk as the master boot sector or master boot record, which contains the master boot code, which is the code that enables the computer to start to boot, and the partition table, which is a four-entry table.

BOOT UP SEQUENCE OF A COMPUTER (IBM CLONE)

1. ROM/BIOS
2. POST
3. Switches or CMOS data
4. Pathway or drive specifications—normally A: then C:
5. Master Boot Record ([Cyl = 0, Head = 0, Sec = 1)
6. Bootable Partition
7. Boot Record
8. Io.sys
9. DBLSPACE.BIN
10. MSDOS.SYS
11. CONFIG.SYS (optional)
12. COMMAND.COM (shell command in config.sys may change this)
13. *AUTOEXEC*.BAT (optional)

Data Integrity

Files may also be identified by a computer-generated (i.e., calculated) value known as a *Cyclical Redundancy Checksum* (**CRC**). This is especially important for forensic investigators as images may be validated by comparing the original CRC value with the imaged files. This process, initiated when data has been transmitted between computers, involves computer calculation on the data transmitted. Upon receipt of the data, an identical computation by the receiving computer is conducted. If the calculations reach different conclusions, the receiving computer will request the retransmission of data. This process may also be utilized on all storage media on which compressed data is stored. This verification process is especially important in criminal cases where validity of evidence is contestable.

MD5 HASH AS A VERIFICATION TOOL

Although there are an infinite number of files which may be created and stored on any given system, there is only a finite number of hash values available. Thus, it has been argued by some defense attorneys that the dawning of increasingly sophisticated machines will eventually lead to the creation of two disparate files with the same generated hash value. However, Brian Deering (NDIC) analogizes the chance of randomly generated matchng has values to hitting the Pennsylvania Lottery Super 6 − 5.582 × 10^{41} (or 558,205 billion, billion, billion, billion) times before this will occur. Thus, it does seem *computationally infeasible to produce two messages having the same message digest http://theory.lcs.mit.edu/~rivest/ Rivest-MD5.txt.*

MD5 Hash

Like the CRC discussed above, the MD5 Hash is a verification tool which may be employed in computer investigations. Developed by RSA, this 128-bit number is an identifier which acts as the equivalent of digital DNA. The odds that two different files have the same value is 2^{128}. Some forensic tools have utilities which search for particular files by hashes. HashKeeper™, a program developed by the NDIC (National Drug Intelligence Center), keeps a listing of a variety of known files. Investigators should develop their own hash files for their toolboxes. Keep in mind, investigators are usually interested most in the *unknown*. Thus, any mechanism which allows investigators to reduce the number of files for evaluation is a godsend.

CONCLUSIONS

The investigation of computer-related crime is increasingly necessary in today's technology dependent society. Administrative apathy and inadequate resources have resulted in poorly run investigations marred by an over-reliance on automated forensic programs or evidence contamination, corruption, or destruction. Although resources do not appear to be forthcoming, administrators must establish forensic computer science capabilities, evaluating the feasibility of partnering LE personnel with civilian experts and relying on the cooperation of corporate entities. Such collaboration is essential for the successful prosecution of computer-related crime. Proper training must begin with a basic understanding of computer structure and data management. Indeed, administrators must recognize that the practice of sending officers to one-week software certification courses may soon be self-defeating as forensic computer science garners credibility as a discipline.

TERMS DISCUSSED

ASCII	file allocation units	password protected
BIOS	file slack	physical drive
bits	head	physical file size
boot sector	hexadecimal	Read Only Memory
CD-ROM	hidden files	secondary storage
CD-RW	logical file size	sectors
clusters	Master Boot Record	semi-permanent
CRC (Cyclical Redun-	(MBR)	storage
dancy Checksum)	MD5-Hash	static memory
cylinder	overt files	tracks
FAT	partition table	volatile memory

DISCUSSION QUESTIONS

1. What are some of the traditional problems associated with computer investigations?
2. In the most basic sense, what is the structure of information storage?
3. How can the integrity of data be verified by investigators?
4. What does FAT represent, and why is it important in computer investigations?

DEVELOPING COMPUTER FORENSIC SCIENCE CAPABILITIES

9

INTRODUCTION

Now that we have identified some of the very basic components and terms associated with disk structure, we must now identify the procedures, policies, and practices that constitute the development of an effective forensic computer science unit within a department. Like other units found within LE agencies, the development and regular review of standard operating procedures **(SOP)** is essential as technology changes. As recommended by the IOCE (International Organization on Digital Evidence), these SOP should be reviewed annually, due the changing nature of technology. This ensures that personnel, training, equipment, and procedures continue to be appropriate and effective (SWGDE, 2000). In addition, these SOP should be consistent with current scientific knowledge as to emphasize validity and reliability.

The IOCE also suggests that these SOP should be clearly articulated and readily available. They include recommendations for discussing appropriate software, hardware, and specific investigative procedures. However, some experts argue that such formalization may be dangerous, arguing that written procedures may be subpoenaed and thus hazardous to LE investigations. Therefore, administrators must exercise caution in the preparation of such procedures. Every conceivable deviation or such should be documented—and language should be as flexible as possible. (Remember: every crime scene and criminal investigator is different. Thus, data recovery tools, data capture tools, data duplication tools, and data analysis tools vary per investigation.) Such a plan should address the development of a computer laboratory, pre-search routines, crime scene procedures, and evidence analysis. Although most departments do not have the resources to assemble a full-time investigative team, a "barebones" laboratory with the appropriate computer hardware, software, and storage capabilities should be developed as soon as possible, as it is literally impossible to successfully prosecute computer-related crime without proper analysis and custodial accountability. However, such development is often overlooked, because many departments have tended to focus on quick fixes, collecting digital evidence with no consideration of analysis capabilities or legal ramifications surrounding improperly handled data.

Like other sorts of criminal evidence, computer components and data should be kept under lock and key to maintain the integrity of the evidence in question. Such locks, like the one pictured here, prevent unauthorized access and may negate chain of custody challenges. (Courtesy of *SLED*)

While perfect departments in perfect worlds would immediately assemble the best (and most expensive) equipment and a library of software to rival Microsoft, law-enforcement agencies across the United States are not privileged with this luxury. As such, the following categories are not intended to be concrete—in fact, they are intended to represent the minimum requirements for an effective and efficient computer crime unit. In the software section, for example, readers should be aware that there are a variety of other tools available to computer crime investigators. Those discussed in the text are those that have been independently evaluated by the author unless otherwise noted. Such discussion is not intended to serve as an endorsement for particular products. In fact, investigators should test all equipment and software for themselves, as they will be required to testify as to their validity and reliability in court.

The importance of such validation cannot be overstated as past experience reveals that many investigators do not know the entire functionality of the software that they employ to recover data, proving immediately fatal to courtroom examination (As an example: During one test of a copy of files from a CD to a hard drive, XCOPY corrupted some data. But such changes may not be picked up by the verify option.)[1] In addition, the software programs discussed in this text are primarily reserved for forensic analysis of hard drives or removable media. Network analysis is outside the scope of this text. (It must be noted that complete forensic laboratories should also include a multitude of network specific software for ongoing investigations. Such software should be capable of tracing connections, identifying ISPs, pinging specific IP addresses, and the like.)

TRADITIONAL PROBLEMS ASSOCIATED WITH FINDING DIGITAL EVIDENCE

Unlike traditional investigations in which forensic experts are tasked with analysis of criminal evidence, computer-related investigations often require role multiplicity on the part of investigators. In fact, computer crime investigators are often forced to act as case supervisors, investigators, crime scene technicians, and forensic scientists. Such duality is further exacerbated by characteristics unique to digital evidence. First and foremost, digital evidence is especially volatile and voluminous, susceptible to climatic or environmental factors as well as human error. It may be vulnerable to power surges, electromagnetic fields, or extreme temperatures. Unlike traditional evidence in which analysis of small samples is utilized to preserve the totality of the evidence, assessment of digital evidence requires evaluation of the whole, making investigative mistakes quite costly. In fact, this characteristic may increase the potential of liability for criminal investigators if mistakes result in loss of critical data. Such is not the case with traditional evidentiary matters. (Mishandling of powdered substances or serological material rarely results in catastrophic damage to business operations, as does the destruction of business records or accounting spreadsheets). The sheer volume of digital evidence further complicates its recovery, making it virtually impossible to conduct on-scene analysis. As such, investigators often overlook the significance of certain material or seize information which is not included in the warrant application. (Imagine searching for a stolen diamond ring at Chicago's O'Hare international airport—securing the airport, ceasing all mobility, questioning all individuals present, searching every area, and releasing the scene in a timely manner.)

Digital evidence is also unique in its level of camouflage possibilities, lending itself to concealment by individuals desiring to hide information. In essence, computer ne'er-do-wells may hide incriminating evidence in plain sight without damaging its utility. This is in direct contrast to many types of traditional evidence (imagine hiding cocaine by mixing it with sugar.) In fact, the software community

---

[1]According to many experts, including Dan Mares, software works in the bell curve. This functionality is adequate for average users. However, investigators often confront extreme situations! Thus, it is essential for software to be tested and retested and retested, including as many extreme conditions as possible. Investigators should test their own software library for flaws, creating a range of files from zero bytes to a very large maximum file size. This allows investigators to testify that they are fully aware of the potential failures of their software, and where these flaws are likely to occur.

and other interest groups are actively campaigning and creating tools counter-productive to computer investigations. Traditionally, individuals well-trained in computers could recover files relatively easily, using tools such as Norton Utilities' Unerase, and such. It was a rare occurrence when systems and data were configured with multiple levels of security. The advent of encryption and steganography programs have made the process of recovering data increasingly complex. Currently, adequate tools exist to break through most of these layers. However, one look at hacker and civil libertarian pages reveals a new trend in software—ensuring privacy from all, but especially their self-identified nemesis, the government.

Self-destructive programs are also readily available for private consumption, allowing users to sabotage their own systems upon unauthorized access. This may be likened to a cache of explosives with a triggering mechanism. Unfortunately for law enforcement, these characteristics create an inauspicious environment for the standardization of procedures. Indeed, the method of analysis of computer evidence is always contingent upon case characteristics. In some cases, for example, it may be necessary to shut a computer off to prevent remote destruction, while in others, the action of disconnecting the power supply may result in irreparable damage to computer programs and corresponding data.

Finally, technology is outpacing law-enforcement training. In an ideal situation, investigative units would have individuals devoted exclusively to technological development and training and others equally dedicated to on-site analysis. The first group, of course, would be responsible for passing their knowledge on to their compatriots. Unfortunately, this is almost impossible. As we stated before, departmental resources often preclude adequate training. Even those departments that have substantial resources cannot devote a multitude of investigators to this task. In addition, until a plateau is reached in computer technology

Encryption—has long been used by government officials to protect national security. As far as computers are concerned, many private citizens have utilized encryption programs to protect their own sensitive information. In its most basic form, "encryption" refers to the process of converting a message from its original form ("plaintext") into an indecipherable or scrambled form ("ciphertext"). Most encryption programs use an algorithm to mathematically transform data, decipherable only to those individuals or entities holding an access key. This access key acts as a password. The security of encryption programs varies with the strength of the algorithm and the key.

Steganography—Like encryption, steganography involves the securing of information through the manipulation of data. Unlike encryption, which prevents access to specified data through the use of ciphertext, steganography is designed to hide the data from view.

Whenever possible, investigators should secure funding for digital cameras. *(Courtesy of SLED)*

(which does not seem likely in the foreseeable future), any training passed on would become obsolete moments after dissemination. Thus, significant problems exist regarding the discovery and analysis of digital evidence. Although not insurmountable, these problems are sure to plague computer crime investigators for years to come. However, the development of local, regional, and state computer crime laboratories may decrease these negative repercussions, but investigators may find justifying such expenditures as challenging as evidence recovery.

MINIMUM HOUSING REQUIREMENTS

The first step in the development of computer forensic capabilities is the construction of a computer laboratory. As with other areas in which forensic analysis is conducted, the allocation of private space that is forensically friendly is extremely important. Investigators should attempt to identify (and articulate) an environment that is comfortable to investigators, equipment, and evidence, alike. Once identified, investigators then face the daunting task of acquiring such space from chief executives. Investigators should concentrate their justifications on the necessity of protecting the expensive nature of the materials to be housed therein, and emphasize the vulnerability of electronic equipment. As always, justification arguments should concentrate on areas most important to the chief. One investigator, for example, successfully received the necessary space by arguing that the nature of the work (i.e., pornography, child exploitation, etc.) required privacy to preclude the possibility of litigious activity by coworkers offended (or possibly "sexually harassed") by such exposure. (It appears that the chief in this particular

> ## MINIMUM HOUSING REQUIREMENTS
>
> 1. Cipher combination locks
> 2. High-security combination safe
> 3. Heavy construction metal shelving for evidence
> 4. Bookshelves
> 5. Work areas including tables
> 6. Ergonomically designed adjustable height chair
> 7. Long-term storage capability
> 8. Environmentally controlled work and storage space

case did not want to knowingly create a potentially "hostile" work environment.) By focusing on the bottom line, like the potential expenses associated with replacing damaged components and defending sexual harassment cases, arguments may prove more persuasive to chiefs concerned with dwindling resources.

Investigators should identify the minimum spatial requirements for evidence storage as well as analysis, bearing in mind the sluggish nature of the criminal justice system. Such space should be privately contained and environmentally appropriate, free from dust, debris, corrosive materials, electronic hazards, and extreme temperatures. (Remember, the evidentiary value of computers in traditional evidence rooms has been inadvertently destroyed through carelessness, dust, or unhealthy climate conditions.) Cipher combination locks should be obtained to properly secure the area, as the absence of controlled entry may result in chain-of-custody challenges. Evidence storage areas should be additionally secured, and include fireproof housing. Both areas should include heavy construction metal shelving for the placement of evidence, and bookshelves for the number of manuals and documentary evidence associated with computer-related crime. As in traditional laboratories, appropriate work areas should be established with well-built tables and ergonomically designed adjustable chairs. (This is critical in forensic computer laboratories as the vast majority of analysis is conducted from a seated position.) In addition, all areas of containment should be climate controlled for temperature and moisture, providing a comfortable workspace for investigators and non-destructive environment for evidence.

MINIMUM HARDWARE REQUIREMENTS

Although the acquisition of computer hardware has become more reasonable in recent years, investigators should bear in mind that technology is changing at an alarming rate. Thus, any purchase could become obsolete in a relatively short period of time. As such, the acquisition of said equipment should be characterized by both parsimony and prescience, reserving some funds (whenever feasible) for

Mobile forensic machines like those employed by South Carolina's State Law Enforcement Division (SLED) enable investigators to image suspect media and analyze data on-site. *(Courtesy of SLED)*

the future. At the same time, lab architects should acquire as much forensic equipment as possible, including:[2]

- **Notebook with docking station**—allows investigators to add peripherals such as PSI and ESA cards as opposed to port replicators.
- **Full tower workstation with external drive support**—need full tower, not minicomputer.
- **Large monitor with dual system switch**—enables users to use one monitor for multiple stations at the same time.
- **Forensic disk duplicator.**
- **External Zip and Jaz drives with SCSI adapter.**
- **Tool kit**—screwdrivers, tape, etc. Some computers tend to have proprietary hardware necessitating special tools (e.g., Compaq screws).
- **High resolution, color laser printer.**
- **Assorted media.**
- **Digital Camera.**
- **Flatbed Scanner.**
- **CD-R Burner and media**—enables the inexpensive duplication of significant amounts of data (both evidentiary and laboratory support). Especially useful for routine cases in which small amounts of evidence can be encap-

---

[2]It must be reiterated that these are the *minimum* hardware requirements for a computer forensic laboratory. This list is not intended to serve as, nor does it include, a wish list of forensic equipment, as most local agencies are incapable of financing the acquisition of high-end forensic devices, such as a F.R.E.D.

sulated for courtroom presentation. In addition, it enhances the efficiency of forensic software duplication.

MINIMUM SOFTWARE REQUIREMENTS

As mentioned previously, the identification and analysis of digital evidence poses unique challenges to traditional investigators. Discovery of such information is extremely important for successful case disposition. While hardware provides the necessary framework for data acquisition and analysis, it is ineffective without corresponding forensic software.[3] (Remember: individual investigators should test all software which they employ, to enhance their credibility in court and to ensure that there will be no surprises.) Generally speaking, there are four broad categories of software tools necessary to equip a barebones laboratory:

1. Boot disks
2. **Data preservation,** verification, and duplication tools
3. Data recovery tools
4. Data analysis tools

Boot Disks

Literally speaking, *booting a computer* simply means to pull a computer up by its bootstraps or more succinctly to load a computer's operating system (OS). Prior to loading the operating system, a computer is largely unusable by most people. The operating system provides the medium for users and application software to communicate or interact. Most users do not know that a Power On Self Test **(POST),** initiated when the power supply is activated, is located in the Read Only Memory (ROM) of every computer. This test, which is relatively quick on most computers (increasingly so as computer capabilities are enhanced), ascertains the peripherals attached to a given system. These peripherals include all drives (floppy and hard), video hardware, memory, keyboard, mouse, modem, scanners, printers, etc. Once completed, this program informs the computer where to load the operating system from. Depending on system configuration, the computer then "looks" for the OS (aka *boot sequence*). On many systems, the computer first checks the floppy drive for this information. If not found, the computer then looks for it on the hard drive. Prior to analysis, investigators should consult experts for traditional system configuration.

Also, many computers allow users to change the boot sequence, enabling users to specify the hard drive or CD-ROM, bypassing the floppy. This is especially popular with computer-savvy criminals. Knowing that information contained in the swap file is only changed when traditional booting occurs, they may

---

[3]The author does not make any endorsements, express or otherwise, of individual software packages. Individual agencies should test all software to prepare themselves for courtroom examination. In addition, the lists provided here are far from comprehensive. Rather, they represent those software packages which are most popular.

intentionally reconfigure their system, making it harder to boot from a floppy. In addition, such individuals may manipulate *command.com* in order to circumvent investigations. (For example, a user may reconfigure a DIR into DEL or FORMAT so that an investigator using the suspect system's *command.com* could destroy evidence).[4] Thus, investigators should familiarize themselves with checking and changing CMOS setups controlling the boot-up sequence and always use a clean boot disk made from a clean system.

The importance of a boot disk lies not in starting the computer. Rather, **boot disks** enable investigators to bypass the operating system on the hard disk, enabling investigators to completely image the contents of the computer without interference. (Information contained in file slack may be overwritten during traditional booting processes.) With the advent of **Graphic User Interface** systems (hereafter, GUI, pronounced "gooey," like candy), the potential for overwriting potentially critical evidence has increased exponentially. GUI programs, like Windows™ (i.e., point-and-click systems), increase user friendliness while sacrificing available disk space. Thus, booting Windows™ is detrimental for computer forensic technicians (i.e., data found in free and swap space may be lost forever by traditional boot processes). As such, boot disks are perhaps one of the most important tools in an investigator's evidence kit and forensic laboratory. Investigators can make their own or purchase the entire range of DOS diskettes. In addition, a thorough preliminary investigation should reveal relevant software, drivers, etc. needed for booting from a floppy. Investigators should know, for example, any compression or storage-enhancing capabilities on a suspect drive. This knowledge enables investigators to adequately prepare boot disks. These disks need to include: write-blocking programs (those which "lock" the suspect drive, preventing any changes); any specialized software that involves hardware management, such as Super Store, Double Space, Sticker, etc.; any appropriate drivers, including scanners, printers, network interfacing cards, soundboards, DVD, CD-ROM or CD-R drives, etc.; network access and fax enabling software; keyboard enhancements; GUI's (i.e., Windows, Macintosh, etc.); supplementary file systems (i.e., HPFS, FAT, NTFS, NFS, etc.); and an updated virus scanner as a Terminate and Stay Resident (TSR) program. In addition, investigators may wish to include additional programs or batch files containing routine collection procedures based on case characteristics.

Data Duplication, Verification and Preservation Tools

Traditionally, suspect drives and disks were copied at the directory level. In fact, this practice is still utilized in the private sector by some IT personnel. However, this procedure lacks forensic robustness, as it only captures recognized files, ig-

---

[4]Even inexperienced users could boobytrap their system with relative ease. Perhaps the easiest way is to hack into a system's *command.com* file. This allows the user to alter internal DOS commands, while instructing the computer not to see it. For example, an individual could reconfigure the DIR (directory) command to DEL (delete). Thus, in the event that a third party attempted to display the contents of the drive using DIR, everything on the specified path would be erased. Although some forensic tools would defeat this, they would be ineffective in the hands of an inexperienced investigator.

Case scenario: In one case, an inexperienced investigator who wished to impress his chief with his computer "expertise" reformatted a suspect's hard drive erasing the entire contents, including potential criminal evidence of a child pornography ring. His first (of many) mistakes was acting under the assumption that the suspect was less intelligent than him. His second was not booting the drive from a clean disk. And his last, and most fatal, was attempting to copy the contents of the drive onto a Jaz with the COPY command. You see, the suspect had reconfigured his *command.com* file to prevent the copying of his files.

noring fragments of information that may be found in deleted files and slack space. **Imaging** programs are designed to correct this fault by providing a bitstream image of the suspect drive, bit-for-bit, byte-for-byte. It enables investigators to perfectly duplicate a suspect drive onto a form of removable media (type of media will vary based on the spatial characteristics of the suspect drive). This is essential for courtroom purposes. Investigators should *always* work from an im-

STEP-BY-STEP—MAKING A RELIABLE BOOT DISK

With the introduction of DOS (Disk Operating System), the process of making a bootable floppy became much easier. (This is not to suggest that other operating systems present the same ease.) The first step in determining the appropriate method is the determination of the file system preferred. Investigators need to identify the destination system for their investigation (i.e., ensure that their investigative software is compatible with the operating system). Investigators need to be completely familiar with the investigative software that they employ. If officers are unclear as to the investigative software or operating systems discussed, experts should be contacted.

Creation of a DOS boot disk is relatively simple. (Investigators should have several boot disks available. Variations of operating system, software employed, and associated hardware change the requirements for analysis.) Using MS-DOS 6.0™, insert a new (i.e., unused) diskette into a known (i.e., preferably departmental for court validation) computer. These diskettes should be new and unformatted. As such, the first command will instruct the computer to format the disk for the FAT file system and install MS-DOS™. The correct command is: **FORMAT A:/S.** This format will include *IO.SYS* and *MSDOS.SYS,* and allow investigators to access system, hidden, command, and read-only files.

Users cans also make boot disk in a GUI environment by going to START, then PROGRAMS, then MS-DOS prompt (*c:\windows* is the default), then type **<A:FLOPPY>**, and then depressing **<ENTER>**.

```
System memory has been flushed.

Captured Drive Identity
Manufacturer's model name: Maxtor 31536H2
Drive Serial Number: N21F8GYC

      *  N  2  1  F  8  G  Y  C  *
Total Drive Capacity: 14655MB, 30015216 sectors
Drive Physical Geometry: CHS=16383,16,63

Captured Drive Boot Record
Drive Logical Geometry: CHS=1868,255,63

Total Number of Partitions 2
Partition #1:
    Partition type primary NTFS (07)
    Partition volume label ""
    Partition starting sector number 63
    Total size of the partition 4128642 sectors
Partition #2:
    Partition type logical drive NTFS (07)
    Partition volume label ""

    Partition starting sector number 4128768
    Total size of the partition 25880652 sectors
Target Drive Identity
Manufacturer's model name: Maxtor 93652U8
Drive Serial Number: E803SEKC

      *  E  8  0  3  S  E  K  C  *
Total Drive Capacity: 34837MB, 71346240 sectors
Drive Physical Geometry: CHS=16383,16,63
```

Popular imaging programs like ByteBack and Safeback are relatively easy to use and are bootable from a floppy. *(Courtesy of James Doyle/NYPD, ret.)*

age, preserving the original evidence. This counters many defense challenges and negates the possibility of data destruction or manipulation (both accidental and intentional). (Remember: preservation of the original enables investigators to make additional images at their leisure.)

There are a variety of imaging products readily available for law enforcement. Investigators should carefully select at least two that they are most comfortable with. As with all forensic software, it is essential that multiple tools are available, as the tool that investigators most rely on will be the one that fails when they least expect it. Investigators should also consider the utilization of both independent *verification* programs and those that are included within imaging packages.[5]

---

[5]While some imaging tools provide mechanisms for checking their own output, investigators should be aware that many of them change the boot record. For example, Safeback's verification process changes the boot record when used with defaults. In fact, Safeback has been known to change bootable slave drives into non-bootable ones (Mares, 2000). Unfortunately, many investigators are not aware of this, as the program is designed to bypass boot records so that these changes are not readily apparent. Relatively speaking, these changes are inconsequential. However, investigators *must* know the entire process or face impeachment in court. Thus, investigators should test the software themselves, thoroughly preparing themselves for court testimony. Defense attorneys questioning investigators on these changes may inadvertently enhance the reputation of the investigator they are trying to destroy.

Verification programs are those programs which read disks a track a time, beginning with head 0 and progressing to the last head, calculating a algorithmic signature represented by unique file identifiers. While comparisons focusing on *Cyclical Redundancy Checksums* (CRC's) have traditionally withstood courtroom challenges, investigators should consider the utilization of programs capable of comparing MD5 Hashes, as they issue 128-bit identifiers (see Chapter 8).

Some of the most popular imaging software employed in forensic analysis includes: *Ghost*™, *ByteBack*™, and *Safeback*™. *Ghost*™, a relatively inexpensive program, allows investigators to make duplicate images of hard drives and logical partitions. However, many investigators caution that this program requires some knowledge on the part of users. For example, investigators need to know which switches to throw to create this pristine image. However, investigators may avoid possible mistakes by simply creating a batch file which specifies switch configuration.

ByteBack™, a program created by Tech Assist and available at *www.toolsthatwork.com*, is increasingly popular among LE agencies. In addition to providing bitstream images, *Byteback*™ is capable of addressing damaged media, scanning for physical flaws and reporting all bad sectors, and automatically reconstructing partition tables and boot records (i.e., will read physically damaged drive. If you command it to do zero retries, it will skip over damaged heads, sectors, etc. However, the user must invoke the reporting command, so it reports the action of skipping.) Because the program works in physical sector mode it also supports multiple formats, including Linux, Unix, NFTS, Fat16, and Fat32, and enables investigators to determine file formats and read partial sectors. Like *Ghost*™, it also fits on a standard floppy, making it especially desirable for onsite analysis. Unlike *Ghost*™ and some automated forensic packages, it allows for Direct Access and includes a four-terabyte limit, enabling investigators to bypass the BIOS and image everything together, respectively. Finally, it incorporates the MD5 standard into most program operations, and allows for verification at every step. One disadvantage to the program is that it will not write to streaming media (i.e., tape).[6] However, this criticism is becoming increasingly passé, as alternative media become more efficient.

By far, *Safeback*™ is the most popular imaging program utilized by investigative agencies. Created exclusively for forensic investigations, this package was not created as a disk manager. Like *ByteBack*™, this program copies both the physical hard drive and logical partition tables, as well as providing MD5 verification. Unlike *Byteback*™, this program will write to streaming media. However, this program, now owned by New Technologies, Inc. (NTI), is expensive, and only individual licenses are issued. (Unlike most forensic software companies which issue more generalized licenses, NTI reserves software for individual officers as opposed to agencies or machines.)

---

[6]Some investigators have reported that the program has problems with some SCSI drivers. However, the author did not verify this, and Tech Assist appears willing to correct any problem identified by users.

The imaging of diskettes is also extremely important in forensic investigations. Although many investigators utilize traditional methods of copying employing DOS's **<COPY>** command or Norton Utilities' *Diskedit*™, these programs do not provide bitstream images. *DISKIMAG*™, part of the *Maresware Suite*™ (also spelled Marsware), is designed exclusively for the imaging of storage media regardless of format or type. It enables investigators to maintain the same level of duplication for jurisprudential considerations involving diskettes. Unlike the DOS command **<COPY>,** it targets the entire diskette including file slack and multiple data streams. In addition, the image it creates uses the same serial number as the origination diskette. In addition it allows investigators to manipulate sectors and tracks on a floppy. *DiskEdit*™, on the other hand, will not allow this, and will produce a different CRC for copies and originals.

Independent verification programs which are popularly used for forensic purposes are also included in the *Maresware Suite*™, available at *www.maresware. com.* The first of these, *CRCKIT*™, provides 32-bit CRC and a 16-bit checksum of an individual file, and can be utilized to verify that data is free from manipulation. The second, *DISK_CRC*™, also produces a 32-bit CRC of a hard disk or a floppy, but also includes an option to create an MD5 (128-bit) hash of the disk. This program may be utilized to process entire physical drives, and is capable of processing a variety of operating systems, including Linux and MacIntosh. Finally, it can be used to process unusual disks that do not have standard boot sectors. However, it cannot be used on logical disks. Like other manual programs, either of these may be placed in a batch file.

Other imaging/verification possibilities include a new hardware device manufactured by Guidance Software, the makers of *EnCase*™ (discussed below). According to the manufacturers, *FastBloc*™, allows for direct data acquisition from Windows at speeds up to 2-3 times the speed of native DOS acquisitions. It allows for non-invasive Windows acquisitions and subsequent verification, as opposed to the more technical DOS environment. Finally, it allows for previewing information through a direct IDE connection, and enables the reading of IDE hard drives with a fast, flexible SCSI interface. However, images obtained with *FastBloc*™ are only compatible with the *EnCase*™ forensic software. Like NTI products, these products have been criticized for being expensive, and requiring regular (and costly) updates.

Almost all of these programs provide for the security of the hard drive during imaging. Investigators must also ensure that evidentiary originals are secured against accidental or intentional manipulation. *Write-blocking* programs are designed to prevent changes to a specified drive. *PDWRITE* from Digital Intelligence, for example, secures the drive under analysis—preventing any data from being changed. Other programs, designed primarily to disable the keyboard attached to a suspect machine, include Maresware's™ *DISABLE*™. When placed in the config.sys file or the autoexec.bat file of a bootable floppy, this program will disable all keyboard functions and alerts the user to the presence of seized evidence. (Placing it in the autoexec.bat of a WIN98 or higher boot disk does not guarantee automatic disabling.) More importantly, this program allows investigators to personalize such alerts, displaying individual contact information.

Data Recovery Utilities

Once verified images have been obtained, it will be necessary for analysts to re-cover digital information. Fortunately, much criminal evidence is obvious to even novice investigators. However, investigators should remember that unobvious places may also contain critical data. As such, forensic laboratories must have software capable of revealing obscure information. Like other areas of forensic software, investigators should employ both manual and automated programs to reveal hidden and deleted files and unlock encrypted files. By far, the cheapest, and most respected, manual disk management program available on the open market is *Norton Utilities*™. Manufactured by Symantec, *Norton Utilities*™ allows users to automatically or manually recover erased files (*Unerase*™); view and edit the entire contents of a disk or floppy in text, hexadecimal, or directory mode (*Diskedit*™); evaluate file slack (*Diskedit*™) and search for identified text. In addi-tion, it provides an extensive glossary and help files for novice users, and has both GUI and command line accessibility.

While *Norton Utilities*™ provides users with encryption abilities[7] and allows in-vestigators to restore deleted files and reveal those that are hidden, it does not provide the mechanism for password cracking to those same investigators. Thus, all forensic laboratories must include effective **password cracking programs.** Perhaps the best known and heavily touted among investigators is the *Password Recovery Tool Kit*™ (Access Data™). This program provides locksmithing tools for a variety of popular software, including: Microsoft Word™, Excel™, Lotus 1-2-3™, Paradox™, Symantec Q&A™, Quattro Pro™, AmiPro™, Approach™, QuickBooks™, ACT™, WinZip™, Professional Write™, DataPerfect™, Microsoft Access™, CCMail™, MicrosoftMail™, Quicken™, Dbase™, Ascend™, Lotus Organizer™, Microsoft BOB™, PKZip™, PGP™, Microsoft Scheduler™, VersaCheck™, Symphony™, Word Pro™, Microsoft Money™, BestCrypt™, Microsoft Outlook/Exchange™, Norton's Diskreet™, TaxWise™, Novell NetWare™, and WindowsNT™.

This program may be used independently or integrated with other forensic software. In addition, it allows for the importation of specialized word lists, and also provides for the exportation of word lists, enabling investigators to use a sus-pect drive against itself (i.e., by creating a dictionary comprised of every word on the suspect machine including passwords). Elcom™, a Russian newcomer to the market, also manufacturers a similar product also named *Password Recovery Tool kit*™ and provides for the purchase of platform-specific software. While the de-bate rages over which is the fastest, both run circles around non-forensic pass-word crackers. Unfortunately, neither has the capability to defeat passphrases (nor does any other product, as it would be virtually impossible to identify every pos-

---

[7]Norton Utilities allows users to create *virtually encrypted disks*. Every file in these disks is encrypted—displaying only gibberish until passwords are entered upon startup. Once a computer is shut down, these disks "close"—returning their contents to a nonsensical format. Thus, investigators who inad-vertently (or intentionally) shut off a machine without due regard may find it extremely challenging to regain access. Some software programs even come equipped with privacy safety mechanisms. Just like screen saver passwords, they require password access after an interval preset by the user.

Hardware imaging solutions, provide an audit trail for investigators
which may be introduced in court.
(Courtesy of James Doyle/NYPD,
ret.)

sible word combination). Although many administrators may initially balk at their respective price tags, their ability to quickly crack most encrypted files is essential for any computer forensic laboratory.

Compression Utility software is the final category of recovery software necessary for forensic laboratories. Popular programs like *WinZip*™ and *PKZip*™ enable users to mathematically compress data. Essentially used to compact data for ease in the storage and transmission of data, these programs are increasingly popular, as they increase the efficiency of network transfers of large files. Thus, forensic laboratories should have a collection of the most popular compression utilities, including, but not limited to, *WinZip*™ and *PKZip*™.

Data Analysis Tools

Only after data recovery and restoration may analysts turn to the arduous task of data analysis. As with other areas of computer forensics, both automated and manual products are available for evidence analysis. Generally speaking, automated analysis tools are designed to be useful to virtually anyone, including unskilled investigators. In the words of a seasoned examiner, "anyone can pick the low-hanging fruit" (Mykyten, 2000). Case characteristics and situational variables will dictate the level and sophistication of the search necessary. Certainly, cases involving threats to national security are such that an exhaustive examination of all available materials are all but mandated. Simple cases involving 40 counts of child pornography in which the criminal evidence clearly resides on a suspect's desktop may not require such detail. Unfortunately, many investigators have become too reliant upon such tools, and fail to comprehend the nature of their operations, leaving them susceptible to courtroom impeachment. Thus, it is essential that analysts understand the process of the software selected.

Regardless of approach, data analysis tools may be grouped in five general categories: indexing, text searching, viewers, time/data verifiers, and file managers. Perhaps the most commonly used analysis software in local agencies are *file viewers,* such as *Quick View Plus*™. These programs allow front-page viewing of multiple files (including those that are archived), enabling investigators to quickly identify questionable graphics files. Many may also be integrated into other programs, and are accessible through traditional menu programs in popular applications such as *Word*™ and *Excel*™. **Text Searching** software is also a critical forensic tool, enabling investigators to search for specific words, phrases, and strings appropriate to individual cases. *Time/***Data Verification Tools,** such as Maresware's™ *TRUETIME*™ verifies system time, and interprets julian dates.

Finally, file managers, like *XTreePro Gold*™, can be utilized to locate files on hard drives and networks. This program allows analysts to read the suspect programs and files in their native form. It also provides both ASCII and HEX , search by text, date, and file name. Perhaps the greatest strength in this program lies in date searches. While other programs allow for text and file searches, few allow investigators to search chronologically. This is especially important in cases which hinge on alibi defenses. It may provide investigators with lifestyle patterns of suspects or provide documentation which implicates or clears them in a given investigation (e.g., suspect claims s/he was at work, yet files created during those hours prove otherwise—check with employer). However, this particular program is no longer commonly available for DOS, and requires more than one boot disk. Thus, investigators may wish to invest in forensic suites, both manual and automated.

Maresware™, a software suite created by Dan Mares, a former criminal investigator with the Internal Security Division of the IRS, operates from a DOS boot or a DOS box (command window under a GUI OS), and includes a variety of forensic analysis tools including both 16 and 32 bit programs. Designed to sort voluminous files for evidentiary analysis, the suite enables users to manipulate awkward data files for ease in viewing and reporting—making sense of binary data and allowing for the importation of data into GUI programs like Excel™. In addition, it enables users to identify valid file extensions even if they have been manipulated and evaluate files in hexadecimal format, revealing hidden or corrupted data. Like automated programs, it allows the analysis of file attributes, but allows users to dictate operations—tailoring individual investigations to appropriate case characteristics. Generally speaking, the suite is both a comprehensive disk management and a forensic analysis tool. It includes a variety of programs which enable users to perform more sophisticated analysis of suspect data, while enhancing the efficiency of traditional command-level platforms. Perhaps most importantly, extensive training is available for interested parties, and customization of programs is often available upon request. Finally, individual programs are consistently updated at little or no expense—enhancing functionality for individual users and providing warm fuzzies for the chief.

EnCase™, by Guidance Software, is a fully automatic program touted for its user-friendly (some say idiot-proof) nature. A comprehensive package, *EnCase*™ includes mechanized imaging, verification, and analysis capabilities, all within a GUI environment. In addition, it automatically identifies and displays all graphical image files in gallery format, unzips and searches zip files, and provides a tree-like view of the registry. Newer versions provide for the integration of other programs, like password crackers, and enables hexadecimal viewing. By far the most popular program found in local agencies, *EnCase*™ is useful in the majority of routine investigations. Like other forensic packages, however, it is quite costly to law enforcement, and the price of upgrades is significant. In addition, it has been criticized for being too user-friendly, and providing a false sense of security to unskilled investigators.

The *Forensic Toolkit*™ by Access Data is similar to *EnCase*™ in that it provides for the searching, viewing, and analysis of digital evidence in a GUI environment. Although it does not provide imaging capabilities, it is compatible with images acquired with a variety of other packages, including *Encase*™, *Snapback*™, and *Safeback*™. Among other utilities, the program provides hashing verification, known file filtering, encrypted file identification, deleted file recovery, and INSO viewing (full and thumbnail). And, of course, the program is interoperable with Access Data's *Password Recovery Tool kit*™.

Miscellaneous Software

Once analysis has been completed, investigators must develop mechanisms for interpreting and relaying highly technical information to lay persons without losing robustness of evidence. While many automated programs present information in a digestible format, investigators should also have presentation-specific software (e.g. *PowerPoint*™, etc.) available for non-traditional or unique cases, as well as a collection of popular applications (e.g. *MSWord*™, *Excel*™, etc.). In addition, forensic laboratories should be equipped with *wiping software:* 1) so that criminal contraband can be permanently removed from suspect machines (after final disposition); and, 2) so that confidential, classified, or sensitive material can be permanently removed from departmental equipment prior to disposal through sale or recycling. Several programs meeting the Department of Defense standards regarding declassification of hard disks and cleansing of floppies which are available have already been discussed, including: Maresware's™ *DECLASFY*™, Tech Assist's™ *ByteBack*™, and Access Data's™ *WipeDrive*™. In general, these programs are designed to rewrite disks multiple times. *DECLASFY*™, for example, operates by writing the entire disk with hex zeroes then ones, then random characters or sym-

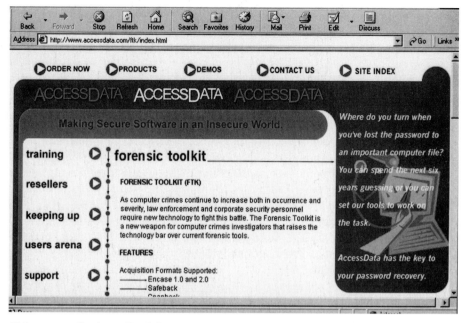

GUI programs like AccessData's Password Recovery Toolkit are popular among many investigators due to their user friendly nature and their password cracking capabilities, of course. *(www. accessdata.com)*

bols. (The entire procedure may be performed three times, resulting in nine over-writes.)

Virus software is also essential in a forensic laboratory, as it protects both evidentiary matter and departmental equipment from destruction. Relatively inexpensive, programs like *McAfee's Virus Scanner*™, catch traditional viruses and provide users with timely updates as new threats emerge. Finally, it is recommended that forensic laboratories employ anti-theft software on their equipment, as the replacement of such equipment is often outside the limits of departmental resources. Programs like Maresware's™ *BRANDIT*™, enables the branding of a physical hard drive with up to 5 lines of identifying information.

● MISCELLANEOUS DOCUMENTS AND LITERATURE

Perhaps the cheapest aspect in the development of a computer crime laboratory involves the compilation of a computer library, including a variety of miscellaneous hardware, software, and operating system manuals, most particularly DOS. Unfortunately for many investigators, a familiarity with DOS is essential for any computer forensic investigator. (Although DOS is anathema to many, the fact that most suspect computers (especially at the local level) operate with a DOS platform requires all investigators to immerse themselves in . the world of DOS, at least to the extent that they can navigate around a PC from a command prompt.

This is important for court challenges as to an investigator's capabilities and, perhaps more importantly, many crucial disk utilities do not work from a GUI (graphical user interface). In addition, GUI platforms should be avoided as much as possible, because they may write to the drive, destroying potential evidence). Thus, all computer laboratories should include a complete set of DOS manuals, and elementary DOS texts (e.g., *DOS for Dummies,* etc.). In addition, ASCII charts and other interpretative schemes should be available, as well as a computer-specific dictionary. These items aside, investigators should attempt to collect every software and hardware manual that is reasonably available. (One person's trash is another's treasure is especially true in computer forensics.)

Much of this information is readily downloadable from the Internet, and may be compiled on computer storage devices to save space and increase efficiency. Investigators should keep in mind that a future seizure may include offbrand, outdated, or otherwise unusual equipment. Finally, a comprehensive list of contact people which includes LE agents, legal counsel, private sector practitioners, and vendor representatives should be readily available.

CONCLUSIONS

Although departmental resources are often strained, the development of computer forensic capabilities is necessitated due to the emergence of a new type of criminal evidence. Increasingly, administrators are tasked with the development of such capabilities. Thus, computer investigators must identify the minimum requirements, including necessary housing and equipment. The information contained within this chapter should provide some guidance. Environmentally controlled work and storage space, recovery and analysis hardware and software, and computer training represent the minimal elements necessary for the establishment of a barebones forensic laboratory.

TERMS DISCUSSED

boot disk	imaging	steganography
data preservation	password cracking pro-	text searching
data verification tools	grams	write-blocking
encryption	POST	
Graphical User Inter-	standard operating pro-	
face (GUI)	cedure (SOP)	

DISCUSSION QUESTIONS

1. What factors should be considered by administrators in developing SOPs for computer investigations?
2. What are some of the problems traditionally associated with finding digital evidence?
3. Generally speaking, what are the five categories of software which may be useful in an investigation?

10

COMPUTER INVESTIGATIONS: PRE-SEARCH ACTIVITIES

Regardless of case characteristics, the construction and maintenance of a technologically-sound forensic laboratory is the foundation for successful case disposition. Once in place, a forensic laboratory is critical for the analysis of computer-related evidence and courtroom presentation. However, even the best forensic laboratory and analyst may be rendered moot if the investigation is conducted in a haphazard manner or exhibits disregard for legal specifications. Thus, pre-analysis activity is equally important and worthy of comparable attention to detail. This includes all pre-search activities (i.e., warrant preparation, intelligence gathering, assembling an execution team, planning the search, and assigning responsibilities) and on-scene processing (i.e., executing the warrant, securing the scene, evidence collection and preservation, and the transportation of evidence).

As stated, all phases of evidence identification, collection, preservation, and analysis are necessarily interdependent, and will directly impact the success of a criminal prosecution regardless of case characteristics. Computer crime investigators, like their non-technological counterparts, should remember that advance planning ensures the success of evidence collection. Proper intelligence gathering, for example, enables the investigative unit to collect the right experts, evidence containers, forensic software, and the like, while providing a blueprint for the corresponding warrant application. Thus, all investigators should carefully evaluate the scene in question, and familiarize themselves with case parameters. Tools specifically designed to facilitate the collection of this type of evidence include **Title III** of the Omnibus Crime Control and Safe Streets Act of 1968 and the **Electronic Communications Privacy Act,** which *requires* telephone companies, Internet Service Providers (ISPs), and other communication carriers to provide technical assistance to carry out a legitimate law-enforcement mission. Technological aspects notwithstanding, investigators may also rely on proven techniques for intelligence gathering, such as surveillance, undercover reconnaissance, informants, criminal histories, known photographs, and the like. Utility checks or architectural archives, for example, may be helpful in securing blueprints, floor plans, or maps of the area in question—essential not only for scene security, but also for their illustration of electrical and telephone outlets.

As much as possible, an investigator should attempt to determine the location, size, type, and number of computers at a suspect scene. This is especially critical in voluminous searches for warrant preparation. **Dumpster diving** (i.e., the processing of trash) may provide a wealth of information in developing a schematic of suspect machines as individuals, even those criminally minded, will often discard this type of information or even incriminating evidence. In addition, their refuse may be helpful in gathering passwords or personal information on suspects. Investigators should be cautioned that even the most innocuous of material may provide assistance in a computer crime case (i.e., packaging material, discarded media, system reports, software manuals, post-it notes, social facts for password cracking, etc.).

Social engineering and **informants** may also be used to secure this type of information, providing investigators with pertinent information such as type and number of computers and storage devices, operating systems employed, as well as schedules of applicable personnel and their personal histories. Surreptitious role-playing may be especially effective, as individuals routinely give out sensitive information to representatives of the telephone company, service or security provider, or computer/network support staff. Once this information is obtained, investigators should prepare their tool kit accordingly—adding additional media, cords or connections, and appropriate drivers to their boot diskettes. However, this does not suggest that other items be removed! Rather, investigators should take the opportunity to double up certain types of media known to be at the scene. Remember, the best time to get the equipment needed is *before* you arrive!!

WARRANT PREPARATION AND APPLICATION

Intelligence gathering is critical to the development of a comprehensive warrant. Operating systems, storage devices, and hardware specifications must be included in warrant applications. Such articulation insures that searches are tailored to the particulars of the case at hand, and that evidence collected within the parameters of the warrant will withstand future judicial scrutiny. As with other issues in the investigation of computer-related crime, there are no givens in computer search warrants. Each case will vary based on scene characteristics and corresponding judicial jurisdiction. Although they are within the same system, Federal circuit courts have issued widely differing opinions. Thus, investigators must be aware of the corresponding legislative and jurisprudential climate in their area, and structure their application accordingly.

As warrants provide a cornucopia of legal issues at the trial level, the importance of warrant preparation cannot be overstated. Thus, any warrant application should be reviewed by as many specialists (i.e., computer investigators, legal counsel, etc.) as possible prior to magistrate approval. This ensures that it will include all of the relevant protections and language. In addition, it ensures that all equipment, media, and incidentals which may prove evidentiary are included. Finally, it breeds a familiarity on the part of the investigator which ensures judicial approval. (Unlike other criminal search warrant applications, which are routinely processed without much scrutiny, investigators should painstakingly point out the essentials to any judicial officer. This includes explaining terminology and defining case characteristics. This makes the warrant itself more defensible in court. However, it does not negate the possibility of issues related to the actual execution of said warrant.) Remember, the first step in the preparation of any warrant application is the operationalization of the crime itself and, more specifically, defining the role of the computer in it. Such characterizations necessarily outline the scope of the corresponding search and seizure and are essential for the establishment of probable cause.

Probable Cause

As in non-computer cases, three elements of probable cause must be clearly articulated to an appropriate magistrate in order to secure a warrant: **probable cause** that a crime has been committed; *probable cause* that evidence of a crime exists; and, *probable cause* that extant evidence resides in a particular location. Thus, successful applications clearly demonstrate the rationale for the criminal investigation and the justifications of the requested search and/or seizure. Such considerations will dictate the scope of the warrant. For example, demonstrations that the computer in question represents the instrumentality of the crime will provide investigators with broader search powers than will one in which the computer was simply a repository of evidence. It is recommended, then, that investigators clearly establish not only the role played by a suspect computer or its components, but any reasonable role *they might have played*. This will grant them greater discretion in the search and seizure of equipment. In cases of child pornographers, for example, investigators could reasonably argue that the seizure of the defendant's monitor and printer is necessary to view the images as the defendant would. (It is strongly recommended that investigators attempt to include graphic files in all search warrant applications as a cornucopia of child pornography is often found inadvertently. In non-pornography cases when the original warrant is predicated on criminal behavior in which evidence is not normally found in graphic images, examiners may be able to articulate their rationale for looking at these types of files, by explaining methods of hiding data through file extension manipulation, steganography, and the like.

ON-SITE VS. OFF-SITE SEARCHES

Based on case characteristics, investigators must determine if on-site or off-site searches will be conducted. Each type has its advantages and disadvantages. On-site searches allow interviewing of witnesses based on developing evidence, yet may be impossible if there are multiple computers or large drive computers or excessive media. On the other hand, off-site searches allow investigators to proceed at their leisure, ensuring that evidence is not overlooked. However, legal issues may arise. Thus, investigators must clearly articulate (prior to scene arrival) what items are to be seized and which require on-site evaluation.

Seizing Equipment

Probable cause notwithstanding, investigators must also justify the **seizure** of equipment which does not necessarily represent an instrument of the crime. As warrants are issued under the provisions found within the Fourth Amendment, it is essential that investigators clearly substantiate any requests for seizures of equipment. This will minimize claims of unconstitutional deprivations. It is highly recommended that investigators request explicit permission to seize all hardware and storage devices that are constitutionally justifiable as on-site analysis might negate the utilization of some forensic approaches. (Investigators should be aware that such requests are often denied in cases where equipment is essential for business operations.) As always, fruits of the crime, criminal contraband, and those items criminally possessed may be seized without judicial authority.

No-Knock Warrants

If exigent circumstances dictate it, a request for a "no-knock" warrant should be included in the application. As always, exigent circumstances would include the nature of the offense (violent v. non-violent), the potential for evidence destruction, the sophistication and maturity of the target, and the absence of resident. With the vulnerability of computer data, investigators should be able to present a case to the magistrate for rapid entry if the suspect has prior knowledge of the search or if they have the technical expertise to destroy evidence. Although these types of warrants are much harder to justify and are closely scrutinized by the courts, investigators should attempt to obtain one in any situation in which case characteristics dictate it.

Secondary/Multiple Warrants

In many cases involving computer-related evidence, multiple warrants may be required. In cases of stolen components, for example, the *contents* of the suspect computer would fall squarely outside the boundaries of most applicable warrants. Additional warrants may also be necessitated in cases where investigators inadvertently uncover evidence of a secondary crime not included in the original warrant. For example, investigators searching a computer for drug-related spreadsheets who inadvertently uncover images of child pornography will need to obtain a **secondary warrant** to search for additional images. (Although many investigators have attempted to apply the "plain view" doctrine to such material, the courts have not agreed. *U.S. v. Carey* (172 F.3d 1268; 1999 U.S. App. LEXIS 7197; 1999 Colo. J. C.A.R. 2287.) In fact, secondary or multiple warrants are quite common in computer-related investigations, and investigators should be encouraged to seek additional judicial permission whenever the applicability of the original warrant is questionable.

Multiple warrants are also encouraged in cases involving networked computers. However, this may be problematic as investigators may be unaware of the physical residence of the storage facility. If unknown, investigators should inform the magistrate that there may be an additional location. In some cases, magistrates will agree to expand the scope of the warrant to include non-specific areas contingent upon discoveries at the scene. In those cases where such permission is denied, investigators should request additional warrants once the physicality is determined. As a general rule, investigators should raise the possibility of off-site storage in the original warrant to strengthen any subsequent applications. Finally, additional warrants may be necessitated in cases involving locked or encrypted files, as heightened expectations of privacy apply. This is true even in warrantless consent searches if a suspect refuses to identify the password for protected areas.

Summarily, investigators should be cautioned against broad or generalized on-site searches. Warrant applications should be characterized by a degree of specificity such that a reasonable officer can clearly differentiate between searchable and non-searchable areas. Although some investigators proclaim the merits of vagueness and obfuscation, suggesting that this increases their investigative authority, such generalities may lead to the judicial nullification of the original warrant. Remember: it is far easier to obtain a secondary warrant based on emerging facts, than to build a case in which all of the evidence has been discarded due to a faulty warrant. (Luckily, many criminals will commingle criminal evidence or contraband and legitimate documents, an area outside the umbrella of Fourth amendment protection.)

PLAN PREPARATION AND PERSONNEL GATHERING

The case supervisor should develop a preliminary plan of attack prior to assembling the relevant investigators. Once a team is in place, a brainstorming session(s) which exhaustively analyzes all of the issues involved in the particular case should be held to clarify roles and responsibilities and generate a comprehensive strategy. As always, written plans are highly recommended as they enable investigators to study them in depth, providing them with a global perspective of the mission at hand, while clearly delineating individual tasks. (It is also recommended that these plans be accompanied by bulleted checklists and marking instruments, as mechanisms for individual accountability have proven most effective in other areas.) At a minimum, such plans should follow the five-paragraph military order **SMEAC** (see box), and will vary depending on case characteristics determined during preliminary intelligence gathering.

On-Scene Personnel

As with traditional investigations, the deployment of personnel and the allocation of responsibilities are critical to the success of any investigation. In computer-related investigations, there are seven general categories of players. It is important to note that these categories are not mutually exhaustive or exclusive, and certain individuals may experience duality of expectations. In addition, the list provided is intended to serve as an optimal guideline. However, investigators

S.ituation—clearly define the who and what of the investigation. This includes number of individuals and computers, types of equipment, geographical location, and perhaps most importantly, the background of the suspects and any dangerous situations which may arise.

M.ission—what is the optimal case scenario? What do investigators want to happen? For example, is it desirable to conduct the search while others are present? If so, surveillance prior to arrival is necessary to ascertain prime hours.

E.xecution—How will the mission be accomplished?

A.venues of approach and escape—How will investigators enter the scene? How will investigtors exit? In the event of an emergency, what is the safest escape route? Where should the media be directed to? Remember that all cases are different. Some may require the use of SWAT. In those cases, civilian personnel should be kept away from the scene until it is secure. Case supervisors should provide detailed maps to investigators prior to scene arrival. Preferably, these maps should include the location of doors, elevators, obstacles, parking facilities, and the like. Suspects or suspect equipment should be clearly identified on each map.

C.ommunications—How will investigators communicate at the scene? How will investigators communicate to the department? Who is the primary point of contact? All of these things are extremely important in any criminal investigation. But in computer cases, where cellular phones and traditional radios may create electromagnetic fields and static electricity, it is essential.

should recognize the necessary limitations imposed by departmental resources, and plan accordingly.

Case Supervisor(s)

Without exception, on-scene supervisors should be the most experienced, with minimum qualifications including: acting as an investigator in a variety of previous cases and situations; the ability to assume control and command respect; and the ability to effectively communicate to varying populations in a professional and articulate manner. In departments, which do not have experienced computer investigators, assignment of a civilian expert and experienced criminal investigator as co-case supervisors is recommended. (Although this kind of situation has proven incendiary in other types of cases, most officers are willing to defer to the technological expertise of computer experts.) Individual responsibilities for this position(s) include, but are not limited to: information dissemination; interaction with media; personnel scheduling and team compilation; equipment preparation; and, of course, overall supervision. Both LE and civilian experts employed in this capacity should remain onsite until scene closure. (Some texts argue that civilian experts are unnecessary beyond initial entry and scene securement.)

Arrest Team

Although individuals involved in computer crime are often dismissed as nonviolent or physically weak, all execution teams should be prepared for the worst-case scenario. Certainly case characteristics may indicate a lower vigilance threshold, but all executions should include an armed contingent experienced in arrest situations. This team's responsibilities should include arresting suspects, and subsequent custodial transportation.

Scene Security Team

Usually comprised of patrol officers, this team's primary responsibility lies with scene security. As in non-computer criminal investigations, the ability to prevent evidence contamination should be considered a top priority. As such, it is important that these individuals create a visible (preferably uniformed) barrier against scene contamination, evidence destruction, and media impropriety. Although this is more often than not a thankless task, the members of this team should be carefully selected by the team leader.

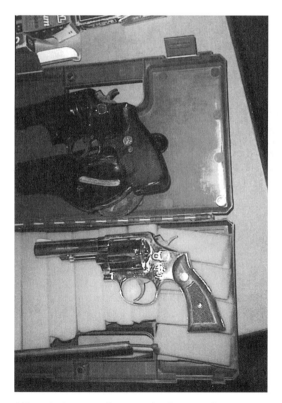

Although they are often perceived as non-dangerous, many computer criminals pose the same risk as traditional suspects. These guns, found in a computer-related search, prove that investigators should be wary of all suspects, not just those on the street. *(Courtesy of James Doyle/NYPD, ret.)*

Interview and Interrogation Team

Although the number of individuals assigned to this team will vary based on case characteristics, this team should be comprised of members experienced in information gathering. As the name implies, this team is responsible for interviewing witnesses and interrogating suspects. As such, it is essential that these individuals possess exceptional communication skills, especially because the traditional interviewee in these cases may have advance warning. The importance of an adequately staffed interview and interrogation team in computer-related investigations cannot be overstated. In fact, many child pornographers have confessed at the scene when confronted with evidence of their activity, while others have willingly provided passwords and the like to avoid possible damage to their equipment. (Interestingly, many computer criminals do not realize the legal ramifications of their actions, naively believing that their computers will be returned to them unchanged and that their lives will return to normal.)

Sketch and Photo Team

Like the interview and interrogation team, individuals assigned to this team should be carefully screened for investigative experience. These individuals should be as meticulous as possible, as these sketches may be subpoenaed. In addition, their documentation may be used for recreation or reconstruction purposes. Their responsibilities include diagramming and photographing the entire scene, including criminal evidence, and, when possible, videotaping the activities of the on-scene investigators.

Physical Search Team

Case characteristics including the size of the crime scene and the multiplicity of machines will dictate the number of individuals assigned to this unit. In large searches, one officer per room should suffice, as case supervisors should limit the number of personnel on a scene to the absolute minimum to curtail possible scene contamination. The primary responsibility of this team is to identify and mark any and all potential evidence. They are *not* responsible for the collection of such evidence. These individuals should be well versed in types of computer evidence, possible locations, and such. (Although some authors (e.g., Clark & Diliberto, 1996) suggest that these officers do not need to be "computer experts," this author suggests that all team members be selected for their familiarity with computers.)

Seizure Team

Unlike other areas of the investigative unit, assignment to this particular responsibility should be reserved for experienced computer investigators! These individuals are responsible for **bagging and tagging.** Due to the fragility of evidence, it is absolutely essential that individuals handling this step be experienced computer investigators. This team is responsible for imaging the drive, dismantling the computer, and labeling and recording of all relevant evidence. This team should be present at all times during scene processing. (Remember—seizure is the *last* step!) Ideally, this team is comprised of at least two investigators who have extensive computer forensic training. Since this is not possible in most departments, the team should be comprised of at least one seasoned investigator and one computer expert. This is important because computer experts are not usually aware of the legal aspects of investigations, particularly those dealing with chain of custody and the preservation of criminal evidence. (Many civilians are experts at finding hidden data, but are unable to articulate the process implemented.) Thus, officers must be present to ensure proper documentation.

Regardless of team assignment, it is imperative that notification of responsibilities and scheduled activities occur as soon as possible. Such forewarning, including written instructions and expectations, enables team members to prepare themselves and collect the necessary equipment, as well as providing an opportunity for asking questions. Final pre-raid briefings should address any concerns, and should include cautionary admonitions. All team members should be reminded that technological climate aside, traditional procedures for crime scene investigation remain sacrosanct. Thus, officer safety and evidence preservation, respectively, remain top priorities, and conventional distrust of suspects should guide their on-scene behavior.

PREPARING A TOOLKIT

As with non-computer related investigations, the preparation and maintenance of a forensic toolkit is essential for task accomplishment. Such toolkits should be compiled with materials and equipment found within the in-house forensic labo-

As stated throughout the text, the investigation of computer-related crime is similar to the investigation of non-computer-related crime. Thus, much of the material necessary for traditional scene processing, including evidence labels, is also necessary in computer cases. *(Courtesy of James Doyle/NYPD, ret.)*

ratory, but are hardly universal. Case characteristics and scene demographics uncovered during intelligence gathering will dictate the specific elements to be included, as well as the necessary quantity. **Toolkit** preparation should always be initiated with the collection of basic materials found in traditional criminal investigations, and culminate with the assemblage of those unique to computer investigations. Investigators should remember that the value of equipment is only appreciated when it is not available. (Remember, it is impossible to be *too* prepared, so it is not only acceptable, but preferred, to compile more equipment than necessary.)

Traditional Equipment

1. **Evidence Tape**—used to mark the perimeter of the crime scene, it not only prevents entry by individuals external to the investigation, but also induces caution among on-scene personnel.
2. **Packing Tape**—used to secure evidence containers.
3. **Evidence storage containers and labels**—although standard evidence labels are appropriate for computer-related evidence, special care should be devoted to the packaging materials used in these investigations, as evidence may be especially vulnerable. (Although the optimum packaging material (i.e., original) is often unavailable, investigators may solicit similar materials from computer stores, large corporations, and universities.) Additional packaging materials include: diskette sleeves for protecting floppies; a multitude of folding boxes and paper bags; and anti-static peanuts.
4. **Miscellaneous writing and labeling materials**—used to label evidence, maintain the chain of custody, and document scene characteristics.
   a. Materials to sketch the crime scene (i.e., graph paper, ruler, pencils, etc.).
   b. Blank forms, including inventory, evidence booking, search warrant templates, etc.
   c. Writing utensils (pens, markers, highlighters, etc.). Indelible markers, such as laundry pens, are especially useful for marking floppies.
   d. Labels.
   e. Note cards (usually 3 × 5).
   f. Stick-on circles for marking evidence.
   g. Adhesive numbers or large labels for marking cards and cables.
5. **Sanitary materials**—used to prevent evidence contamination, and to protect investigators from unsanitary environments. Such materials include: rubber gloves, bleach, and disposable wipes.
6. **Flashlight**—used in the event of a power outage or to illuminate dark areas (particularly useful under desks, behind equipment, and the like).
7. **Extra batteries**—used to ensure continuity of investigative equipment, including, but not limited to: cameras, flashlights, cellular telephones, tape recorders, etc.)
8. **List of contacts**—(including software support, computer experts, hardware manufacturers, magistrate's office, support organizations (HTCIA, FCIC, etc.).

9. **Mobile carts or evidence transport units**—used to transport multiple containers and heavy equipment and transport investigative equipment.

10. **Wireless communications**—used as mode of communication and point of contact while on-scene. (Investigators should not use suspect phone.)

11. **Photographic Equipment (camera, batteries, extra film)**—used to produce visual documentation of crime scene. Such equipment should be provided to investigators as well as scene photographers, while the latter should be equipped with magnification capabilities. As always, scenes should also be videotaped if departmental resources permit.

12. **Non-magnetic screwdrivers and hex wrenches**—used to open computer boxes. Often overlooked, such tools are necessary for getting to the guts of the computer. However, investigators should be aware that in rare cases electric screwdrivers emit enough magnetic fields to erase data, and manual tools are preferred.

13. **Small diagonal cutters**—used for cutting nylon wire ties which are commonly utilized to secure multiple wires for organizational purposes.

14. **Hammer or nail puller**—used for removing nails which secure multiple wires.

Computer-Specific Equipment and Materials

1. **Multiple boot disks**—used to avoid self-destructive programs employed by the suspect and to minimize changes to a suspect drive (i.e., during the routine boot process, disk space is reassigned and file slack may be overwritten). It is highly recommended that investigators maintain custom boot disks which will boot to controlled specifications. At an absolute minimum, investigators should have a Windows 98 boot disk with imaging capabilities.[1] Investigators should include a Terminate and Stay Resident (TSR) virus shield on their investigative systems and on any boot disks taken to the scene. Some examples include McAfee's *VSHIELD* and *FPROT*. Investigators should remember to update this file on a regular basis. Unlike other programs traditionally found on boot disks which do not necessitate updating, the virus protection should be the most current. Boot disks should also include storage enhancement programs and popular drivers for computer peripherals. A custom boot disk should boot to controlled specifications.

2. **Backup hardware and miscellaneous computer peripherals**
   a. External devices and corresponding media to capture image of suspect drive. May vary based on case characteristics (i.e., size and number of sus-

---

[1]**Reminder:** The importance of a book disk does not lie in starting the computer. Rather, boot disks enable investigators to bypass the operating system on the hard disk, enabling them to completely image the contents of the computer without interference. (Information contained in file slack may be overwritten during traditional booting processes.) With the advent of Graphic User Interface systems, the potential for overwriting potentially critical evidence has increased exponentially. GUI programs, like Windows, increase user friendliness while sacrificing available disk space. Thus, booting Windows is detrimental for computer forensic technicians—data found in file slack and swap space may be lost forever by traditional boot processes.

pect drives, amount of data, etc.) and departmental resources. Such devices may include: Bernoulli drives, optical disks, Jaz drives, Zip drives, and secondary hard drives.

b. Color scanner—used to record potential evidence which may not be seized.

c. Color printer and an assortment of computer paper—used to capture potential evidence residing in print buffers in those cases where on-scene printers are not included within the specifications of the applicable warrant. Printers may also be used to print additional forms, labels, and the like.

3. **Anti-virus software**—used for the documentation and validation of suspect machines and the prevention of infection of forensic machines.

4. **Imaging software**—used for the preservation of the original evidence. As mentioned previously, all forensic analysis should be conducted on the forensic image, ensuring the integrity of the suspect data.

5. **Application software.**

6. **Forensic software**—used for on-site evidence analysis (discussed in greater detail in the previous chapter).

a. **Viewers**—enable investigators to quickly scan the contents of large numbers of computer files, providing, among other things, a rapid mechanism for identification of criminal contraband.

b. **Text editors**—enables investigators to quickly search for keywords applicable to the current investigation.

c. **Hex editors**—enables investigators to view files in hexadecimal formats and quickly search for files which may have been intentionally manipulated or which have been erased or deleted.

d. **Password crackers**—enable investigators to circumvent many security measures employed by the suspect.

e. **Verification software**—used to demonstrate the validity of the imaged drive.

f. **Time/date programs**—verify the system time on the suspect machine.

g. **Wiping programs**—enables investigators to completely delete (i.e., wipe) files representing criminal contraband if seizure is not possible.

h. **Locking programs**—ensures data integrity, preventing intentional or accidental manipulation of data.

i. **Fuzzy logic tools.**

j. **File cataloging and indexing**—compartmentalizing evidence for ease in further analysis and organization.

k. **Recovery**—enables investigators to retrieve data from corrupted media, including hidden and deleted files.

7. **Extra media**—used for a variety of purposes including: copying potential digital evidence and creating additional boot disks.

8. **Extra cables, serial port connectors, and gender changers**—used for connecting forensic units to suspect machine.

9. **Extension cords and/or power strips**—used to connect machines to power supplies.

10. **Surge protectors and/or UPS (uninterruptible power supply)**—used to ensure electrical and telephonic continuity to prevent possible destruction of computer data.

11. **Open purchase order**—although difficult to secure, optimal situations provide open purchase orders as the unexpected may occur. While investigators are strongly encouraged to provide for any possible situation and prepare investigative toolkits accordingly, they are often confounded by those situations which they had deemed *impossible*.

CONCLUSIONS

Although many departments lack sufficient resources to adequately staff full-time computer crime units, traditional procedures for criminal investigations may be utilized by supervisory personnel in high-tech cases to ensure proper evidence collection and analysis. Partnering civilian computer experts with seasoned criminal investigators enables even the smallest department to confront computer-

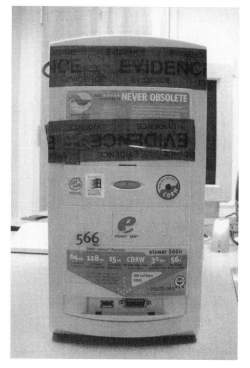

To avoid accidental contamination of evidence, drive openings should be inaccessible. Evidence tape, included in investigator toolkits, may accomplish this goal. (Courtesy of James Doyle/NYPD, ret.)

related crime. Careful planning and meticulous oversight, negating many disadvantages created by budgetary constraints, provide a platform for successful prosecution.

TERMS DISCUSSED

bagging and tagging
dumpster diving
Electronic Communications Privacy Act
hex editors

informant
no-knock warrants
probable cause
secondary warrants
seizure

SMEAC
social engineering
Title III
toolkit

DISCUSSION QUESTIONS

1. What does the acronym SMEAC stand for, and how does it apply to computer investigations?
2. What are the seven general categories of personnel which are necessary for crime scene processing in computer-related cases? What roles and responsibilities characterize each?
3. What items should be placed in on-scene toolkits? Which are mandatory and which will vary due to case characteristics?

11

ON-SCENE ACTIVITIES

The investigation of computer-related crime requires the same level of preparation and evaluation as do traditional ones. They are neither more intensive nor more demanding on average than non-technological investigations. They simply require different skills on the part of investigators. As such, the investigative process should mirror conventional methods. Careful handling of evidence, attention to detail, and professionalism should remain paramount considerations, and the unexpected should be expected in all cases. (As discussed in the preceding chapter, pre-search activities often establish the solvability of a particular case. Haphazard investigations are rarely successful, regardless of case content.) Every investigation, for example, should begin with the development of a plan to accomplish the mission at hand, as well as to secure personnel and evidence. Minimal requirements of such plans should include: approaching and securing the crime scene; documentation of scene activities; discovery and identification of potential evidence, the collection and retrieval of such material; and, finally, the processing or analysis of potential evidence.

APPROACHING AND SECURING THE CRIME SCENE

The first step taken at the majority of crime scenes involves the execution of the search warrant (i.e., *knock, notice, and document*). As in other cases, investigators must announce their presence, their interest, and their intentions, unless extraneous considerations exist which suggests heightened vulnerability of evidence or enhanced risk to the security of team personnel or civilians. (Careful pre-search planning should reveal potential threats, and requests for no-knock warrants should be included in warrant preparation.) To prevent any questions as to their practices, it is highly recommended that this (and the remainder of the investigation) be videotaped whenever possible. Such documentation provides authenticity to their claims, and more importantly, refreshes the memory of investigators when final case disposition is extended. This process can be called *Knock, Notice, and Document*.

The next step in any investigation is the securing of the crime scene. As in non-computer cases, scene security is perhaps one of the most important, yet often overlooked, factors in the successful prosecution of a suspect. Questions arising from chain of custody, scene contamination, and officer error can all but negate the most compelling of scientific evidence. Thus, it is essential that due regard be given to this step of the investigation. Unlike traditional crime scenes which are often identified and secured by patrol officers, the majority of computer-related crime scenes are such that advanced planning is possible. As such, scene security measures are often tailored to unique case characteristics and are determined prior to scene arrival. Knowledge of case characteristics also enables investigators to determine their method of evidence canvassing (i.e., circular, grid, sector, or triangulation).

Upon scene, several actions must take place simultaneously at an absolute minimum (Remember: there are no absolutes in computer forensics, or police work in general for that matter. Case characteristics will dictate proper procedures and determine potential problems. Thus, the following is not intended to serve as an all-inclusive list. Rather, it represents the absolute minimum activities which should occur upon scene arrival).

1. Dangerous individuals or safety hazards must be immediately recognized and contained.
2. All computers must be located and secured.
3. All personnel must be removed from the immediate area of the evidence.
4. Network connections must be ascertained, and appropriate action taken. (Depending on the particular case, the network administrator may prove to be quite helpful in this respect. S/he may immediately disable network access, preventing possible remote destruction).
5. All suspects should be immediately separated, and escorted to a predetermined location.
6. All computers should be protected by a police officer. This is necessary to ensure that the computer is not manipulated in any way—remotely or not. While many of the concerns involve remote destruction, it is not always possible to sever network connections immediately. Thus, some computers may remain vulnerable to outside actions.

As securing computer crime scenes includes consideration not only of traditional hazards, but also electronic threats as well, it is imperative that investigators identify threats that might exist from non-traditional sources and/or remote locations. Potential hazards may include booby-trapped drives and remote access. Hacker systems, in particular, should be approached with due caution. Luckily, these systems, on average, are relatively easy to identify. Work spaces littered with food and beverage debris, evidence of an individual spending large portions of time with their computer, may signal the presence of a hacker system. Homemade systems, an assortment of atypical computer devices, or open computer boxes (i.e., computer casings, not cardboard containers) are additional beacons. Other hints in or around computer areas may include the presence of hacking literature (e.g., *Phrack, Legion of Doom Technical Journal, Activist Times Incorporated, P/HUN*) or war dialers, while software cracking programs, Trojan horses, and philes from Cult of the Dead Cow located on a suspect device are a sure sign. (Once the actual analysis of a system begins, investigators may also wish to look at the size of the autoexec.bat file, directories labeled "bats," "batches," "belfry" (i.e., home for the real flying rodents) or the like,[1] and caches of hacker sites—often identified by the unique language or orthography found within them (e.g., use of the numeral "0" in place of the letter "O," "Z" in place of "s," "ph" in place of "f," etc.). (Mares, 2000).

DETERMINING THE NEED FOR ADDITIONAL ASSISTANCE

Once the scene is secured, team supervisors must evaluate the capabilities of the personnel present during warrant execution. Assuming that proper pre-search routines included adequate intelligence gathering, this step may not be necessary, although team leaders should be prepared for the unexpected at all times, as criminal investigations tend to adhere to Murphy's Law. Even the most prolific computer crime investigators, for example, confront certain systems outside of their expertise. Thus, outside assistance should be requested if any of the following systems are to be analyzed, and departmental personnel lack certification.

1. **Mainframes** are usually found in large organizations or governmental institutions. They are usually contained in one area with sophisticated air conditioning and power systems. When serving warrants on **mainframes**, investigators should seek the assistance of the system programmer. If the one onsite is not reliable or is actually a target of the investigation, investigators should contact the manufacturer. They usually have technical support available 24-hours a day.
2. **Minicomputers** are similar to mainframes which require a specially trained staff to maintain. Again, if investigators are not comfortable with the current administrator, they contact the manufacturer or vendor.
3. **Specialty and Hacker Computers**—usually identified by its appearance, a hacker or specialty computer may be characterized by drives without covers, unusual connections, various external media, or cluttered work space. Often times, hacker systems, in particular, will be surrounded by food wrappers, soda cans, ash trays, and the like, betraying the user's lifestyle. These systems should be approached with great caution, as hackers take pains to protect their own systems from intrusions. Investigators who have no experience with these systems should call an expert for assistance. At the minimum, investigators should secure the computer from any and all suspects. In addition, investigators should ascertain the presence of modulating capability, prohibiting contacts with telephones.

---

[1] A knowledgeable computer criminal might create a number of batch files which can perform all sorts of unusual and nefarious tasks. That person might store all of the .bat files in one subdirectory for ease of access. She may have even named the subdirectory belfry, in which to store all the bats (Mares, 2002).

● SCENE PROCESSING

Once the scene has been thoroughly secured and all necessary personnel have been employed, the next step in any criminal investigation involves scene processing. Although case characteristics may alter the significance or length of each individual step, the single most important aspect of scene processing in all cases is proper documentation, as investigative tactics and collection procedures may be dissected in open court. This is especially true in computer cases. Defense attorneys, relying on the traditional stereotype of technologically retarded officers, may attempt to discredit investigators by grilling them not only on procedures, but also on the justification of these procedures. Unwary investigators may find themselves unprepared to answer technologically direct questions. As such, investigators should carefully document *every* step taken during the investigation. At a minimum, such non-computer-specific documentation should include:

- the date, time, and location of the search and a chronological timeline of all investigative steps taken during the process
- the identity of all individuals present at the scene upon arrival
- the identity of all investigative personnel assisting in scene processing (including names, ranks, and badge numbers of all officers)
- names, positions, and contact information for non-departmental personnel
- descriptions and locations of all computers, devices, or media located throughout the search (including CPUs, monitors, keyboards, external storage devices, etc.)
- physical condition of all computer equipment located at the scene, including visible damage (this may be especially important to protect the corresponding department from allegations of abuse)
- presence of and status of network connections and the presence of a dial tone in cases where modems are used for connection purposes
- identification of all material or equipment which is seized
- detailed description of the scene
- status of all computers at the scene, including a description of what the computer is doing (i.e., off/on, connected to the Internet, open documents and programs, etc.)
- chronological timeline of all investigative clues and developing leads; date, time and description of any investigative software used, and a brief justification
- whether the potential for external destruction (including mechanical, weather, magnetic) exists
- a detailed chain of custody report

In addition, investigators at the scene should document any computer-specific information available which does not require intrusion, such as: open documents, desktop, tree structure, system ID, and time/date of computer clock.

Capturing the entire process on videotape is *highly* recommended, although it is not necessary to enable the audio recording capability. (In fact, audio record-

LIVERPOOL JOHN MOORES UNIVERSITY
LEARNING SERVICES

MINIMUM THINGS TO DOCUMENT

1. Date, time, and description of computer, including physical damage.
2. Identifying information on all investigative personnel.
3. Identifying information on all individuals present (i.e., potential witnesses, suspects, etc.).
4. All investigative clues uncovered and developing leads.
5. Investigative software used.
6. Chronology of all actions taken.
7. Type and status of network connection.
8. Verification of network connection.
9. Status of computer.
10. Computer activity (including open documents, active software).
11. Computer desktop.
12. System date/time.
13. Tree structure (if possible).
14. Image verification.
15. Chain of custody.

ings are highly discouraged as conversations between or reactions of investigators may contain profanity or comments viewed as inappropriate or unprofessional by a civilian jury.) This practice allows officers to revisit the scene as often as necessary. In addition, it makes a permanent record of all of the actions that were taken, and all of the evidence that was uncovered. This may prove especially important if the computer evidence is somehow altered or destroyed during or after the investigative process. A computer screen depicting child pornography which is caught on tape, for example, may prove invaluable if the data is erased through remote detonation or careless handling. Finally, it provides a pictorial representation of the appearance and position of objects at the scene and supports the testimony of investigating officers.

Such documentation may provide them with inalienable credibility with judicial officials, and, perhaps more importantly, jurors. In addition, such practices provide the chain of custody necessary for evidence validity. This may be especially important in cases where violations of the Electronic Communication Privacy Act (discussed in Chapter 7) are alleged. Thus, every step of the investigation should be clearly articulated. (In addition, proper pre-search activities should inculcate the specifics of the case, and, most importantly, the limitations of the applicable search warrant. Investigators should be very clear on the types of evidence which are searchable, and those which may be seized *prior* to scene processing.) This is especially important in computer investigations as case characteristics and evolving evidence all but negate traditional notions of routinization. (*Remember:* any of the following variables may alter the methodology of scene processing: computer operating systems; status of computers; status of network connections; types of network connections; active software applications; advance knowledge of or on-scene discovery of self-destructive programs; assessment of other types of computer vulnerability (e.g., electrical surges, weather considerations, etc.); and warrant permissibility (i.e., breadth and scope).

Photograph/Video

As stated previously, the golden rule for any successful criminal investigation should be: *document, document, document.* Photographs and videos are an integral part of the documentation process, and should occur at every stage of scene processing. As in traditional crime scene investigations, it is absolutely imperative that the complete computer crime scene be photographed prior to evidence collection. (To reiterate, complementary videographic documentation is highly encouraged.) This allows investigators to fully document their actions and the state of the evidence during scene processing. This may nullify defense arguments that officers contaminated or corrupted criminal evidence. Regardless of approach, investigators should pay extra attention to the configuration of computer equipment, including connections, and most importantly, the back of the computer. This practice serves several purposes. First, it enables investigators to fully document to the court the manner in which the scene was processed. Second, it serves as a refresher for investigators called to testify months or years after the fact. And, finally, it enables investigators to duplicate the original state of the computer in court. These photographs should include close-ups and distant shots, and evidence should be illustrated in a contextual manner, using common objects as references. (*Remember:* photographs and videotapes may either serve as an alibi or signal an investigator's death knell. Investigators should be instructed to act as if they were performing live for the public or the jury—because they are).

Computer-Specific Things to Photograph

1. Entire system configuration.
2. Front, back, and sides of computer.
3. Electrical wires, outlet configuration, and cable connections.
4. Corresponding media.
5. Printer status.
6. Attached hardware and peripherals.
7. Computer screen—this is essential as the data stored in RAM will be lost once the computer is unplugged.
8. Connection to the phone.
9. Any unusual characteristics (i.e., hiding places, written passwords, etc.).

Non-Computer-Specific Things to Photograph

1. Entire scene.
2. Bookshelves—may give clues as to the level of sophistication of the suspect, possible passwords, and the like.
3. Desks, area surrounding computer.
4. Notes, stickies, paper products surrounding computer.

Sketching the Scene

Sketching a crime scene is essential in any criminal investigation. It provides an overview of the state of the scene, and acts as corroboration for investigative field notes and scene photographs. Because extraneous objects may be omitted from crime scene sketches and not from photographs, sketches represent a more focused illustration of the applicable evidence. All sketches should include: name and rank of investigator; time, date, case number, and crime classification; name, rank, and/or identification of any and all persons providing assistance for the artist (i.e., those assisting with measurement, etc.); and, orientation of all evidence, including compass direction, landmarks, position in building, etc. In the interest of efficiency, original sketches should be made in pencil and investigators should not attempt to draw everything to scale. The documentation of measurements, and the like, will allow for sketch clean-up at a later time. (However, investigators should remember that even rough sketches may be subpoenaed, and are treated as permanent recordings.) Measurements should extend along fixed and identifiable points, and objects must remain stationary during the measurement process.

Identifying Potential Evidence

Perhaps the most challenging of all aspects of computer crime scene processing is the identification of potential evidence external to the computer itself. Often times, investigators, in their haste to identify evidence residing on a suspect drive, will overlook trace evidence and other forms of information which may be critical to a successful investigation. As such, traditional scene practices like reviewing paper documents at the scene, dusting for fingerprints, or looking for hair and fiber may be sensible actions. In addition, this type of evidence is essential for physically placing the suspect at the scene. Assuming that the scene has been physically and electronically secured and that there is no immediate threat to human life, investigators should gather **trace evidence** prior to seizure of electronic evidence. As always, investigators should take due regard to ensure that such evidence is not altered or destroyed by careless handling of keyboards, power supplies, and the like.

In addition to trace evidence, investigators should also be alert for the presence of other types of material which may circumstantially link a suspect to a particular crime or reveal clues which further or advance an investigation (e.g., passwords). Computer printouts, software packaging, and post-it notes might contain criminal evidence, as even computer criminals use paper for record-keeping purposes. Software manuals, for example, may provide a wealth of assistance in criminal investigations, as they are often a popular place for hiding passwords. These manuals and the contact numbers for technical support found within them might also prove critical for investigators faced with software which is outdated or outside their expertise. Finally, these manuals or packaging might indicate the types of software residing upon a suspect system, signaling the sophistication of the user and the appropriate level of caution to be exercised by investigators; and, alerting investigators to hidden programs. Thus, investigators should exhaustively search for documentary evidence, both direct and circumstantial, and other non-computer specific materials at the scene in addition to targeted systems.

Computer components, the most recognizable of all computer evidence, includes hard drives, keyboards, monitors, modems, printers, graphic cards, assorted storage devices, etc. In most investigations, a plethora of direct and circumstantial evidence may be located on a suspect hard drive. The presence of a library of pornographic representations of children, for example, may directly link a suspect to peddling in child pornography, while a review of cache files may circumstantially link him to a multitude of sites facilitating the transfer of such material. Both types of evidence might also be contained in computer peripherals like printers, where evidentiary documents are directly linked to a specific computer with individual characteristics (i.e., dot matrix with indelible "I", etc.); or circumstantially used to discuss class characteristics of printed material (i.e., laser, ink jet, dot matrix, daisy wheel, thermal printers, etc.). (As such, investigators should use caution not to disable or disconnect a printer which is currently running until the evidentiary value is ascertained. In addition, printers which are currently disabled should be powered on as print buffers might contain criminal evidence).

Direct and/or circumstantial evidence might also reside on storage media in the same manner as it does on the hard drive. **Magnetic Tape Storage Units,** mostly used as backup devices for large amounts of data, for example, may contain large portions of hard drives. They may also be useful in the collaboration of

Many suspects will attempt to thwart investigations by destroying computer equipment. Fortunately for investigators, they will often forget to destroy corresponding media. In this case, the suspect had copied photographs of his underage stepdaughter onto media found at the scene. (Courtesy of James Doyle/NYPD, ret.)

evidence collected at the scene, negating challenges by the defense that the hard drive was manipulated or altered by law enforcement. Disks and diskettes, including Jaz, Zip, CD-RW, etc., may also serve the same function, and all should be treated as potential evidence regardless of written labels. However, investigators should be aware of the limitations of the corresponding warrant and the particular jurisdictional climate in which it was issued. A good rule of thumb in all computer investigations (especially during the warrant preparation) is to include *assorted media* in the list of items to be searched and/or seized. Whenever authorized, investigators should seize *all* disks and diskettes. In searches predicated on a warrant authorizing the seizure of *related media* only, investigators should randomly sample several diskettes to ascertain the accuracy of their labeling scheme. Such sampling should also include those items appearing to be audio recordings (i.e., music CDs), as a case can be made that they might contain criminal evidence (i.e., hiding in plain sight is often best). (Remember: Actions which are reasonable in nature and scope are more likely to withstand judicial scrutiny.

Assorted computer components might also prove valuable as circumstantial evidence. The presence of active modems (modulators/demodulators) or network connections, for example, clearly illustrates the computer's ability to communicate with others, while the presence of a CD burner demonstrates the device's capacity for mass production of copyrighted material. Investigators should also be alert to those items which are not directly attached to a suspect system. Assorted computer paraphernalia, like extra hard drives, computer cords, connection devices, or power strips, might reveal the recent presence of a computer at a scene in which the computer was removed by the suspect prior to the search. Although circumstantial at best, this type of testimony coupled with corroborative evidence like eyewitness testimony may result in the successful prosecution of a suspect.

Locating Evidence

As stated, not all the evidence involved in computer-related investigations is computer-specific. In fact, items which appear to bear little relevance to case characteristics may be those which are most critical to the investigation. Paper documents, crumpled sticky notes, well worn books, materials found within or around computer work areas may prove to be critical for successful prosecution. Thus, even those investigators who are largely unfamiliar with computer-related criminal activity or the evidence that surrounds it can employ traditional crime scene investigation tactics, with some variations, by focusing on some of the following areas:

Desktops—Desktops may be a virtual cornucopia of evidence including messages, memos, monthly bills or statements, notes, ledgers, computer media, and equipment, manuals, containers, radios, tapes, televisions, and numerous office supplies. (Remember: Much of this information has traditionally been overlooked in computer seizures. While it may seem a mundane task initially, the potential of finding incriminating evidence may make this task gratifying.)

Monitors—Computer monitors have proven a popular place for passwords. This is especially true for multiple system users. Because some systems require different passwords for security purposes and others require users to change their passwords frequently, many users simply tape them to their monitors. Other items which may be taped to a computer monitor include web addresses, phone numbers, appointments, and the like. (Monitors should also be carefully evaluated to ascertain if the monitor itself has images burned onto its surface. Although this applies more to monochrome monitors and is, in fact, most unusual in this era of screen savers and advanced technology, investigators should study the screens of all suspect machines.)

Keyboards—Notes and passwords may also be taped to the computer keyboard. Investigators should always inspect the underside of the keyboard and other computer components, as suspects have been known to tape passwords, diskettes, and the like, in these locations.

Telephone—Like monitors and keyboards, telephones have proven a popular place for passwords, appointments, phone numbers, and the like. Some individuals have even taped codes for voice messaging to the receiver.

Wallets or Purses—While some evidence found in purses, such as electronic organizers or Palm Pilots, may seem obvious; investigators should be careful in searching the entire contents carefully, making notes along the way. Information such as student IDs, credit card numbers, birthdates or pocket organizers may be useful in cracking passwords. (Remember:, many individuals tend to pick one combination of letters or numbers for all their password needs. Thus, slips of paper, social security cards, driver's license, may carry information vital to cracking protected systems.)

Clothing—Just as traditional crime scene investigation involves a search of the suspect's clothing, so should tech investigations. In the computer-oriented world in which we live, computer media have often replaced briefcases. Thus, critical evidence may be found within a suspect's coat or shirt pocket in the form of a computer diskette.

Trash Cans, Recycle Bins and other Garbage Containers—Alert investigators have been known to discover valuable evidence in refuse containers. Hard copy printouts of computer produced documents may include incriminating evidence. In addition, handwritten notes may reveal passwords, location of files, or criminal networks. Even documents which have been shredded may prove invaluable to investigators as some devices fail to separate the shredded documents —neatly folding the shredded item on top of itself. Thus, a little scotch tape and some patience may go a long way! Other items found may include the perforated edges of computer paper and computer packaging products. These items may be important indicators of what type of computer equipment should be at the scene, sometimes alerting investigators to their absence. Investigators should carefully evaluate all paper products for possible evidence. Although this may seem a daunting and often thankless endeavor, computer diskettes, spread sheets, and password listings are but a few of the items which have been found carefully taped to the pages of novels, medical books, software manuals, and computerized printouts.

Printers—Much like hard drives or other storage media, hard disk print buffers and print spooler devices retain data until it is written over. Thus, the last image printed by a laser printer may be retrievable, while traditional ribboned printers (found primarily on older machines) maintain evidence on the ribbon itself.

Inside the computer—As expected, the majority of evidence in a computer-related crime resides within or upon a computer component. While the recovery of such evidence will be discussed in the next chapter, investigators should be aware that all storage devices and input/output devices are potential gold mines of information. Thus, non-technical investigators or non-specialists should treat all computer components and paraphernalia with utmost caution.

Seizure and Documentation of Evidence—Bagging and Tagging

Once evidence has been identified, it is necessary to determine if the evidence is actually seizable. While some things may be seized on their face (i.e., contraband, fruits of the crime, items criminally possessed, etc.), others may not. Investigators, especially those inexperienced in computer investigations, should read the applicable warrant carefully, familiarizing themselves thoroughly with its specifications and limitations, *prior to* its execution. Whenever possible, each individual investigator or team of investigators should physically maintain in their possession a copy of the warrant throughout the duration of the investigation, as techno-warrants may be quite lengthy. As with traditional investigations, personnel should collect and preserve all evidence with extreme caution—assuring court admissibility. If, for example, an item is found which appears to contain criminal evidence but is not included in the warrant, its seizure should only occur if the original warrant is formally amended or (more likely) a secondary warrant is issued. (Remember: waiting an hour for a judge's signature may seem inconvenient and more than a little annoying, but it pales in comparison to the days, weeks, months, or even years of work that can be dismissed in a jurisprudential second.)

Once the determination is made that evidence may be seized, the collection process should be initiated with the **imaging** (i.e., duplicated byte for byte, bit for bit) of drives onto clean media (i.e., hard drive, Zip, CD-RW, etc.), preferably new. It is absolutely essential that this process be conducted on all hard drives prior to analysis or removal with clean boot disks previously prepared. These boot disks, designed to control the boot process and bypass specialized software found in the CONFIG.SYS and AUTOEXEC.BAT files on the suspect drive, should include any and all system drivers, applicable software, virus protection, and write-blocking programs. (Remember: write-blocking is necessary to negate challenges of corruption or contamination). Verification of such images should also be conducted prior to evidence removal as forensic analysis should only be conducted on such images, preserving the original evidence in its entirety.[2] Many software

---

[2]Although common sense should tell investigators to properly check to see if the CD-R that they created is readable, many rely on the copying program's statements. Thus, a good rule of thumb for investigators is to thoroughly check and recheck all copied files and imaged drives prior to scene release. In addition, CD-R's should be tested independently, as some programs show copied files in their directory, but give no indication of the functionality of such copy.

packages, some commercially available, provide both imaging and verification utilities.

To pull or not to pull remains one of the greatest debates in the field. While circumstances vary and no rule is absolute in computer forensics due to diversity in operating systems and case characteristics, most argue that it is usually best to pull the plug from the back of the computer, unless the computer in question is connected to a network. (Remember: never do anything to the seized computers prior to making an image and ascertaining the viability of such image and *always* work with an image, preserving the original evidence in its original form.) Secured computers (i.e., safe from destruction—remote or actual) which are on should not be turned off until the scene is photographed and properly documented, unless the imminent hazards to data outweigh the need for documentation. The current state of the computer and the monitor should be carefully noted prior to powering down. Some investigators also suggest copying all open documents to a floppy prior to powering down. They should not simply turn the power off on the computer! In some cases, investigators have unwittingly turned the computer off, destroying potential evidence. This is especially problematic if the suspect is using an uninterruptible power supply, and is working solely in memory.

However, circumstances may be such that remote manipulation or destruction of data is a distinct possibility. In these situations, investigators will have to evaluate the advantages and disadvantages of imaging drives prior to disconnecting them. If, for example, investigators are unable to disconnect a target computer from a network interface, they may wish to sacrifice the memory in RAM and pull the plug in the back of the computer. (Remember: if it is determined that a computer should be disconnected, always pull the plug from the back of the computer itself. This saves investigators the extended time it may take to locate the power outlet, and, more importantly, eliminates the possibility that they may miss an uninterruptible power supply.) Regardless of approach, investigators should be aware that powering down may lead to more complicated analysis at the lab. (On Windows 2000, for example, a simple check mark in the *Advanced* section of the *File Properties* window enables encryption of files and entire folders, while running invisibly in the background. Thus, if the user chooses to encrypt documents and temporary files, pulling the plug would lead to automatic encryption of working files. Although password crackers could be utilized, investigators must consider the possibility that those files would be permanently inaccessible.)

As always, documentation is essential. All case notes, materials, etc. should be written in ink, requiring initialized verification for subsequent alteration or modification. In addition, notes should be of a comprehensive nature—enabling any investigator to clearly articulate the process, procedures, and investigative steps undertaken throughout initial scene processing. Although often overlooked, the importance of comprehensiveness can not be overstated. As the criminal justice process is often slow and convoluted, individuals may be asked to testify in cases with which they are completely unfamiliar. In addition, proper documentation will eradicate many of the judicial headaches that may be encountered under cross-examination.

IMAGING AND VERIFICATION SOFTWARE

As stated in previous chapters, all software programs have been criticized in some form or fashion. Thus, investigators are *strongly* encouraged to test all software packages employed in their investigations to such an extent that they are confident in their knowledge of their limitations, criticisms, and strengths.

Safeback—Many law enforcement agencies prefer this program above others since it was created exclusively for forensic investigations. Unlike other programs, this package was designed to provide a duplicate copy (or image) for forensic purposes and was not created as a disk manager. Although relatively expensive in comparison to other imaging programs, it copies both the physical hard drive and logical partition tables. In addition, it allows investigators to use a variety of removable media including DA Tapes, Jaz, Zip, and hard drives.

Ghost—A relatively inexpensive program, Ghost allows investigators to make duplicate images of hard drives and logical partitions. However, many investigators caution that this program requires some knowledge on the part of users. For example, investigators need to know which switches to throw to create this pristine image. Notwithstanding, this program is a valuable tool for the experienced forensic tech.

> Both *Ghost* and *Safeback* have switches which must be enabled to make a pristine image. Some investigators have claimed that SafeBack changes the boot record when used with defaults, and that the CRC is designed to bypass boot records so that this is not seen. Although these changes (if they exist) would be forensically inconsequential, investigators must know the process prior to challenges in court.

Anadisk—Unlike Ghost and Safeback, Anadisk is designed exclusively for the imaging of storage media regardless of format or type. It allows investigators to maintain the same level of duplication for jurisprudential considerations involving diskettes. Unlike the DOS command COPY, it targets the entire diskette including file slack and multiple data streams. In addition, the image it creates uses the same serial number as the origination diskette. In addition it allows investigators to manipulate sectors and tracks on a floppy. DiskEdit, on the other hand, will not allow this.

CSCDUP-CSC, FastCache Disk Drive, and CD-ROM Duplicator Package—According to the National White Collar Crime Center, this package enables the user to copy hard drives (IDE, SCSI); magneto-optical Drives, CD-R and CD-ROM (IDE, SCSI); DOS-compatible image files stored on network servers, and SCSI tape drives. However, it does not provide a pristine-image, as it does not copy logical partitions.

Bagging and Tagging.

Like any scientific evidence, great care must be exercised when collecting and preserving crime scene evidence. The chain of custody and continuity of possession must be maintained at all times for court admissibility. Investigators should adhere to standard operating procedures for custodial evidence collection—keeping in mind that routinization enhances witness credibility and evidence validity. Although policies and procedures vary by department, certain things remain constant.

Once images have been taken and verified, investigators should carefully label all components of the computer system and corresponding computer media and connections. Investigators should place coordinating labels on both ends of every cable and the corresponding outlets. Empty outlets should always be labeled as such to simplify physical reconfiguration at the lab or in the courtroom. Empty disk slots should be filled with a floppy containing a disabling program and taped closed to secure the read/write heads in the floppy drives during transport and to prevent accidental access by non-investigative personnel. (Investigators may write-block drives in the autoexec.bat or use programs like Maresware's *DISABLE* which will disable a computer's keyboard, lock the computer upon start up, and alert the user that this device is forensic evidence.) This process, and the remainder of the evidence collection, should be videotaped whenever possible. If using traditional methods, investigators should carefully photograph all of the evidence after labeling, paying particular attention to the back of the computer. This enables investigators to recreate the entire system in the lab, and more importantly, in the courtroom.

Packaging of hard drives and other computer components should be undertaken with great care, and be consistent with traditional collection methods. Latex gloves, for example, should be employed as to not contaminate fingerprints or other potential trace evidence, and a detailed shipping manifest which includes the date and time of shipping, the contents of each box, and the name or identification of the individual loading each box should be created. (This process is essential for maintaining the chain of custody, and should ease the loading and unloading of often voluminous evidence.) Each individual piece of evidence should be carefully marked by the officer or investigator who collects it, and all components from a single computer system should be packaged together. This marking should never damage or impair the value of evidence or limit the number or type of examinations which may be conducted by experts. Although some investigators have adopted the practice of scratching initials, date, and the like on objects recovered, this is not recommended in computer cases.

As mentioned previously, computer components and media are more fragile than some traditional forms of evidence. Thus, marking materials should be non-destructive or intrusive. Computer wires and connection ports should be carefully labeled with colored tape prior to removal or disconnection. Computer diskettes and covered components may also be marked with colored tape and stored in appropriate sleeves. Minimum information should include the investigator's initials,

As with traditional crime scenes, proper documentation of the scene is extremely important. Computer evidence requires additional photographs, and particular attention should be given to the state of the computer prior to seizure. Such documentation includes, but is not limited to: computer connections, screen activity, etc. (Courtesy of James Doyle/NYPD, ret.)

date found, and location of evidence. When available, original packaging is the best form of container. (Investigators may also wish to include extra packaging materials in their evidence kits.) Other appropriate forms of containment include static-free paper products. In a pinch, standard paper envelopes may be used, but all packaging materials should be carefully labeled to maintain the chain of custody.

As stated, the maintenance of the chain of custody is essential for any successful prosecution. However, it is not the only consideration in computer-related investigations. Contamination and corruption, a consideration in all criminal cases, may be more so in computer cases, because of the fragile nature of the data. Thus, traditional methods are not always appropriate. Like blood and other liquid evidence which is vulnerable to environmental factors, computer media may be inadvertently destroyed if exposed to extreme temperatures or careless handling. As a general rule, the following factors must be considered in computer-related investigations:

GENERAL CHECKLIST FOR EVIDENCE PRESERVATION

Resources permitting, agencies should strive to create computer-specific evidence rooms. This prevents the potential for evidence corruption, contamination, and destruction. These environments should be climate controlled, dust free, and large enough to store equipment for extended periods. The following list is provided for agencies without these capabilities.

1. Temperatures should reach no higher than 90° F and no lower than 60° F.
2. Environments should (as much as possible) be dust-free. Additional security may be provided by paper packaging or coverings.
3. Environments should be free from magnetic fields. If possible, computer evidence should not be stored in proximity to electromagnetic fields. (A compass may be used to test for magnetic fields.)
4. Environments should be free from corrosive elements, such as those commonly found in arson investigations (i.e., accelerants, etc.).
5. Evidence should be stored on non-plastic shelving, preferably wood.
6. Environments should be static-free. Simple precautions may include avoidance of carpet, plastic shelving or containers, excessively dry environments, etc.
7. Upon arrival at storage facility, tags and identifying materials should be verified and properly marked for easy identification.
8. Evidence should be stored together so that investigators may find all components quickly and easily.

Temperature—Heat poses one of the greatest threats to computer evidence. Investigators should take care not to place computer components or media near excessive heat or direct sunlight. Although hardware is not as susceptible, media are especially vulnerable to intemperate environments. Several well-documented cases have been hopelessly lost because investigators left computer evidence in their cars. Obvious damage included warped diskettes, melted tapes, and the like, but further damage may occur when damaged media are not immediately recognized and introduced into other computer equipment. Lost data and damaged equipment are but two of the possible results from exposure. The fallout of such disregard may include lost cases, thousands of investigative dollars wasted, and perpetrators set free.

Magnetic Fields—Any type of magnetic field poses a potentially calamitous risk to computer media and hardware. Even low-level magnetic pulses, such as those emitted from car radios and transmitters, create an environment hazardous to computer-related evidence. Such situations may cause information erasure. Other hazards may include electric motors, speakers, magnetic clips, or even refrigerator magnets. (Due to the sheer volume of potential evidence, some investigators have attempted to photocopy computer media as a form of scene documentation. This may prove fatal to an investigation. *Do not* photocopy any computer evidence. Photographic or videotaped evidence is not only preferred, it is a necessity!)

Static Electricity—An additional hazard to computer components or data involves static electricity. Traditional plastic evidence bags, for example, may generate levels of static electricity dangerous to computer media. Because of the magnetic components previously discussed, static electricity which may appear to be little more than a nuisance in other situations (e.g., clinging garments, low-level shocks, etc.) can irreparably damage critical evidence. Thus, evidence should be collected in paper evidence bags. Some manufacturers of collection materials have even developed special containers for this very purpose. Static electricity may also pose a danger to circuit boards and exposed wires. Investigators may not recognize this danger until computer equipment does not function properly. Unfortunately, by then, it is too late. Static electricity and the destruction of data in cases with exposed wires are not the only dangers. High voltage and exposed wires also pose a significant risk to human life.

Oil, dirt and dust—Investigators have long known that introducing foreign elements to a crime scene may irrevocably contaminate or corrupt potential evi-

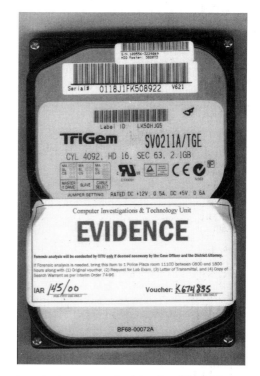

In order to preserve the integrity of the evidence, investigators should clearly label each item. Evidence labels, like the one shown here, are ideal in computer cases in which evidence may be quite fragile. (Courtesy of James Doyle/NYPD, ret.)

dence. Accordingly, evidence techs have traditionally taken precautionary measures such as gloves, hair and shoe coverings, and the like. However, these things, while protecting traditional forms of evidence, create unacceptable levels of static electricity to computer evidence. Investigators should be acutely aware of the dangers posed by common oils found on palms and fingertips. Special care should be exercised when dealing with damaged media or exposed tape, heads, or drives. (*Remember:* Contamination is contagious—exposing other elements to damaged or corrupted components may spread the problem.)

Additional Environmental Characteristics—Although the fragility of computer equipment may appear obvious, past cases reveal that this is not the case. Investigators have been known to stack heavy objects on top of computer equipment, damaging the hard drive and destroying criminal evidence. Others have been known to place computer equipment in dusty or dirty environments. (*Remember:* If you would not be comfortable in an environment, neither is the computer.) Attempt to place related materials singularly on appropriate shelving in a climate controlled, dust-free environment.

Scene Departure and Transportation of Evidence to Lab

Once the evidence has been properly collected and loaded into appropriate vehicles for transportation, investigators should follow traditional procedures for exiting a crime scene (i.e., physically securing the scene, removal of recovery equipment, etc.). Prior to leaving, investigators should re-photograph the crime scene to avoid allegations of police misconduct (Mares, 2002). Upon arrival at the lab, shipping manifests should be checked over carefully, and all items should be properly accounted for. (In addition, investigators should note the condition of the boxes upon unloading, erring on the side of caution.) These manifests should remain with the evidence at all times, and should, in fact, be treated as evidence in and of themselves. Once accounted for, all incoming evidence should be entered into the appropriate evidence control systems and assigned to a location or examiner to await analysis.

TERMS DISCUSSED

batch files	mainframes	minicomputers
computer components	magnetic tape storage	trace evidence
imaging	units	

DISCUSSION QUESTIONS

1. Why is proper scene documentation so critical in criminal investigations? What are some basic guidelines?
2. What are some unusual situations that may require additional or specialized assistance?
3. Generally speaking, what are the basic steps of crime-scene processing?
4. Where should investigators look for evidence in computer-related cases?
5. What are some unique concerns in preservation of digital evidence?

12
DATA ANALYSIS

While many investigations will focus primarily on evidence stored on a suspect CPU, others will concentrate exclusively on a variety of storage media, and still others will include a combination of both. In all cases, automated or manual recovery efforts are appropriate (we will not rehash the argument as to which is better, although many investigators may be tempted to use automated programs due to their quick and painless operation). Whatever the case may be, investigation of floppies should be separate from CPU processing. Due to the voluminous nature of some cases, it is imperative that investigative procedures remain the same (as much as possible) across investigations. This will ensure a continuity across investigations, and enhance testimonial validity. In addition, it will reduce confusion and increase the efficiency and subsequent effectiveness of the search. (However, agencies must be cautioned that formal policies may actually be detrimental to successful prosecution in some cases. Thus, departments should scrupulously develop generalized policies which encompass provisions for unique circumstances.

Regardless of software employed, investigators must thoroughly capture a complete schematic of the suspect system, keeping detailed notices to assist them with often delayed courtroom presentation. Such documentation must include any and all changes to the data collected, including justifications for modifications. In addition, this documentation should include a schematic of evidence volatility, providing justification for deviations from SOP. (As in all criminal investigations, evidence should be categorized by its inflammability, corrosive, or volatile characteristics). Keep in mind that all analysis activities should be conducted with a forensic machine, due to the possibility of intentional sabotage or accidental contamination or destruction.

ASPECTS OF DATA ANALYSIS

As stated previously, every computer investigation is different, but one rule remains the same: *document, document, document!* Other than that, procedures may vary depending upon departmental resources, expertise of personnel, and exigent circumstances. Again, each agency should develop its own investigative policy (formal or informal), and follow it as closely as possible. This is not to suggest, however, that one policy can completely account for all circumstances that may arise. Rather, it may be analogized to a coach's playbook, changing weekly after the competition has been rated and evaluated.

Having articulated appropriate disclaimers, investigators may find the following steps useful:

Document

The importance of documentation can not be overstated. Judicial oversight and defense challenges require that scrupulous attention be directed towards the documentation of any and all activities conducted on a particular piece of evidence. As such, analysts should continue the documentation process which was initiated by the evidence technicians or on-scene investigators by retrieving and updating the evidence logs. At a minimum, lab analysis should include: the name, rank, and identifying information for any individual tasked with the analysis of such evidence; the condition of the evidence upon delivery to the analyst; the date and time of evidence arrival and return; and the name, rank, and identifying information of the person delivering such evidence. (As with traditional criminal investigations, any investigator or individual wishing access to the evidence *must* sign the evidence out. Once this process is completed, investigators or analysts may retrieve the digital information that may reside therein.

As stated previously, contemporary criminal behavior often requires the analysis of computer materials. Using a variety of software packages, it is now possible to thoroughly analyze all of the information on each piece of storage media. Depending on the amount of media under analysis, this process can be quite cumbersome. In addition, case characteristics may preclude the most comprehensive manual search. Indeed, many investigators prefer to use automated programs like Expert Witness due to its ability to quickly analyze large disks. In addition, case characteristics may be such that it is unnecessary to search every single file (although it is always recommended). For example, in a child pornography case, where hard-copy photographs were accompanied by desktop child pornography and a directory entitled "child porn" which contained 400 depictions of child pornography, a thorough search of slack space and file swap may not be compelling in the case at hand. However, it may contain addresses, phone numbers, or other evidence which may incriminate others. Evidence notwithstanding, investigators should properly document all forensic software utilized, analysis techniques employed, damaged or compromised media (i.e., bad sectors, physically damaged diskettes, etc.), and evidence recovered. This documentation process should continue throughout the investigation process, and should not be completed until final case disposition has been achieved.

Establish Forensically Sterile Conditions

All media used in the analysis of computer evidence must be forensically sterile for courtroom purposes. Investigators must be able to testify as to the condition of all media prior to the imaging process. As such, it is highly recommended that all media used for imaging purposes be brand new and forensically wiped prior to analysis, as some manufacturers have sold refurbished equipment as new.

However, due to limited resources, this process may not be possible for poorly funded agencies. In this case, used media should be forensically wiped clean of data using software meeting DOD standards. This will prevent data corruption from previous use and data contamination from destructive programs. In addition, the condition of all physical drives should be verified prior to analysis. Media which contain damaged areas (i.e., sector, clusters, etc.) should not be utilized. However, it must be reiterated that new media which has been forensically wiped is *highly* recommended.

Ensure Legitimacy and Capabilities of Analysis Tools

Licenses for all forensic software that is expected to be employed in the analysis of suspect media should be verified prior to actual analysis. This process, often overlooked, is critical for witness credibility. (Imagine the embarrassment that would result if it was revealed that software employed was not properly licensed and was being illegally used by law enforcement authorities.) Unfortunately, many investigators fail to appreciate the importance of nuances found in many licensing agreements, using unlicensed shareware programs indiscriminately or making duplicate copies of single-user forensic suites.

Investigators should also validate any forensic software to be used, testing the software at the extremes and familiarizing themselves with its capabilities (Mares, 2000). (Too often, investigators simply trust the documentation provided by the manufacturer.) Again, this practice is critical for courtroom testimony. Although many defense attorneys are not currently knowledgeable about forensic software and practices, this is sure to change. Thus, investigators must be able to articulate the limitations of the analysis tools and the steps that were taken to identify them.

Investigators should always verify that proper imaging has occurred prior to analysis. (Courtesy of James Doyle/*NYPD*, ret.)

Simplistic practices could include, for example, the intentional manipulation of data in a multitude of places on a variety of levels, such as hiding data in unused clusters and file slack or using an editing program to intentionally mark clusters as bad or delete files.

Physical Examination

Just as on-scene investigators noted the condition of the suspect equipment, so should the forensic examiner. This physical examination should note any damage or markings and record class characteristics, such as make, model, etc. In addition, attached peripherals, wires, or storage media (e.g., floppy disk) should also be noted. This enhances the credibility of the chain of custody.

Creation and Verification of Image

Assuming that an image was not secured at the crime scene, analysts should create one prior to any forensic analysis. (Remember: all examinations and analysis should be conducted on this image, leaving the original forensically pure.) In ideal situations, images should only be created on forensic machines. This preserves the integrity of the original evidence, prevents data contamination, and establishes the veracity of the subsequent analysis.

Assuming that BIOS passwords do not interfere with the investigation, the imaging of drives should always be initiated by booting the suspect drive from a previously verified forensic floppy as some users will configure their system to make modifications or erase data if third-party access is determined.[1] (As discussed in Chapter 9, there are a variety of imaging programs available to law-enforcement investigators, and all forensic labs should be equipped with at least two. Analysts should choose the one with which they are the most comfortable.) This forensic floppy should contain the applicable operating system, as well as a means for locking the hard drive prior to imaging. (This mechanism, often referred to as write-blocking, prevents the destruction, contamination, or corruption of original media and can be accomplished with many of the popular imaging programs, disk management software, or simple DOS commands.) Forensic boot disks should also include applicable **storage enhancement** programs (e.g., Stacker™, DoubleSpace™, PKZip™, etc.), drivers for external media and printers, and an assortment of drivers and software programs determined from good pre-seizure surveillance or by evaluation of the suspect's CONFIG.SYS and AUTOEXEC.BAT files.

Investigators may also wish to consider including batch files which generally evaluate all computers for court purposes. This is especially important for those officers conducting manual analysis of forensic evidence. Such batch files would make life easier for an investigator who is processing several drives at once and those who do this type of analysis on a daily basis. In addition, they may provide a platform of consistency that validates their procedures to the court. Generally

---

[1]During the boot process of a computer, the operating system is loaded first, followed by other programs. These programs allow users to interact with the computer in a specific manner. As such, these programs should also be included on a boot disk to prevent destruction of data (possibly evidence) located in file slack and ROM.

speaking, this batch file would enable investigators to establish a step-by-step preliminary investigative process which runs programs in a specified order. This saves time, and, perhaps more importantly, establishes a general process for all investigations. This may prove critical under cross-examination. (For example, a defense attorney may question the applicability of the plain view doctrine if a search for transactional information reveals child pornography. If an investigator can demonstrate that s/he always sorts documents by file extension or that a thumbnail program is always executed against a suspect computer, s/he may successfully defeat the challenge.) In fact, batch files may be created to incorporate all of the forensic software employed, including: write-blocking, imaging and verification, disk management, time/date authentication, virus scan, etc. In addition to any batch files or independent forensic tools, boot disks should always include virus protection in order to protect departmental computers. However, investigators should *never* "cure" the virus on the suspect media!! The importance of preserving original evidence can not be overstated. This step simply allows investigators to protect their own systems. Thus, investigators should include a Terminate and Stay Resident (TSR) virus shield on their investigative systems and on any boot disks employed. Some examples include McAfee's VSHIELD and FPROT. Investigators should remember to update this file on a regular basis. Unlike other programs traditionally found on boot disks which do not necessitate updating, the virus protection should be the most current.

In the rare case that investigators cannot remove a suspect drive (i.e., permission to seize is not granted, suspect drive is intrinsically necessary for system maintenance, etc.), they may be confounded by the presence of a **CMOS password.** Currently, CMOS RAM, traditionally stored in a Motorola module used for permanently storing setup information, is found in the peripheral controller buffer via an external battery (often a coin-size Sony "lithium disk"). In many Intel chip sets, excepting the Pentium II boards, the PIIX4 component acts as the host, offering an additional 128 bytes via ports 72h/73h and allowing for the read/write protection of sectors 38h to 3Fh with a "write once bit." (This protection can be set via software, but needs to be reset through a hardware reset.) Thus, to bypass BIOS passwords, investigators must erase or circumvent the CMOS RAM. While many inexperienced investigators have panicked in this situation, others believe that they can attack, and eventually crack, them. This has proven extremely short-sighted in some situations. While some of these passwords have been cracked using "social engineering" or default passwords, many have not. In these situations, investigators who are even slightly apprehensive should stop and contact an expert. CMOS passwords are not invincible, and may be circumvented using a variety of methods, including, but not limited to: jumping, **pulling the battery,** default passwords, social engineering, and suspect interrogation.[2]

---

[2]While there are other hardware solutions to defeating a CMOS password, they are extremely invasive, and go beyond the introductory parameters established in this text. Once again, it must be emphasized that this text is not intended to serve as a primer for computer forensics. Rather, it is intended to provide a brief overview of the issues involved in the investigation of computer-related crime.

Jumping the CMOS Password

While other types of passwords may be defeated using traditional password cracking software, CMOS passwords often require hardware manipulation on the part of the investigator. CMOS (or "boot) passwords are designed to be the first line of defense for users, preventing individuals from booting the computer's operating system. Therefore, it is impossible to circumvent with traditional means. However, one effective means of circumventing the CMOS is to simply "jump" it. (To locate the correct jumper, investigators may wish to read the motherboard's manual.) **Jumpers,** located either by the BIOS or elsewhere on the motherboard, may be utilized to bypass protections found in the CMOS. *Jumping* the CMOS involves the manipulation of hardware in which the password is cleared after the jumper has been reset. In these cases, investigators should look for the jumper often labeled "Clear RTC" or "Clear CMOS" or "PWRD." Once located, this jumper can be manipulated by turning the computer off for a couple of minutes, and then restarting after returning the "jumper" to its original position. (Some motherboards will automatically turn themselves back on after flashing the BIOS.) However, if no manual is available, and the jumper is not obvious, investigators must identify the jumper through basic trial and error. Things to look for: jumpers which are isolated; those that are located near the BIOS; and those which may be switched. Investigators should only change one jumper at a time. In the event that the jumper is not adequately defined or the investigators is not familiar with system configuration, other approaches should be considered. For example, if a Dallas clock ending in A (ex. DS1287A) is present and a clear jumper cannot be located, investigators may ground the 21st pin to clear RAM.

Short Circuiting the Chip

Like the pulling of the battery, the short-circuiting of the BIOS chip will enable investigators to defeat the boot process. Generally, this process involved the short-circuiting two pins of the BIOS chip for a few seconds. Although not recommended, this process can be accomplished with a paper clip or electric wire. Common examples include: CHIPS P82C206—(square) pins 12 and 32 (the first and last pins of the bottom edge of the chip) or pins 74 and 75 (the two pins on the upper left corner); OPTIF82C206 (rectangle)—pins 3 and 26 (third pin from left side and fifth pin from right side on the bottom right; Dallas DS12885S, Benchmarq bq3258S, Hitachi HD146818AP, Samsung KS82C6818A, pins 12 and 24; and Motorola MC146818AP, pins 12 and 24 or 12 and 20. In all cases, investigators should remember to turn the computer off during the process.

Pulling the Battery

Investigators may also pull the CMOS battery, as the memory will be lost after a period of time. In these cases, the battery should be disconnected for at least 24 hours. (If time permits, investigators should wait a longer period of time just to be sure). This entails opening the case on the central processing unit (CPU), and removing the CMOS battery. (However, this approach may not be possible in cases where the battery is soldered onto the CPU.) Unfortunately, such action could result in damage to other portions of the CMOS which are essential to evidence recovery. Thus, investigators should be extremely careful when using this approach. (Investigators should also remember that notebooks often have two batteries: one buffering battery exchange; and one that supplies the clock and CMOS RAM). If investigators find that any of the above practice has resulted in modification of memory and hard drives, it will be necessary to manually reconfigure the system. Although this practice is different on some computers, many allow users to enter the setup program by depressing [F2]. Other systems may require the combination [Ctrl] [Alt] [Esc]. (If neither of these is successful, a simple call to the manufacturer may provide the solution.) Fortunately, most systems will prompt the user once they recognize that they are misconfigured. Investigators should pay careful attention to the information provided during the boot process, and any information which may be located upon the hard drive's cover. Important—this new configuration may also require the Windows installation CD (i.e., it may find new hardware).

Default Passwords

Like other areas of data security, CMOS passwords may also be circumvented in many cases through the use of default passwords installed as backdoors by the manufacturer (see above). Fortunately for law enforcement, many OEMs employ these standardized default passwords (often extremely simplistic) which are commonly available on the net.

Social Engineering/Brute Force

By far, the most time consuming (and exasperating) method of circumventing CMOS passwords involves the use of social engineering and brute force. This methodology requires meticulous investigation by law enforcement authorities. As mentioned previously, it involves traditional investigative practices, requiring the manual input of every possible personal computation. Such analysis begins and ends with the information compiled through the investigation of the suspect.

Key Disks

Some computers allow a BIOS bypass by inserting a **key disk** in the floppy disk drive while booting. Toshiba laptops, for example, enable users to bypass the

---

SOME STANDARDIZED BIOS PASSWORDS

AWARD BIOS—AWARD SW; AWARD SW, Award SW, AWARD PW, award, awkward, J64 j256, j262, j332, j322, 01322222, 589589, 589721, 595595, 598598, HLT, SER, SKY_FOX, aLLy, aLLY, Condo, CONCAT, TTPTHA, aPAf, KDD, ZBAAACA, ZAAADA, ZJAAADC, djonet,

AMI BIOS—AMI, A.M.I., AMI SW, AMI_SW, BIOS, PASSWORD, HEWITT RAND, Oder

Others—LKWPETER, lkwpeter, BIOSTAR, biostar, BIOSSTAR, biosstar, ALFAROME, Syxz, Wodj

Note—in some European keyboards, the American underscore (i.e., "_") is actually represented by a "?"—so AWARD_SW would become AWARD?SW

BIOS by creating a key disk. To create a key disk, take a standard floppy, and change the first five bytes of the second sector (the one after the boot sector) using a hex editor to 4B 45 59 00 00. (The first three bytes are the ASCII for "KEY"). This will enable the investigator to set his or her own password.

Image Verification

All images should be verified prior to analysis. Fortunately, most imaging programs provide verification capabilities. This verification is necessary to avoid evidentiary challenges of contamination or corruption. As discussed in Chapter Nine, a variety of levels of verification are available, and while CRC comparisons have traditionally remained unchallenged, the MD5 hash and the SHA (Secure Hash Algorithm) are much more robust.

Logical Examination

Once a verified image has been created, investigators should logically examine the contents for criminal evidence. (In many cases, analysis of physical drives may not be necessary.) This includes the verification of **partition tables** and disk information (i.e., storage, hidden files, etc.). (Remember: There may be only one bootable partition per drive, located at cylinder = 0, head = 0, sector = 1.) This process may be conducted with fully automated programs or manually with programs like *DiskEdit*™. This procedure is essential as computer hard disks and floppy diskettes are structured in such a way that evidence can reside at various levels within the structure of the disk. Because the intentional modification of disk structure and obfuscation of data is commonly discovered in the investigation of computer-related crime, investigators should be equipped with programs to view partition information, clusters, sectors, drives, directories, and hidden and **erased files.** Such views may reveal the presence of hidden files or even entire partitions. A logical analysis, for example, enables investigators to look for spatial discrepancies between logical and physical drives, possibly revealing hidden partitions.

Restoration of Files

As previously discussed, criminals may hide any and all incriminating data residing on their computer. Luckily, the majority of criminals are either technologically incompetent or technologically naïve, often "hiding" data in obvious places (i.e., changing file extensions, creating innocuous file names, marking clusters as "bad" or deleted, etc.) file while assuming the totality of deletion. Thus, all forensic laboratories should be equipped with software capable of recovering deleted, erased, and **compressed files.** While fully automated forensic suites include these capabilities, investigators should be comfortable with manual recovery programs like *Norton Utilities*™ *Unerase* and understand the process that the operating system employs to erase files. DOS platforms, for example, will change the first character of a file name to the Greek Sigma (denoted by hexadecimal E5) to "inform" the computer that the space originally designated for this file is no longer needed, (This also enables investigators to identify all deleted files.) DOS then zeros out what a specified cluster pointed to and proceeds to zero out the remaining links to the original chain in the FAT. Norton's *UnErase*™ attempts to recover these files by replacing the Sigma with a valid ASCII character, identifying the number of clusters necessary, locating the corresponding unallocated clusters, and updating the FAT. This process, however, is not always as successful as investigators would like. In fact, the ability to recover deleted files depends on a variety of factors including time lapsed since deletion, usage of system, etc. Thus, investigators may also use a disk editor to reconstruct files by manually employing the same methods.

Although a relatively elementary and unsophisticated approach to hiding data, some suspects may also attempt to hide data by simply using the operating system's "hidden" attribute or by altering the applicable file extensions.[3] For example, child pornographers may "hide" pornographic images by designating them as text files (i.e., JPG to TXT) by simply changing their name. They may also hinder recognition of a file by using a hexadecimal editor to change the file signature, a sequence of bytes at the beginning of a file that specifically indicates the type of file. Although the file will be unreadable until the signature sequence is restored, investigators may employ programs like *Maresware's HexDump* and *DISKCAT*™, identifying and reconciling contrary file signatures. However, other situations are a bit more complicated.

In some cases, investigators may confront untenable situations in which the data has been intentionally and "permanently" destroyed by employing "wiping programs." These programs, commercially available, remove multiple layers of data, and may require special chemical processing. Such handling is almost always outside the budgetary constraints of any investigative agency, and is only employed in cases which involve national security. However, many popular wiping programs do allow recovery of some portion of information for the savvy investigators. For example, *BCWIPE*™ destroys slack space and file swap, but fails to remove the volume label from the disk. It also fails to wipe the last two sectors of the drive, allowing viewing by a collection of viewers like *Norton Utilities*™. In addition, renamed files are designated by a wipe extension.

Finally, data may be concealed through the use of sophisticated software which is designed exclusively to hide data in plain sight using the least significant bit (LSB). One such category of software, steganography, allows users to effectively hide the content of selected files in others. Popular software programs like *S-Tools*™ and *StegoSuite*™ enable users to hide images and text within wave and graphic files. Thus, file viewers which typically allow investigators to physically view the contents of a document would only display the *container* (i.e., the picture or sound file) and not necessarily the suspect data (**Steganographic** messages have two parts: the **container,** which is the file which conceals data; and, the **message,** which is the actual data.) Due to the randomness of algorithmic ma-

---

[3]File extensions are identifiers designated by DOS located after the period which indicate the type of file included therein. For example, the extension DOC in the file ILOVEYOU.DOC would indicate that the file was textual in nature (i.e., a word processing document).

STEGANOGRAPHY

The practice of hiding information from discovery is not unique to the computer age. The word actually is a derivative from the Greek *steganos* for hidden words, where it was a common practice to place wax over words to hide them from detection. Steganography was also practiced by the Chinese who would tattoo messages on the bald head of soldiers, and allow the natural regrowth of hair to conceal the messages. Contemporary practices are far more sophisticated. However, they still rely on the ignorance of investigative authorities for their success.

nipulation employed in steganography programs, there is no commercially available software which will detect the presence of files imbedded in other files. Unfortunately, this requires investigators to manually evaluate all graphics and wave files (i.e., they must use the suspect program to evaluate all appropriate files, looking for a positive response).Thus, investigators must look for the presence of steganography software to discover the very presence of hidden images. Investigators may discover these types of files by looking for files created with S code or by looking for unusually sized applications. (Investigators should consider that the best containers are busy programs, like complex photographs, while the worst are simple ones, like a two color image. In addition, sound files (e.g., WAVE, etc.) sometimes prove to be a bonanza for law enforcement, as suspects may place a continuous stream of data in a sound file, forgetting that there are periods of silence.) Unfortunately, recovery of these programs may be further complicated by secure passwords.

List of Files

As part of the documentary process, investigators should list all files on the suspect drive after the recovery of erased, deleted, hidden, and compressed files. Disk editors are particularly useful here, as they provide tree structures which display all files and their origination path.

Examine Unallocated Space for Data Remnants

Often times, investigators may find additional evidence residing in unallocated clusters which were not intentionally manipulated by suspects. As discussed in Chapter 8, DOS and Windows™ operating systems use fixed clusters depending on the size of the disk (i.e., an entire cluster is used for any given file regardless of the file's size).[4] Thus, files of a size not sufficient to fill the designated space of a cluster are still allocated the entire space on a cluster, leaving unused or *slack*

---

[4]It should be noted that NT uses a much smaller default cluster of either 4 or 8K

space. Consequently, remnants of files which may have contained criminal evidence may be recoverable. Although remnants of graphic and image files may not be particularly helpful, vestiges of text files may contain evidence including passwords. Fully automated programs like *EnCase*™ are designed to evaluate slack, and several manual programs like *GetSlack*™ may be used to perform the same function as well as providing a mechanism for contextual analysis. Again, case characteristics will dictate the forensic methodology employed.

Unlocking Files

Unlike the CMOS password, software and document passwords do not affect the startup of the computer and may be encountered by investigators on a variety of different levels. These passwords, designed to prevent access to special documents, programs, or compressed files, actually serve to encrypt information. In order to circumvent these types of passwords, cracking dictionaries or software is the tool of choice. These password programs are actually compilations of dictionaries and characters. They attempt to "guess" the password by inputting combinations of standard words, common characters, and lower and upper case levels. These password-cracking programs operate by comparing hash values of files. Thus, pass-phrases are almost impossible to crack. However, some powerful software cracking software like Access Data's *Password Recovery Toolkit*™ allow investigators to create dictionaries from the suspect drive, simply by entering the imaged drive. Although time consuming, this may allow the recovery of such pass-phrases.

Unfortunately, not all passwords can be cracked. Strong encryption programs like PGP and Triple DES have proven resilient to all available crackers. In fact, PGP is so confident in their ability to remain unbreakable, that they have made their source code available to the public. It is programs like these that have prompted Congress to propose third party key requirements (i.e., forcing users to provide a third person with their password). Having said this, however, it may still be possible to identify passwords through intensive analysis. Some forensic utilities, for example, enable investigators to *sniff* the hard drive the same way that hackers have sniffed identifications and passwords (e.g., Access Data and Entomb). Remember, passwords may actually be secreted away on the computer, thereby providing investigators an opportunity to find them. These passwords may reside in slack space or swap files or may be attached to other files as attachments or riders (i.e., Multiple Data Streams). Thus, investigators may wish to create a dictionary out of the file swap or slack space. (Most forensic crackers allow for the importation of investigator created dictionaries.)

If time is of the essence, investigators may also wish to manually evaluate these areas and identify anomalies. In other cases, it may be possible to identify other passwords on a suspect computer in traditional ways. For example, investigators may identify Word files that are password protected, and crack them using traditional methods. Once investigators have secured one password, they may try it on those files that are heavily encrypted, such as PGP files. (It is often surprising how individuals will use the same password for a variety of files.)

Brute Force/Social Engineering

If the above techniques have not produced any measure of success, investigators may also try developing a profile of the suspect or the suspect computer and manually attempt password cracking. Many individuals use common or everyday words to secure their documents. Other favorites include pet's name, pet's breed, mother's name, father's name, siblings, birthdays, social security numbers, favorite sports team or figure, school name or mascot, place of birth, favorite color, boy/girlfriend's name, spouse's name, suspect's middle name, literary figures, favorite television program or movie, etc. Think of your own passwords. Chances are that someone who knew you well would be able to guess them in their entirety or at least guess the root of the password. Thus, social engineering is a good method for all criminal investigations, especially computer-related investigations.

Program Defaults and Program-Specific Crackers

Investigators may also find it useful to compile a list of standardized defaults for password location. For example, in *Simple Accounting for Windows*™ 6.0 and 7.0, the password resides in the .ask file. In *Simple* 6.0 entity name is at offset 290–434 and the password is contained in 38 bytes from offset 252–289. For *Simple* 7.0 the password is still in the 38 bytes right before the entity name in the .asc file but the offset is different. Investigators may find it useful to contact vendor support to identify program particularities, eventually developing their own list. Investigators may also find that the Web provides a plethora of this sort of information for the diligent. Finally, investigators may wish to compile a library of program-specific password crackers. These programs reveal or circumvent the password by simply locating it with the same program defaults. These include: *WordCrack*™, *ZipCrack*™, etc. However, investigative agencies which have the financial wherewithal to purchase the comprehensive forensic suites may not find this necessary.

Examination of User Data Files

Once all data have been preserved and/or recovered, investigators should then examine the contents of those files that are within the parameters of the warrant and consistent with case characteristics (i.e., warrants issued in drug cases, for example, may not allow for the examination of graphic files). File viewers and text searching utilities are especially useful for this purpose. File viewers, for example, allow investigators to view the front page of all documents. In addition, many allow users to quickly identify graphics files regardless of assigned file extension. This is particularly helpful to investigators searching for child pornography. Text searching utilities, on the other hand, enable investigators to search through innumerable documents for words or phrases consistent with their evidentiary expectations. Moreover, many utilities provide *fuzzy logic* capabilities, in which input derivatives are also identified. These tools usually provide investigators with data location (cluster, sector, and offset), and allow investigators to pipe the information to an evidentiary file. However, they can prove relatively useless if the keyword list employed is poorly prepared.

According to many investigators, the construction of an adequate keyword list is one of the most difficult, and potentially time consuming, tasks necessary in computer investigations. Such lists must be consistent with warrant specifications and particular to case characteristics. Effective lists may be described as a balance of vagueness—vague enough to identify all files that may contain criminal evidence, but not so vague that false hits are numerous. Investigators should avoid common terminology and look to case particularities to identify appropriate terms, including characteristics of the suspect or victim (i.e., name, nicknames, etc.) and aspects of the crime (i.e., location, methodology, etc.). In cases involving child pornography, for example, investigators may wish to avoid terms like "kid" or "sex", because of the potential for false hits.

Investigators should also examine the contents of the autoexec.bat file. Reliance upon automated recovery programs overlooks the obvious—the suspect's computer may be booby-trapped in some way. In addition, important information of a non-destructive nature may reside there. For example, commands in the autoexec.bat may indicated that routine back-ups were made, leading investigators to search for additional media.

Piping of Evidence

Although the majority of evidence recovered in a computer case is admissible only in that form, investigators should make hard copies of any file which may be introduced. This includes word-processing documents, spreadsheets, graphics, movie clips, rogue programs, etc. Investigators should also be careful to make hard copies of directory and subdirectory trees. Finally, all results should be sequentially numbered. It is highly recommended that investigators employ the Bates numbering system, as judicial officials are familiar with its schematics.

Examine of Executable Programs

Examination of executable programs is essential for evidentiary validity. Identification of Trojans, for example, may prove critical in child pornography cases where the suspect argues that s/he was unaware of the images residing on the computer. Because programs like *Back Orifice, Deep Throat,* and *NetBus* allow total remote access to compromised machines[5], investigators must account for their presence, or lack thereof. While some software is commercially available to identify such programs, they are most often program specific. For example, *NetBuster* identifies and locates *NetBus* only. Unfortunately, most of these Trojans were developed by computer hackers, and can prove quite tricky to find. *Back Orifice,* for example, was created by the Cult of the Dead Cow at a hacker's conference (DEFCON7), and later versions allow users to hide the program virtually anywhere. Thus, it is essential that investigators familiarize themselves with the process for Trojan identification.

---

[5]Generally speaking, these types of Trojans come in two parts: the *client* and the *server.* The *client* portion of the program is the one which allows users to remotely access other machines, while the *server* is the portion which *serves* (i.e., provides) information to the client. Most often, the *server* is surreptitiously delivered and executed by unsuspecting victims.

EXAMINING DISKETTES

Like the investigation of computer hard drives, there are no absolutes in the processing of removable storage media. However, informal, generalized guidelines similar to those discussed above may be employed. (Agencies should be hesitant to formally introduce investigative procedures due to the volatile and intangible nature of computer forensics, and the absolutism often demanded in judicial setting.)

Document, document, document—As mentioned previously, the one constant in computer forensics is the need for documentation. At a minimum, documentation should include: the name and rank of all investigative personnel involved in the analysis; time, date, and place of analysis; methodology employed; physical description of media; and all files found on each. This may be done in a variety of ways. The best known (i.e., DOS) is probably the most cumbersome. While this method is relatively easy (a variation of directory, subdirectory, and hidden commands), the printouts tend to be overwhelming. Other programs such as *PowerDesk*™, *Norton Utilities*™, and Maresware's *DiskCat*™, simplify data and beautify possible exhibits, while enabling investigators to search for files by name, date, size, or type. As stated previously, hard drives are not the only source of computer evidence. Storage media, in particular, may be a virtual treasure chest for the experienced investigator. However, the same protections that were necessary to protect the robustness of evidence found on the hard drive apply in the case of floppy diskettes.

In order to identify potential evidence on computer floppies, investigators must first protect the data on the disk from corruption or destruction. The easiest way to do this, of course, is to write-block the entire disk by sliding the plastic lock tab located on the bottom left of a standard 1.44-mb diskette down. To further protect the evidence, it is strongly recommended that investigators also slide a plastic tie through the slot and secure it. This will prevent any accidental manipulation of data. In fact, investigators should be trained to treat all diskettes as if they were unlocked, further ensuring the sanctity of the data. Once the evidence is protected, investigators should image the disk. This can be done with a variety of file management software programs such as *Norton Utilities*™ and *AnaDisk*™. As with the analysis of the hard drive, all forensic analysis should be conducted on verified forensic images. Once such images are obtained, the procedures for evidence recovery are very similar to those employed with the hard drive.

Returning Equipment

Once analysis has been completed, all material or equipment which has proven to be irrelevant or superfluous should be returned upon request as the courts have recognized that the deprivation of computer equipment and data stored therein may provide unacceptable hardship to individuals and corporations, especially in situations where no opportunity is afforded for duplication (Winick, 1994). Indeed, with the increasing reliance upon computer technology, individuals or corporations may face significant economic hazards including bankruptcy. As such, they have argued that continuing deprivation constitutes unreasonable police action once evidence recovery is achieved. In fact, only those computers or equipment which fall under legal forfeit may be held without risk of violating the PPA or incurring civil liability (*Mora* v. *United States,* 955 F.2d 156 (2nd Circuit, 1992). However, it is permissible, and necessary, to "wipe" all contraband from returned equipment.

● A WORD ABOUT DOS

As previously discussed, investigators should maintain a variety of forensic tools, including both automated and manual programs. Both are necessary, although many investigators appear to be overly reliant upon one-stop programs like *EnCase*™. In fact, automated analysis tools are designed to be useful to virtually anyone, including unskilled investigators. In the words of a seasoned examiner, "anyone can pick the low hanging fruit" (Mykyten, 2000). Case characteristics and situational variables will dictate the level and sophistication of the search necessary. Certainly, cases involving threats to national security are such that an exhaustive examination of all available materials is all but mandated. Simple cases involving 40 counts of child pornography in which the criminal evidence clearly resides on a suspect's desktop may not require such detail. Irrespective of the tools selected, a familiarity with DOS is essential for any computer forensic investigator.

Although DOS is anathema to many, the fact that most suspect computers (especially at the local level) operate with a DOS platform requires all investigators to immerse themselves in the world of DOS, at least to the extent that they can navigate around a PC from a command prompt. This is important for court challenges as to an investigators capabilities and, perhaps more importantly, many of the disk utilities necessary for evidence recovery do not work from a GUI (graphical user interface), as GUIs require writes to the suspect drive for operation. Daunting at first, many officers find that practice makes perfect, and that DOS commands and parameters are similar. Below are several of the most common DOS commands encountered during investigations. The list is not intended to provide a complete tutorial in DOS-based systems. Rather, investigators are strongly encouraged to purchase additional texts on DOS. Through anecdotal experience, many investigators new to the field have found the *DOS for Dummies* particularly useful. In addition, the list is most relevant to MSDOS version 6.22, although most of the commands are consistent with earlier versions of DOS.

Investigators should remember that DOS commands will default to the drive in use unless otherwise specified, and that the execution of command lines simply requires the depression of the **<Enter>** key. In addition, investigators should bear in mind that **Internal commands** are loaded into memory from the *COMMAND.COM* file upon startup. As such, these commands are always available. **External commands,** on the other hand, must be stored on the disk in order to be executed. Perhaps the most useful (and certainly the most commonly used) of all internal commands available from the command line in DOS is the help command. This screen is available for all DOS commands, and involves typing the name of the command with a forward slash (/) followed immediately (no spaces) with a question mark. For example, typing **dir/?** at the C prompt **(C:/>)** would display a screen that listed some of the commonly used options (i.e., switches) available for viewing the contents of drive C. If a user wished to preview the contents of drive A, the simple command would read **dir A:**. Since DOS is usually configured to run an entire command without pausing, a user would usually wish to specify pauses between screens. The subsequent command, then, to reveal the page-by-page contents of Drive A would read **dir a: /p** or **dir a:/p**. In addition, users wishing to look beyond the root directory system may use the **/s** switch to look at a directory tree including subdirectories.

Other common internal commands available from the prompt include:

Changing directory—**<cd>**—this allows users to change the directory from the root to a specified path including drive, directory, and subdirectory. Thus, if an investigator wanted to view the contents of a subdirectory entitled "documents" found in the directory "MSWORD" on A drive from the C prompt, they would type **cd a:\msword\documents.**

Copying files—**<copy>**—this command enables users to copy a file from one location to another. As always, if no destination is specified, the default locations would be the current path. Generically speaking, the command line would read **COPY filename destination** Specifically, the command line **COPY alphabet a:** would copy the file **alphabet** to the root directory in the A drive. Users can also be more specific in pathnames. For example, if an investigator was copying all relevant files into a file named **evidence** located on the A drive and s/he wished to copy the document *cocaine1* located on the C drive to this location, s/he would type **COPY cocaine1a:\evidence.**

Date/Time verification—**<DATE TIME>**—these commands enable investigators to verify the suspect system's time and date. This is a very important step in evidence validation. The command line for this is very simple. At the prompt, type either **Date** or **Time**.

Deleting Files—**<DEL>**—as a general rule, investigators can not make changes to the original hard drive of a suspect's computers. However, there are some circumstances which may require the removal of contraband material prior to the return of a machine. (Keep in mind that additional programs, such as Maresware's RMD are more effective in permanently removing contraband.) Very similar in structure to the COPY command, the generic command line would be **del pathname/filename.** Thus, to remove the file **sweet13** which is located on the C drive in directory **photographs,** and investigator would type **del c:\photographs\sweet13.**

Verifying modifications and data access—**<C:\DIR /v>** adding the **<|s>** would give this information down the subdirectory level **<C:\DIR /v /s>.**

Investigators may also find it useful to look at system files located on a suspect drive or evaluate file attributes during an investigation. Config.sys, for example, will provide investigators with system specifications, while using the attribute command will reveal the presence of **hidden files.** They may also find it useful to evaluate the information contained in batch files on a suspect drive, especially those which are automatically executed. Summarily, investigators must be comfortable in the world of command lines, and avoid incompetence through complacence.

TERMS DISCUSSED

CMOS password
default passwords
compressed files
erased files
external commands
hidden files

internal commands
jumpers
key disks
partition tables
pulling the battery

steganographic
(container)
steganographic
(message)
storage enhancement

DISCUSSION QUESTIONS

1. What are the basic steps in data analysis?
2. What are some basic strategies for defeating CMOS passwords?
3. Why should investigators be comfortable within a DOS environment?
4. What are some of the advantages and disadvantages to automated forensic packages?

CONCLUSIONS AND FUTURE ISSUES

13

As stated previously, the advent of technology has vastly changed the modus operandi of certain criminal elements. Indeed, advances have changed the very physical environment in which crime occurs. Whereas physical environments traditionally presented necessary spatial and demographic limitations, the intangibility of electronic communications and commerce exponentially increases illicit possibilities while negating the efficacy of conventional preventive measures. Thieves no longer must concern themselves with the necessary risks associated with the physical removal of massive amounts of stolen merchandise, including their physical presence or the collection of co-conspirators, transportation device, and storage locations. Vandals may generate mass destruction totaling billions without ever leaving the comfort of their home or office. The recent *Code Red Worm,* for example, cost companies over $2.6 billion worldwide, while estimates place the damages associated with the *Love Bug* as high as $8.7 billion *(www.news.findlaw.com/legalnews/s/20011106/n06338921.html).* In fact, the emergence of wireless technology has created an almost ethereal criminal network, in which ghostlike entities emerge ephemerally to wreak their deviant havoc and escape to their digital netherworld. (Such translucence coupled with corresponding perceptions of invincibility has even proven seductive to seemingly average individuals, creating a new breed of first-time criminals.) As such, every aspect of the criminal justice processing of the same must display levels of ingenuity comparable to the virtuosity exhibited by these emerging entrepreneurs. Unfortunately, such has not been the case.

TRADITIONAL PROBLEMS AND RECOMMENDATIONS

Clarification of Computer-Specific Criminal Behavior

For the most part, the investigation and prosecution of computer-related crime has been hindered by a lack of nomenclature, due primarily to the reluctance of the Supreme Court to interpret emerging legislative actions. As such, investigators, prosecutors, and even trial courts have no basis for determining the legality of questioned behavior. This is especially true in the application of child pornography legislation, most specifically, the CPPA. However, such is also the case in cases that are predicated on traditional codification, but contain technological elements. Thus, universal definitions of computer-related crime must be established.

Establishing Technology-Neutral Legislation

The development of computer-specific legislation must be undertaken in a manner that ensures uniformity in application and interpretation irrespective of jurisdictional climate. At the same time, emerging legislation must be generic enough to encompass advances in technology, assuring that application to tomorrow's technology is possible. Just as the applicability of the *Wire Act* has been questioned regarding its implementation for Internet crimes committed via cable modems (as opposed to telephone communications), the advent of wireless communications poses new questions altogether. Thus, legislators should develop technology-neutral legislation, which narrowly defines (and emphasizes) elemental issues like intent, while providing a broad platform for methodology employed. In addition, such legislation should identify traditional challenges in the analysis of digital evidence and provide justifications for the potential of protracted examination of computer materials (i.e., voluminous nature of computer containers, password protected information, damaged media, lack of resources, etc.).

Establishing Accountability for Internet Users

Legislation must also be enacted that ensures confidentiality for those who seek it for legitimate purposes, but that denies blanket anonymity. This would allow legitimate surfers the luxury to browse the Web anonymously for all practical purposes, safely concealing their identities from criminals and government officials alike, while providing a mechanism for LE to pursue those predators, criminals or terrorists who attempt to mask their illegitimate activities. This is especially important in the wake of the events of 9/11. It is imperative that our interest in the globalization of information and communication not supersede the interests of national security. Unfortunately, such a balance is difficult to achieve.

Democratic principles mandate elevated expectations of privacy in private activities which are often counterproductive to law enforcement interests. Moreover, the foundations of open markets and capitalist ideologies require a communication tool which provides a medium for worldwide dissemination, heretofore unavailable prior to the introduction of the World Wide Web. Thus, the development of enforcement-friendly legislation which encourages economic growth consistent with an emerging global market and which does not stifle individual expression is a difficult task at best. Legislatures must also struggle with issues of state sovereignty, taking care that the role of the Federal government is that of mediator, not dictator.

Increasing Public Awareness and Research Capabilities

Traditionally, computer-related crime has not garnered significant attention from most sectors of society, which fail to recognize the insidious nature of the phenomenon. Thus, a comprehensive effort must be undertaken to educate all levels of the community, including politicians, teachers, law-enforcement officials, individual consumers, and children. Such awareness must include the potential of computer crime, creating an appreciation of the dangers inherent in such activities (i.e., everyone must see both the threat and the exponential growth associated with computer crime). Once established, this collective understanding should result in additional funding for computer-related initiatives and increase public reporting and cooperation. In addition, baseline measurements of prevalence and typologies of offenders should be established. One possible solution would be to amend one of the two empirical measures of crime: the FBI's Uniform Crime Report (UCR) and the National Crime Survey (NCS). This would enable officials to classify incidents and offenders, increasing the efficiency and effectiveness of subsequent investigations. (Without such baseline data on incidents, offenders, forensic problems, and case outcomes, identification of regional or national trends is all but impossible, and the development of evidence analysis capabilities is unlikely.) Moreover, available information should include a comprehensive national directory of technical experts, forensic examiners, academic resources, and external granting institutions, as well as local information including a who's who of electronic crime investigators, unit managers, prosecutors, laboratory technicians, manufacturers, and expert witnesses. Such a compilation of data, when presented as an online clearinghouse, should encourage information-sharing among investigators and agencies alike.

Increasing Inter-Agency and Intra-Departmental Cooperation

Although the law enforcement culture has long been characterized by a lack of communication and cooperation among agencies, the lack of resources available to combat computer-related crime mandates increasing the number of multi-jurisdictional task forces and central reporting stations. While LE agencies have recently formed such collaborative efforts, much is left to be done. Local agencies, in particular, should develop formal alliances with better funded, better trained, state and Federal agencies. The Federal government, on the other hand, must make resources available to these same municipal administrators seeking technological assistance. This includes concentrated dissemination of grant solicitations, as well as technical guidance of same. Task forces already in place should independently seek external funding, and should include at least one individual versed in the art of grant writing. Utilization of central reporting stations (both regional and national) should be increased, as duplication of effort dramatically decreases the efficacy of even the most dedicated of efforts. Such clearinghouses should mirror (and work in concert with) the Federal system in which regional U.S. Attorneys' offices are required to report all ongoing investigations to one central location (i.e., the Computer Crime Section of the Department of Justice). To further conserve resources, these stations should serve multiple tasks, such as serving as a 24-hour support line, equipped to handle general legal inquiries and provide onsite management assistance for electronic crime units and task forces. (Inter-agency collaboration notwithstanding, investigators must also secure cooperation *within* their own department, increasing awareness of the potentiality of digital evidence and its corresponding vulnerability. Furthermore, investigators must obtain executive support so that resources may be allocated without reservation. Until such a time, computer-related criminal investigations will remain substandard.)

Developing Relationships Between Investigative Agencies and the Private Sector

All levels of the law-enforcement community must also seek out and establish partnerships with the high-tech industry for a variety of reasons. First and foremost, law enforcement agencies will remain overworked, understaffed, poorly funded, and technologically deficient due to the continuing struggle for external funding. High-tech corporations, with their unlimited resources and highly trained personnel, may alleviate some of this problem by donating equipment and expertise to their local agencies. In addition, these entities may be called upon to develop software requisite to the law enforcement mission like IP tracking systems, editing and searching tools, and general investigative utilities. Partnerships which emphasize ethical accountability may also result in the development of materials which preclude the proliferation of inappropriate material through filtering and professional accountability. For example, the Electronic Commerce and Consumer Protection Group (which includes AOL, American Express, AT&T, Dell, Visa, Microsoft, IBM, etc.) is currently developing jurisdictional regulations to address consumer protection in a global marketplace. Their goals include the development of a code of conduct among e-tailers to facilitate e-commerce within a secure environment and the retention of data to identify online predators. Finally, such teamwork will necessarily result in increased reporting of criminal victimization among corporate targets making it easier to develop baseline data for empirical measurement.

Developing International Cooperation

Due to the increasing globalization of the electronic marketplace, it is imperative that international cooperation be secured. Unfortunately, such collaboration must overcome traditional problems including: cultural stereotypes and multi-cultural tensions; a lack of global consensus on criminal behavior and human rights; a lack of expertise in criminal justice and legal communities; competing interests; a lack of extradition and mutual assistance treaties; a lack of synchronized law enforcement efforts; and, finally, jurisdictional disputes regarding original sovereignty in cases of dual criminality. While some of these traditional barriers may be overcome through perseverance and a universal understanding of the insidious nature of computer-related criminal activity, others may not. However, officials should attempt to establish an increased number of Multi-Lingual Assistance Treaties (MLAT's) which address jurisdictional inconsistencies. Without these, international legal assistance is governed by domestic mutual legal assistance laws and practices, which includes the *letters rogatory* process (a *letter rogatory* is a letter request for assistance from one country's judicial authority to that of another country) (*www.usdoj.gov/criminal/cybercrime/unlawful.htm*, last accessed on 10/01/01). Such practices are not only unworkable in most cases, but they require individualized intervention of Federal authorities, a situation sure to result in increased backlogs and case overload. In the absence of MLATs, Federal authorities should develop formal alliances with enforcement components of other nations. The Organization for Economic Cooperation and Development (OECD), for example, recognized that cultural differences must be overcome when circumstances dictate, publishing a report that evaluated existing laws among international communities and suggesting revisions of same which would establish a minimum list of abuses that all member countries would prohibit and prosecute. Thus, administrators must diligently pursue such collaborations. At a minimum, a generalized understanding with other international communities which allows for investigation and subsequent prosecution of computer crime must be achieved.

Standardization of Accreditation or Expertise

Due to the inexperience of legislative authorities and the inconsistency of judicial estimation, law-enforcement authorities must establish a standard of accreditation and/or expertise of forensic methodologies and examiners. As in any emerging discipline, such standardization would decrease *Daubert/Frye* challenges to the recovery of digital evidence. (Such challenges, issued to emerging or untested scientific methods, require a variety of thresholds, many of which have not yet been achieved in the emerging field of computer forensics.) Thus, the discipline should attempt to identify and address each of the following questions:

1. Can the techniques involved in data recovery be empirically tested?
2. Have they been subjected to peer review and publication?
3. Does the theory or technique have the potential for a high rate of error?
4. Does the technique enjoy a general acceptance within the scientific community?

Such challenges can only be met through the development of professional associations and academic publishing which provide a means of discourse among analysts. (The standard does not require a universal acceptance or rigorous testing by *all* experts in the field, but it does require a mechanism for empirical testing and debate.) Although the resources associated with the development of independent research outlets could prove insurmountable at the present time, practitioners should evaluate the feasibility of amalgamation with established forensic science associations. As an alternative, funds could be solicited from federal monies or technology companies. Such funds could then be invested in an interest-bearing endowment, much like specialized chairs in university settings. Regardless, law enforcement administrators and legislators should develop innovative strategies to increase revenues available to law enforcement to establish high-tech investigative capabilities.

It must be noted that the standardization of computer forensics cannot be accomplished overnight. Like all recognized disciplines, it must be founded on a solid framework of scientific inquiry. Computer forensic "doc-in-a-box" organizations that tout certificates of accreditation are most often self-serving entities more concerned with capitalism and free enterprise than law enforcement interests. Self-proclaimed "experts" may actually hinder prosecutorial efforts by utilization of unrecognized methodologies. In fact, true experts are much harder to find than the multitude of individuals who have anointed themselves as the computer forensic messiah. Many of the latter category do not display any evidence of expertise (or humility), while the former are those individuals that recognized their own limitations and concede that technology is far outpacing investigative capabilities. Thus, any development of an accreditation process should utilize those individuals who are respected among their peers, and include a combination of investigators and forensic programmers.[1] Such an entity would bring professionalism to computer investigations, extend awareness among the community, and decrease the likelihood of successful evidentiary challenges.

Miscellaneous

As more and more individuals are using the Internet in their daily lives, it is critical for law enforcement to establish a visible presence on the web. All departments, for example, should create and maintain a departmental web page, illustrating their commitment to contemporary problems and providing a mechanism for community input. In this way, technology can be used to foster positive relations with the community, and establish a system conducive to anonymous reporting (i.e., the same perception of anonymity that encourages criminals creates a comfort zone for those wishing to come forward with information but are reluctant to be identified). In addition, it allows departments to publicize their mission statements, promote departmental initiatives, enhance their ability to update community residents (including the photographic display of missing persons and wanted individuals), and provides a mechanism for communication in emergency situations (i.e., severe weather, etc.).

FUTURE TRENDS AND EMERGING CONCERNS

As illustrated throughout the text, the identification, investigation, and prosecution of computer-related crime is accompanied by a myriad of unique problems. Unfortunately, it is anticipated that these problems will be further exacerbated by emerging technologies. Legal questions regarding decency and privacy are but two of the issues sure to plague future administrators. Advances in wireless communications and encryption technology will further complicate the legal landscape, and the increasing convergence of audio, video, and digital data will present new challenges for criminal investigators.

---

[1]The following individuals were but a few examples of experts which the author had the privilege of conversing with during the preparation of this manuscript. All of them recognized the importance of networking, and all would probably object to the characterization as "expert." Danny Mares, *Marsware;* Joe Mykytyn; Chip Johnson, *State Law Enforcement Division (SLED);* Jimmy Doyle, *NYPD;* Sunny Parmar, *RCMP,* Bruce Simmons, *Mitre).*

Wireless Communications

Although cellular telephones have been around for quite some time, the reduction of costs and the increase in communication quality has vastly expanded their audience and created a society increasingly reliant on technology. Fortunately for law enforcement, tapping into wireless communications has proven far easier than traditional telephonic exchanges (i.e., it is easier to identify a suspect's cellular provider than to predict which pay phone s/he will use). Moreover, it provides data on the cell site of the sender or recipient, and provides a mechanism for locating a particular phone. It is anticipated that this capability will only be enhanced by recently passed regulations by the FCC which require all providers to develop the capability of locating phones within a 40-foot radius for longitude, latitude, and altitude (Dempsey, 1997). However, the increase in wireless communications has also complicated investigations and developed new avenues for criminal behavior. Earth-based gateways of the satellite systems which service the United States, for example, may actually reside outside its jurisdictional boundaries making them almost impossible to police. In addition, the decreasing costs associated with cellular service have encouraged the use of "disposable phones" in the furtherance of a virtual cornucopia of criminal activity, while the sheer marketability of wireless communications has attracted representatives from criminal syndicates.

Data hiding: remote storage, encryption, and the like. As if the advent of wireless technologies was not enough to hinder law enforcement efforts, data hiding practices, precipitated by warnings from privacy advocates, present unique challenges. The increase of remote storage facilities (i.e., virtual islands of infor-

ONLINE STOCK MANIPULATION

The Internet has invigorated the entire industry of stock scams. Now there isn't much scam activity that happens off-line.
   —Kevin Lichtman, president of FinanicalWeb.com.

Con artists looking to make a fast buck have been around forever, as have the suckers who fall for their scams. But the Internet has altered the way the game is played; the bad guys have mastered new techniques for touting frauds on the Web, spamming scams through e-mail and talking up hot investment tips on bulletin boards.

The one-time success of Net stocks and the perception that anyone can get rich on the Internet are making the job of scam artists even easier. Plenty of money-losing Internet companies with minimal track records and hazy business plans have been underwritten by reputable brokerage firms, and their stock prices have shot up hundreds of percent a day. Meanwhile, con artists are peddling copycat companies of their own, and investors can find it difficult to differentiate between companies with legitimate potential and scams designed to part them from their money.

mation unattached and, thus, unregulated by a sovereign state), for example, may be especially troublesome to law-enforcement authorities for a variety of reasons. First, it does not seem likely that the Supreme Court will uphold the constitutionality of search warrants for non-particularized locations of remote areas of data storage (i.e., a search warrant for any location of remote data). Thus, investigators may be unable to access incriminating information. Second, the lack of physicality obscures jurisdictional boundaries, making it unclear as to who is the prevailing legal authority. And, finally, hyper-privacy individuals or businesses may utilize *data stripping* methods, where data is fragmented and placed on various servers.

The emergence of over-the-counter encryption technology may also prove problematic for law enforcement officials. As these packages become more available and consumers become more concerned with privacy and/or security, it appears inevitable that encrypted files, folders, and/or drives will become more commonplace in criminal investigations. Unfortunately, advances in encryption technology coupled with the easing of export regulations may make it all but impossible to access questionable data. However, the events of 9/11 may make the passage of anti-encryption legislation more likely, as it has been discovered that communications between the conspirators were encrypted with PGP.

Finally, the increasing availability of anonymizer-type technology and disposable e-mail accounts may further complicate criminal investigations. Like the other

NEW INVESTIGATIVE TECHNOLOGIES AND THE CONSTITUTION

As with other areas of technology, the introduction of surveillance software and methodologies has resulted in a variety of legal questions unanswered by traditional legislation or judicial action. One such question involves the use of software which captures every action undertaken by an individual user of a suspect machine (i.e., key loggers).

Case in point: Does the implantation of key logging software by government officials violate the wiretap statute? What is the legal standard for obtaining judicial permission (i.e., court order, warrant, etc.)? In a recent crackdown on organized crime families in the Philadelphia area, government agents armed with a warrant copied the contents of a personal computer located at Merchant Services, a company allegedly owned by Nicky Scarfo, Jr. However, they were unable to access the information in a file ("Factors") which was encrypted with PGP. So they obtained a court order to return to the location. Subsequently, they installed a key logger on the same machine, and secured the password necessary to decrypt said file. This resulted in a three-count indictment. Government is refusing to identify the methodology used, stating that it is not important. Scarfo's attorneys, on the other hand, claim that this knowledge is necessary to determine whether a wiretap order should have been secured. (Coughlin and Rudolph, 2001.)

technologies discussed, these tools are becoming more popular as more and more consumers become concerned with the security of proprietary and personal information. While the majority of those individuals employing these mechanisms are concerned with protecting themselves from online predators and fraudsters, many deviants utilize them to hide their activities from law enforcement authorities.

Governing Decency and Virtual Pornography

Courts have been increasingly cautious and consistently ambiguous regarding the level of protection afforded online communications and in defining indecency and vulgarity on the web. However, it appears unlikely that a universal definition will soon emerge as content-restrictive legislation has failed judicial scrutiny. Thus, numerous bills have been proposed which involve the use of "E-chip" blocking software. Such devices would be distributed by ISPs and would serve as information filters. Unfortunately, similar measures have been widely criticized as they are incapable of distinguishing between legitimate, educational information and profane or indecent material. Other proposals which include rating systems for sites are equally unworkable as there is no agency for enforcement. Finally, none of the proposals provide for the regulation of simulated behavior or virtual images.

Until recently, the thought that the computer (or any other device) could enable users to act out fantasies in a real-life context appeared preposterous. However, some authors suggest that individual users may utilize advances in technology to engage in virtual behavior which in the real world may be felonious. Indeed, society has already witnessed inroads into computer-generated images. Movies as early as *Jurassic Park* and *Total Recall* have successfully utilized computer-generated animation, while digital remastering has produced the re-release of George Lucas' *Star Wars* trilogy. In fact, some individuals argue that the use of synthetic actors may be the wave of the future as the technology becomes more available and less expensive. This would allow producers to reduce the rising costs of salaries, while at the same time, providing a "safe" way to conduct dangerous stunts (Johnson, 1994). This same technology could also be used in illegitimate markets—allowing pornography peddlers to go beyond the scope of traditional decency standards. At some point, for example, it will be possible to generate realistic images of children engaging in sexual activity or create snuff films, where the computer-generated "victim" is killed during sexual acts. Some even suggest that the near future will bring technology capable of simulating actual sexual intercourse. Appropriately placed sensors in gloves and body coverings coupled with sophisticated programs and virtual helmets would literally enable the user to experience sexual arousal with an inanimate object.

> *Some promoters of virtual reality see a new, safe, clean way to have sexual encounters. Eventually users will be able to don a suit, gloves, and goggles, and have sex with their computer. Inside the goggles are tiny video monitors that would project computer-generated images, and the suit and gloves would have sensors to react to every move of the user. Users will be able to buy, rent, or make their own*

life-like sex partners, and do with them whatever they please. . . . we don't have the sticky stuff that comes with real life, no more AIDS, no more intersubjective rivalries, no more otherness . . . there's no more (real) sex, and therefore there will be no more failure (Johnson quoting Marshall , 1994).

Such capabilities will necessarily increase the number of individuals acting out fantastical situations that would violate criminal statutes in the absence of abstract dimensions. It may be argued that such increases may result in amplifications in real world situations, creating an environment conducive to the exploitation and victimization of children in particular. Thus, legislation must be created to establish acceptable parameters of computer activity. Unfortunately, civil libertarians will continue to argue that virtual victimization is a legal impossibility, and will continue to promote the eradication of any censorship legislation regardless of design.

CONCLUSIONS

Unquestionably, advances in technology increase the potentiality and renovate the methodology of traditional criminal behavior. Just as the automobile vastly expanded the landscape of the criminal underworld, the advent of cyberspace and the ability to communicate globally has exponentially broadened the potentiality of criminal activity. Although some authors predict that *cybercrimes will peak and then decrease within the next five to ten years* (Parker, 1998: 63), there is no empirical evidence to support this supposition. In fact, the streamlining of proprietary data coupled with society's increasing reliance on computer technology is sure to create an environment ripe for criminal entrepreneurs.

It seems entirely plausible that a certain level of street crime will be supplanted by technological alternatives as the profitability and anonymity of cybercrime become well known. In fact, a marked increase in narcotics trafficking and fencing of stolen property has been noted on the Web in recent years. Unfortunately, the criminal justice system is unequipped to deal with such transference. The lack of appropriate legislation and the lack of resources allocated to this area of criminal activity can only be exacerbated by social and judicial indifference to the dangers of computer-related crime. Thus, it is essential that the potentiality of computer-related crime and the insidious nature of the phenomenon be recognized and addressed by all sectors of the community.

DISCUSSION QUESTIONS

1. What can legislators do to assist law enforcement in the area of computer-related crime?
2. What can law enforcement agencies do to enhance their investigative capabilities?
3. What are some potential benefits and pitfalls of formal accreditation of forensic examiners?
4. What are some emerging issues in the area of high-tech crime? Why are these problematic, and what proactive measures can be implemented to lessen their negative impact?

REFERENCES

CASES CITED

Andersen Consulting LLP v. *UOP and Bickel and Brewer,* 991 F.Supp.1041 (1998)

Bernstein v. *United States Department of Justice,* 1999 9th Circuit 9716686

Coolidge v. *New Hampshire,* 403 U.S. 443, 465, 29 L.Ed. 2d 564, 91 S.Ct. 2022 (1971)

Ex parte Jackson, 96 U.S. 727, 733

FCC v. *Pacifica Foundation,* 438 U.S. 726 (1978)

Fraser v. *Nationwide Mutual Insurance* (decided March, 2001) United States District Court for the Eastern District of Pennsylvania. # 98-CV-6726

The Free Speech Colation v. *Reno* (9th Circuit, 1999)–(198 F. 3d 1083, 9th Circuit 1999) #97-16536)

Ginsberg v. *New York,* 390 U.S. 629, (1968)

Hester v. *United States,* 265 U.S. 57

Hoffa v. *U.S.,* 385 U.S. 293 (1966)

In re Subpoena Duces Tecum, 846 F.Supp. 11, SDNY 1994)

Florida v. *Jimeno,* 500 U.S. 248, 251

Junger v. *Daley,* 1998 WL 388972 (N.D. Ohio, 1998)

Karn v. *U.S. Department of State,* 107 F.3d 923 (D.C.Cir. 1997)

Katz v. *United States* 389 U.S. 347, 88 S.CT. 507; 1967 U.S. LEXIS 2; 19 L.ED. 2D 576

Lewis v. *United States,* 385 U.S. 206, 210

Maryland v. *Garrison,* 480 U.S. 79, 84

Miller v. *California,* 413 U.S. 15 (1973)

New York v. *Ferber,* 458 U.S. 747 (1982)

Olmstead v. *United States,* 277 U.S. 438, 457, 464, 466

Osborne v. *Ohio,* 495 U.S. 103,115 , 110 S.Ct. 1691,1699, 109 L.Ed. 2d 98 (1990)

Rawlings v. *Kentucky,* 448 U.S. 98; 100 S.Ct. 2556; 1980 U.S. Lexis 142; 65 L. Ed. 2d 633.)

Reno v. *ACLU,* 117 S. Ct. 2329

Rios v. *United States,* 364 U.S. 253

Roth v. *United States,* 354 U.S. 476 (1957)

Sable Communications, Inc. v. *FCC,* 492 U.S. 115 (1989)

Stanley v. *Georgia,* 394 U.S. 557(1969)

Steve Jackson Games, Inc. v. *U.S. Secret Service, et al.,* 36 F. 3d 457, 463 (5th Cir., 1994)

Timothy R. McVeigh v. *William S. Cohen, et al.* 983 F. Supp. 215 (1998). District of Columbia

United States v. *Abbell,* 914 F.Supp. 519 (S.D.Fla. 1995)

United States v. *Acheson,* 195 F.3d 645 (11th Circuit, 1999)

United States v. *Barth,* 26 F. Supp. 2d 929 (U.S. Dist. Lexis 18316) (U.S. District Court for the Western District of Texas, Midland–Odessa Division)

United States v. *Block,* 590 F.2d 5335 (4th Cir. 1978)

United States v. *Carey,* 172 F.3d 1268; 1999 U.S. App. LEXIS 7197; 1999 Colo.J.C.A.R. 2287. (10th Circuit, 1999)

United States v. *Charbonneau,* 979 F.Supp. 1177 (S.D. Ohio 1997)

United States v. *Dichiarinte,* 445 F.2d 126 (7th Cir. 1971)

United States v. *Elliott,* 107 F.3d 810, 815 (10th Cir. 1997)

United States v. *Gawrysiak,* 972 F. Supp. 853 (D.N.J.1997)

United States v. *Gutierrez-Hermosillo,* 142 F. 3d 1225, 1231 (10th Cir), cert. Denied, 119 S.Ct. 230 (1998)

United States v. *Hersch,* CR-A-93-10339-2, 1994 WL 568728

United States v. *Hilton,* 167 F.3d 61 (1st Circuit, 1999)

United States v. *Hunter,* 13 F. Supp. 2d 574 (D.Vt. 1998)—privileges

United States v. *Kennerley,* 209 F. 119, 120 (S.D.N.Y. 1913)

United States v. *Kim* 27 F.3d 947, 956 (3d Cir. 1994)

United States v. *Lee,* 274 U.S. 559, 563

United States v. *Lyons,* 992 F.2d 1029 (10th Cir. 1993)

United States v. *Maxwell,* 42 M.J. 568 (1995) United States Air Force Court of Criminal Appeals.

United States v. *Mento,* (#99-4813) (4th, 2000)

United States v. *Meriwether,* 917 F.2d 955, 960 (6th Cir., 1990)

United States v. *Miller,* 425 U.S. 435, 443 (1976)

United States v. *Monroe* (50 M.J. 550 (A.F.C.C.A. 1999)

United States v. *Pervaz,* 118 F. 3d 1 (1st Cir, 1997)

United States v. *Reyes,* 922 F. Supp. 818, 836 (S.D.N.Y. 1996); 798 F. F.2D 380,383 (10th Cir. 1986)

United States v. *Ross,* 456 U.S. 798, 820–22 (1982)

United States v. *Sassani,* 1998 WL 89875 (4th Cir. Mar. 4) (per curiam) (unpublished decision), cert. denied, 119 S.Ct. 276 (1998)

United States v. *Schaefer,* 87 F. 3d 562, 569 (1st Cir. 1996)

United States v. *Stribling,* 94 F.3d 321, 324 (7th Cir. 1996)

United States v. *Thomas,* (74 F.3d. 701, (6TH Cir. 1996)

United States v. *Torch,* 609 F.2d 1088, 1090 (4th Cir. 1979)—seizing hardware

United States v. *Turner* (1st Circuit) *http://laws.findlaw.com/1st/981258.html*

Warden v. *Hayden,* 387 U.S. 294, 304

Weeks v. *United States,* 232 U.S. 383

Wesley College v. *Leslie Pitts, Bettina Ferguson, and Keith Hudson,* 974 F. Supp. 375. (1997)—United States District Court for the District of Delaware

STATUTES

Electronic Communication Privacy Act of 19, U.S. Code: Title 18, Section 2510 18 U.S.C.} 2511(2)(a)(i) Federal Rules of Criminal Procedure - 41(e), 15, 17, 18

WORKS CITED

Adams, Jo-Ann M. (1996). "Controlling Cyberspace: Applying the Computer Fraud and Abuse Act to the Internet." *Santa Clara Computer and High Technology Law Journal,* 12(403): *www.lexis-nexis.com.* Last accessed on 1/11/01.

Andreano, Frank P. (1999). "The Evolution of Federal Computer Crime Policy: The Ad Hoc Approach to an Ever-Changing Problem". *American Journal of Criminal Law, 27* (81): Lexis-Nexis.

Baker, Glenn D. (1993). "Trespassers will be prosecuted: Computer Crime in the 1990's." *Computer/Law* Journal, 12 (61): *www.westdoc.com*.

Baladi, Joe (1999). "Buidling Castles Made of Glass: Security on the Internet." *University of Arkansas at Little Rock Law Review, 21*(251).

Bates, Jim. (1997). "Fundamentals of Computer Forensics." *International Journal of Forensic Computing. www.forensic-computing.com/archives/fundamentals.html.* Last accessed on 20 May 2000.

Center for Democracy & Technology (2000). "Encryption Litigation." *wysiwyg:// 99/http:// www. cdt.org/ cypto/litigation/* (accessed on 5/15/00).

Center for Strategic and International Studies, Global Organized Crime Project (1998). "Cybercrime . . . Cyberterrorism . . . Cyberwarfare: Averting An Electronic Waterloo." Washington, DC.

Chittenden, Maurice (2000). "Security Alert as Theif Grabs Military Laptop." *The Sunday Times News. 5/21/00. www.the-times.co.uk/...pages/sti/2000/05021/ stinwenws01039. html.* Last accessed on 9/2/00.

Clark, Franklin and Diliberto, Ken (1996). *Investigating Computer Crime.* CRC Press: Boca Raton, Florida.

Clarke, Catherine Therese (1996). "Innovation and the Information Environment: From CrimINet to Cyber-Perp: Toward an Inclusive Approach to Policing the Evolving Criminal Mens Rea on the Internet." *Oregon Law Review, 75* (191): 1-46; *www.lexis-nexis.com.* Last accessed on 11/20/99.

Coacher, LeEllen (1999). "Permitting Systems Protection Monitoring: When the Government Can Look and What It Can See." *Air Force Law Review, 46*(155).

Cohen, Fred (2001). "Information Protection." Opening Keynote Presentation of the annual meetings of the Techno-Security conference, Myrtle Beach, SC, April 23, 2001.

Doherty, Kelly M. (1999). "*www.obscenity.com*: An Analysis of Obscenity and Indecency Regulation on the Internet. *Akron Law Review, 32*(259), *http://web .lexis-nexis.com*, last accessed on 1/22/01, 4:04 p.m.

Department of Justice (1997). "Report on the Availability of Bombmaking Information, The Extent to which its Dissemination may be Subject to Regulations Consistent with the First Amendment to the United States Consitution." Office of Legislative Affairs, 29 April 1997.

Dempsey, James X. (1997). "Communications Privacy in the Digital Age: Revitalizing the Federal Wiretap Laws to Enhance Privacy." *Albany Law Journal of Science and Technology, 8*(1): *www.cdt.org/publications/lawreview/1997albany.shtml.* Last accessed on April 10, 2000.

Digital Telephony and Law Enforcement Access to Advanced Telecommunications Technologies and Services: Joint Hearings on H.R. 4922 and S. 2375 Before the Subcommittee on Technology and the Law of the Senate Committee on the Judiciary and the Subcommittee on Civil and Constitutional Rights of the House Committee on the Judiciary, 103rd Congress 6 (1994).

Dittrich, David (1999). "The *stacheldraht* Distributed Denial of Service Attack Tool. Written December 31, 1999. *http://packetstorm.securify.com/distributed/ stacheldraht.analysis.*
Last accessed on 2/12/01 at 2:37 p.m.

DOJ (9/25/00). Texas Woman Pleads Guilty to Operating Ring that Trafficked in Counterfeit Microsoft Software. *www.cybercrime.gov/mos.htm.* Last accessed 10/19/00.

DOJ (9/28/00). Emulex Hoaxer Indicted for Using Bogus Press Release and Internet Service to Drive Down Price of Stock. *www.cybercrime.gov/emulex.htm.* Last accessed 10/19/00.

DOJ (2000). Computer Crime and Intellectual Property Section (CCIPS): Prosecuting Crimes Facilitated by Computers and by the Interent. *www.cybercrime .gov/crimes.html.* Last accessed 10/2/00.

EnCase Legal Journal (April, 2000) *Encase Legal Journal, 1*(3): 1–16. Guidance Software, Inc.

FitzGerald, Nick (1995). "Frequently asked questions on virus-L/comp.virus". *www.bocklabs.wisc.edu/ ~janda/virl_faq.html#B01.* Accessed 15 May 2000.

Fu, Kevin (1996). "Crime and law in cyberspace." DOJ/Training Session, The Sixth Conference on Computer, Freedom and Privacy, MIT, Cambridge, MA.

Geating, Gary (1998). "First Amendment: b) Obscenity and Other Unprotected Speech: Free Speech Coalition v. Reno." *Berkeley Technology Law Journal 13*(389). *www.lexis-nexis.com.* Last accessed on 1/22/01.

Gindin, Susan E. (1999). *Guide to E-Mail and the Internet in the Workplace.* Bureau of National Affairs: Washington, D.C.

Glasner, Joanna (2000). "Typo-loving Squatter Squashed." *www.wired.com/news/ business/0,1367,39888,00.html* last accessed on 11/1/00.

Grennan, Sean; Britz, Marjie T., Rush, Jeff, and Barker, Tom (2000). *Gangs: An International Approach.* Prentice Hall: Upper Saddle River, New Jersey.

Guidance Software (1999). *EnCase™: Secure and Analyze Computer Evidence– User's Guide,* Guidance Software, Inc: Pasadena, CA.

Hall, Mark (2000). "Reno Calls for Network Targeting Net Crime." *Computerworld 34*(3): 17.

Harbert, Tam (1999). "Guard Dog Supreme." *Electronic Business, 25*(5): 56–60.

Icove, David, Seger, Karl, and VonStorch William (1995). *Computer Crime: A Crimefighter's Handbook.* O'Reilly & Asssociates, Inc.: Sebastopol, California.

Jacques, Stephen C. (1997). "Comment: Reno v. ACLU: Insulating the Internet, the First Amendment, and the Marketplace of Ideas." *The American University Law* Review, 46 (1945):

Johnson, David (1994). "Why the Possession of Computer-Generated Child Pornography 4(311). *http://web.lexisnexis.com/universal/docu...zS&_md5+aba61b17 e6c9c7f8aoe836f07b620293.* Last accessed 2/7/01.

Kerr, Donald M. (July 4, 2000). Statement for the Record on *Internet and Data Interception Capabilities Developed by FBI* before the United States House of Representatives: The Committee on the Judiciary Subcommittee on the Constitution, Washington, D.C.: *www.fbi.gov/pressrm/congress/congressoo/ kerr072400.htm.* Last accessed 2/12/01.

Kerr, Donald M. (September 6, 2000b). Statement for the Record on *Carnivore Diagnostic Tool* before the United States Sentate: The Committee on the Judiciary, Washington, D.C.: *www.fbi.gov/pressrm/congress/congressoo/kerr090600.htm*

Kluger, Jeffrey (2000). "Extortion on the Internet." *Time 155*(3): 56 (24 June).

Kerr, Orin S. (2001). *Computer Crime and Intellectual Property Section (CCIPS) and Seizing Computers and Obtaining Electronic Evidence in Criminal Investigations. www.cybercrime.gov/searchmanual.htm.* Last accessed on 1/16/01.

Kovacich, Gerald L. and Boni, William C. (2000). *High-Technology Crime Investigator's Handbook: Working in the Global Information Environment.* Butterworth-Heinemann: Boston, Mass.

LaFave, Wayne R. (1996). "Computers, Urinals, and the Fourth Amendment: Confessions of a Patron Saint." *Michigan Law Review, 94*(8): 253–2589.

Levin, Robert B. (1995). "The Virtual Fourth Amendment: Searches and Seizures in Cyberspace." *Maryland Bar Journal, XXVII*(3): 2–5.

Litton/TASC (2000). *Computer Forensics Investigations.* Litton/TASC: Chantilly, VA.

Mahnaimi, Uzi (2000). "Israeli spies tapped Clinton e-mail." *The Sunday Times: Foreign News,* 5/21/2000, *www.the-times.co.uk/...pages/sti/2000/05/21/stifgnusa 02003.htm.* Last accessed 9/15/00.

Manjoo, Farhad (2000). "Hacker finds hole in Netscape Communicator." *Wired News. www.wired.com/news/technology.* Last accessed 9/15/00 at 2:30 p.m.

Meeks, Brock N. (2000). "FBI's Carnivore has partners: Declassified documents reveal e-mail snoop program details." www.msnbc.com/new/47749.asp?0nm=T19&vpl=1.

Metchik, Eric (1997). "A Typology of Crime on the Internet." *Security Journal, 9:* 27–31.

Mitchell, Stevan D. and Banker, Elizabeth A. (1998) "Private Intrusion Response." *Harvard Journal of Law and Technology.* 11(699).

Musgrove, Mike (1999). "Suit Targets DVD-Copying Software: Industry Group Seeks to Block Breaking of Security System." *www.washingtonpost.com/ wp-srv/Wplate/1999-12/29/0261-12299-idx.html* (last accessed on 1/13/00).

Mykyten, Joe (2000). Personal communications. Duluth, Georgia. 18–23 July 2000.

Noblett, Michael G.: Pollitt, Mark M.; and Presley, Lawrence A. (2000). "Recovering and Examining Computer Forensic Evidence." *Forensic Science Communications, 2*(4): *www. fbi.gov/programs/labs/fsc/current/computer.htm* (last accessed 11/6/00).

Orenstein, David (1999). "Standard in Works for Sharing E-Customer Data: Ability to easily share information alarms privacy experts, despite planned guidelines." *Computerworld,* 11/22/99: pg. 2.

Packard, Ashley (2000). "Does Proposed Federal Cyberstalking Legislation Meet Constitutional Requirements?" *Communications Law and Policy,* 5(505): *www.lexis-nexis.com* last accessed on 2/20/01.

Parker, Donn B. (1998). *Fighting Computer Crime: A New Framework for Protecting Information.* John Wiley & Sons, Inc., New York, NY.

Radcliff, Deborah (1999). "Typing a byte out of crime." *Computerworld, 33*(22): 32–33. (8/9/99).

Radcliff, Deborah (1998). "Crime in the 21st Century." *Infoworld, 20*(50): 65–66. (12/14/98)

Randall, Neil (1999). "How Viruses Work: Understanding how viruses work is the first step in defending against them." *PC Magazine,* pg. 1 (2/9/99).

Rappaport, Kim L. (1998). "In the Wake of Reno v. ACLU: The Continued Struggle in Western Constitutional Democracies with Internet Censorship and Freedom of Speech Online." *American University International Law Review, 13*(765): *www.lexis-nexis.com.*

Reno, Janet (21 January 1997). Keynote Address by U.S. Attorney General Janet Reno on High-Tech and Computer Crime. Delivered at the Meeting of the P8 Senior Experts' Group on Transnational Organized Crime. Chantilly, VA. (*http://www.usdoj.gov/criminal/cybercrime/agfranc.htm* last accessed on 10/3/00).

Rodriguez, Alexander (1998). "All Bark, No Byte: Employee E-Mail Privacy Rights in the Private Sector Workplace." *Emory Law Journal, 47:* 1439–1473.

Sammes, Tony and Jenkinson, Brian (2000). *Forensic Computing: A Practitioner's Guide,* Springer-Verlag: London.

SEARCH (2000). *The Investigation of Computer Crime.* The National Consortium for Justice Information and Statistics: Sacramento, CA.

Shnier, Mitchell (1998). *Computer Dictionary,* Que Corporation, Indianapolis, IN.

Soma, John T., Banker, Elizabeth A., and Smith, Alexander R. (1996). "Computer Crime: Substantive Statutes & Technical & Search Considerations." *The Air Force Law Review, 39*(225). [Lexis-Nexis—*http://web.lexisnexis.com/universe/docu...zS& _md5=754b013cfb0e7bead5108ab532fd080d.*

Spernow, Bill (2001). "A Cutting Edge Look at Enhancing Security for the Enterprise." A paper presented at the annual meetings of the Techno-Security conference, Myrtle Beach, SC, April 23, 2001.

Stambaugh, Hollis; Beupre, David S.; Baker, Richard; Cassady, Wayne; and Williams, Wayne P. (201). "Electronic Crime Needs Assessment for State and Local Law Enforcement." DOJ # 98-DT-R-076. Washington, D.C.: NIJ.

Sterling, Bruce (1994). *The Hacker Crackdown, www.eff.orgpapers/hacker _crackdown/ crack_1.html* (last accessed 8/13/00).

Sullivan, Bob (June 21, 2000). "Protesters to Nike: Just hack it!" MSNBC.*www.zdnet. com...tories/news/0,4586,2592093,00.html.* Last accessed on 2/12/01.

Sullivan, Scott (1999). "Policing the Internet." *FBI Law Enforcement Bulletin.* ps. 18–21 (June).

SWGDE (Scientific Working Group on Digital Evidence) (1999). Digital Evidence: Standards and Principles. A paper presented at the International Hi-Tech Crime and Forensics Conference in London, England, October 4-7, 1999. *www.Fbi .gov/programs/lab/fsc/backissu/april2000/swgde.htm* Last accessed on 11/10/00.

Symantec (1997). *Norton Utilities for DOS:Definitions.*

Taylor, Chris (1999). "Geeks vs. G-men". *Time:* 64 (14 June).

Taylor, Chris (1999). "Hacker's Delight". *Time, 154*(18): 18. (1 November).

Tuerkheimer, Frank M. (1993). "The Underpinnings of Privacy Protection." *Communications of the ACM, 36*(8): 69–74.

United States Department of Justice (March, 2000). "The Electronic Frontier: The Challenge of Unlawful Conduct Involving the Use of the Internet–A report of the President's Working Group on Unlawful Conduct on the Internet."

United States General Accounting Office (1998). "Critical Infrastructure Protection: Comprehensive Strategy Can Draw on Year 2000 Experience." DOC # GAOAIMD—00-1, Washington, D.C.: 8.

United Nations (2000). "United Nations Manual on the prevention and Control of Computer-related Criteria." *International Review of Criminal Policy,* 43–44, *www.ifs.univie.ac.at/~pr2gq1/rev4344.html.* Last accessed 5/31/00.

Winick, Raphael (1994). "Searches and Seizures of Computers and Computer Data. *Harvard Journal of Law and Technology, 8*(1): 75–128.

INDEX